The Economics of Philanthropy

See http://mitpress.mit.edu for a complete list of titles in this series.

The Economics of Philanthropy

Donations and Fundraising

Edited by Kimberley Scharf and Mirco Tonin

CESifo Seminar Series

The MIT Press
Cambridge, Massachusetts
London, England

This book was set in Palatino by Westchester Publishing Services. Printed and bound in the United States of America.

Library of Congress Cataloging-in-Publication Data

Names: Scharf, Kimberley A. (Kimberley Ann), 1961– editor. |
   Tonin, Mirco, 1976– editor.
Title: The economics of philanthropy : donations and fundraising /
   edited by Kimberley Scharf and Mirco Tonin.
Description: Cambridge : MIT Press, MA. [2018] | Series: CESifo seminar
   series | Includes bibliographical references and index.
Identifiers: LCCN 2017058654 | ISBN 9780262038447 (hardcover : alk. paper)
Subjects: LCSH: Charities. | Fund raising.
Classification: LCC HV40 .E36 2018 | DDC 361.7—dc23
LC record available at https://lccn.loc.gov/2017058654

10 9 8 7 6 5 4 3 2 1

Contents

Series Foreword

This book is part of the CESifo Seminar Series. The series aims to cover topical policy issues in economics from a largely European perspective. The books in this series are the products of the papers and intensive debates that took place during the seminars hosted by CESifo, an international research network of renowned economists organized jointly by the Center for Economic Studies at Ludwig-Maximilians-Universität, Munich, and the Ifo Institute for Economic Research. All publications in this series have been carefully selected and refereed by members of the CESifo research network.

Introduction

Kimberley Scharf and Mirco Tonin

In many societies, a large fraction of the population is involved (as donors, beneficiaries, or providers) in philanthropic activities like charitable giving, fundraising, or volunteering. For instance, charitable giving in the United States was estimated at $390.05 billion in 2016, with giving by living donors representing the main share ($281.86 billion, or just over 72 percent), followed by foundations (15 percent), bequests (8 percent), and corporations (5 percent) (Giving USA 2017). At the same time, according to the US Bureau of Labor Statistics (2016), about 62.6 million people volunteered in the United States through or for an organization at least once in 2015, giving a volunteer rate of almost 25 percent. This volume collects papers that seek to enhance our understanding of individuals' motives for giving and volunteering, focusing in particular on how they affect donation outcomes, fundraising decisions, and public policies toward giving.

Academic research on the economics of private charity has traditionally viewed motives for giving as being embedded in formal models of economic behavior with rational agents who maximize their own utility while being constrained by their budget. These frameworks have been particularly useful in that they have allowed economists to understand more about the relationship between group size and private contributions, a topic that has been extensively covered in the literature on the private provision of public goods. Theoretical models of private provision of public goods that are based on altruistic motives for giving (also called selfish motives, or collective consumption motives; see Warr 1982, 1983, and Bergstrom, Blume, and Varian 1986), whereby individuals care only about the total amount of public good provided and private consumption, predict that individual donations are negatively related to group size (i.e., there is free-riding) and that total contributions approach zero as groups become very large. However, the prediction is at odds with the evidence, and so such models have been criticized for having poor predictive power. In chapter 1 of this book, Bergstrom constructs efficient rules that can be used to solve the free-riding problem in the context of the Volunteer's Dilemma. But with or without rules, these models are still vulnerable to the criticism that they neglect to take into account well-documented and possibly important motives for giving based on something other than collective consumption motives—that is, individuals may be motivated to give, directly or indirectly, because they care about their own contribution in its own right. Direct motives for giving would include those based on individuals experiencing some private "feel good factor" or "warm glow" associated with their own contributions (Andreoni 1988, 1990). Indirect motives could encompass many things, including prestige (Harbaugh 1998); individual reciprocity (Sugden 1984); or emotions such as guilt, empathy, and pity. Theoretical models that allow for such direct and indirect motives for giving generate better predictions and deliver results whereby, as free-riding on group size is mitigated by other incentives, total contributions do not go to zero as group size becomes very large.

Chapters 2 and 3 of this volume ask questions about these altruistic, direct and indirect motives for giving. In chapter 2, Ben-Ner and Hu reevaluate the notion that altruism is good for social welfare. Altruists help others, cooperate with others, and support the common good, all socially desirable consequences of altruism, but altruism also has its dark side: strong altruism toward in-group members is often accompanied by discrimination against and antagonism toward out-group members, with many undesirable social consequences. The chapter raises policy issues concerning encouragement of altruism, suggesting that in contemporary society in much of the world, parochial altruism is short sighted, and universal altruism should be encouraged. In chapter 3, Andreoni, Koessler, and Serra-Garcia investigate the impact of empathy and impulsiveness on charitable giving, using a real donation lab experiment. Their findings indicate that greater empathy predicts greater charitable giving; however, in contrast to recent literature, they find a significant negative relationship between impulsiveness and donation behavior. Specifically, when financial resources are scarce, donations are more often made by decision makers who are able to suppress an intuitively egoistic response.

Laboratory experiments, such as the one presented in chapter 3, have been important tools of investigation on the topic of philanthropy, so it is important to examine certain methodological issues that come up when using the lab as an experimental setting to study motives for giving and the channels through which giving occurs. In chapter 4, Menietti, Recalde, and Vesterlund reexamine the classic linear public good game, which is commonly used when studying voluntary giving in the lab. A well-known drawback of this game is that any deviation from equilibrium can be seen as other-regarding and thus prevents the identification of contributions made in error. In this chapter, a class of piecewise linear public goods games (PL-PG), wherein mistakes can be identified, is proposed as an alternative. In that class of games, the payoff structure allows for an interior equilibrium in dominant strategies and is sufficiently flexible to also place the Pareto efficient outcome in the interior of the strategy set. Thus mistakes, in the form of choices that are dominated from an individual and group perspective, can be identified. In contrast to past studies, which suggest quite a bit of confusion in public goods games with interior equilibria (using standard nonlinear functions, these studies demonstrate a low frequency of equilibrium play and average contributions that are relatively insensitive to the location of the equilibrium), behavior in the PL-PG game is very sensitive to the location of the equilibrium. After examining results from different implementations of the game, the research finds a high frequency of equilibrium play; a low rate of mistakes; and mean, median, and modal contributions that track the equilibrium. The advantages of the PL-PG game are demonstrated, and examples of charitable-giving applications of the framework are provided.

Social motives for giving could also be predictors of giving behavior. Chapter 5, by Schwirplies, Behar, and Bose, focuses on the role of social information on donor choices and effectiveness of charity output, a recent topic that has been studied in the context of competition in the charitable sector. They conduct an experiment at six universities in the United States and Canada. Student participants can choose between donating to a charity that fights extreme poverty and the student aid program at their own university. There is a social information treatment that consists of requesting participants to justify their choice. The treatment effect is then tested on donations made to the charity that fights extreme poverty (i.e., the cause that is presumed to have higher social impact). While treatments have the potential to influence donation decisions, their experimental findings are highly heterogeneous across the six universities, so much so that no clear conclusions can be drawn.

The effect of motives for giving on donation choice are critical for charities' fundraising strategies. Marx's contribution, chapter 6, looks at how potential donors respond to a nondirected matching gift. A well-known fundraising technique involves charities obtaining a pledge from a major donor to match the gifts of other donors. These matching gifts have been shown to sometimes increase contributions by other potential donors (see Eckel and Grossman 2008). Marx examines a matching gift that was promoted online and covered all gifts by any donor, new or not. He estimates the effect of this nondirected matching gift using difference-in-difference strategies that compare giving to the charity by day in different months and years. Marx finds that the match more than doubles the amount of funds donated, a much larger effect than has been found for matching promoted through mailings to individuals. The contribution in chapter 7, by Horn and Karlan, is to study the effect of various one-line messages on the propensity to donate at the point of checkout on eBay through a large randomized control trial. They use about 39 million observations and confirm how matching grants work well in enhancing donations, while quantification of impact and scientific evidence are less effective. Further expanding the investigation of fundraising techniques, in chapter 8, Eckel, Herberich, and Meer conduct a field experiment on gift exchange and giving at a public university in order to address one of the most important outstanding questions in fundraising: Are donor premiums (gifts to prospective donors) effective in terms of increasing donations? Donors may be motivated by reciprocity, making recipients of gifts more likely to donate and give larger donations. Or donors may dislike donor premiums, preferring instead to maximize the value of their donations to the charity; in this case donor premiums would be ineffective. To examine these questions, the authors conduct a field experiment in conjunction with the fundraising campaign of a major university. Treatments include a control, an unconditional premium with two gift quality levels, and a set of conditional premium treatments. The conditional treatments include opt-out and opt-in conditions to test whether donors prefer to forgo premiums. Compared with the control, donors are twice as likely to give when they receive an unconditional high-quality gift. The low-quality unconditional premiums and conditional premiums have little positive impact on the likelihood/level of giving, and donors do not respond negatively to premiums, so that rates of giving do not suffer when premiums are offered. In addition, few donors opt out of the scheme when given the opportunity to do so, indicating that they like gifts and suggesting that reciprocity rather than altruism determines the impact of premiums on giving.

Another important part of a charity's fundraising strategy is to take into account uncertain revenue flows, which they face just as for-profit firms do. Revenue uncertainty, however, is especially challenging for charities because of their nonprofit status, which limits their ability to resort to capital markets to buffer themselves against short-run income shocks. This can lead to short-term focused responses on the part of charities, undermining their mission and compromising their medium- and long-run sustainability, which in turn, can cause programs to be disrupted and program aims to be overly influenced by transitory changes. Having to continuously refocus and reorganize activities in response to revenue shocks also entails adjustment costs that are wasteful in the medium as well as in the long run. Charities can deal with this problem in several ways. For example, in bad economic times, charities might be forced to rely more on donations of time instead of money. However, switching from relying on monetary donations to donations of time could have unintended consequences if donations of time and money are complementary, as is found for the United Kingdom in chapter 9. Although a relatively large and growing literature exists that examines the factors associated with monetary donations to charitable causes, the literature on volunteering is scant. Chapter 9, by Brown and Taylor, provides the first empirical study for the United Kingdom that explores the factors influencing unpaid volunteering. The study uses data from Understanding Society—the UK Household Longitudinal Study—which is the most recent representative large scale survey for the United Kingdom. Findings indicate that savings, social networks, and cognitive ability are positively associated with individuals volunteering more time. Conversely, hours spent in employment, commuting, and housework are inversely related to time spent volunteering. The relationship between monetary donations and time spent volunteering is also analyzed, and estimates are that a 1 percent decrease in the amount of money donated to charity is associated with spending approximately 7 percent less time on unpaid volunteering. Another way for charities to reduce their reliance on private donations is by increasing their reliance on public funds. The effects of this are the focus of chapter 10, by Minaker and Payne. Two main questions are addressed in this chapter. The first is: When a charity receives government funding, does it undo the benefits of that funding by changing its behavior for the collection of revenues from other sources? The second is: Do donors change their behavior? Data are analyzed from more than 11,000 applications for foundation grants made by more than 4,500 charities over a 10-year period. Findings are that grants increase total revenues by about 16 percent in the first year of funding, and growth in total revenues continues in subsequent years. This growth is observed for all sizes of charities except those with average revenues that are greater than $500,000.

Other ways for charities to cope with uncertain revenue streams involve adopting fundraising strategies that directly aim to reduce revenue uncertainty (e.g., using subscription models or having in place publicity and appeals mechanisms that can be utilized quickly in the case of an unexpected event). Subscription models try to get supporters to commit to make regular donations. It is one way of securing streams of donations. Chapter 11, by Damgaarde, Gravert, and Villalobos, studies reminder response behavior for membership renewals, which are one way of securing a stream of donations from subscribers. The particular focus is on the effect of reminder responses on additional giving. The study uses panel data consisting of 440,000 member-year observations from a large charity. Findings indicate a negative association between late responders and additional giving, thus providing evidence against a simple transaction cost model as an explanation for variations in reminder response rates. This study is a first step toward designing a more efficient and more targeted reminder process for charities. When uncertain revenue streams are shocked by exogenous events, different remedies might be required that are aimed at informing potential donors that help is needed. In chapter 12, Smith, Ottoni-Wilhelm, and Scharf study this problem in the context of natural disasters, such as the 2004 East Asian tsunami, which attracted a high level of donations. While previous literature has shown that the scale of the disaster is important in driving the aid response, there are inconsistent findings about whether the number of individuals killed or the number affected matters more. Main findings are that both the number killed and the number affected matter equally for whether aid is given; the number killed is more strongly related to the magnitude of the aid response. This chapter also presents new evidence confirming the importance of publicity for disasters, focusing on appeals.

There is an increasing awareness in the field of economics of the need to better understand philanthropic activities. This book addresses a variety of topics related to the economics of philanthropy, ranging from the determinants of giving to the effectiveness of fundraising techniques. It showcases how the collaboration between academics and practitioners—for instance, through the implementation of field experiments or the analysis of administrative datasets—can lead to a better understanding of what drives philanthropy, with mutual benefits. Our hope is that this volume will spur further discussion and collaboration and will stimulate this growing field of research.

References

Andreoni, James. 1988. "Privately Provided Public Goods in a Large Economy: The Limits of Altruism." *Journal of Public Economics* 35 (1): 57–73.

Andreoni, James. 1990. "Impure Altruism and Donations to Public Goods: A Theory of Warm-Glow Giving." *Economic Journal* 100 (401): 464–477.

Bergstrom, Theodore, Lawrence Blume, and Hal Varian. 1986. "On the Private Provision of Public Goods." *Journal of Public Economics* 29 (1): 25–49.

Eckel, Catherine, and Philip Grossman. 2008. "Subsidizing Charitable Contributions: A Natural Field Experiment Comparing Matching and Rebate Subsidies." *Experimental Economics* 11 (3): 234–252.

Giving USA. 2017. *Giving USA 2017: The Annual Report on Philanthropy for the Year 2016. Researched and written by the Indiana University Lilly Family School of Philanthropy.* Available online at www.givingusa.org.

Harbaugh, William. 1998. "What Do Donations Buy? A Model of Philanthropy Based on Prestige and Warm Glow." *Journal of Public Economics* 67 (2): 269–284.

Sugden, Robert. 1984. "Reciprocity: The Supply of Public Goods through Voluntary Contributions." *Economic Journal* 94 (376): 772–787.

United States Bureau of Labor Statistics. 2016. "Volunteering in the United States, 2015." February 25. https://www.bls.gov/news.release/volun.nr0.htm.

Warr, Peter. 1982. "Pareto Optimal Redistribution and Private Charity." *Journal of Public Economics* 19 (1): 131–138.

Warr, Peter. 1983. "The Private Provision of a Public Good Is Independent of the Distribution of Income." *Economics Letters* 13 (2–3): 207–211.

1   Efficient Ethical Rules for Volunteer's Dilemmas

Ted Bergstrom

As you stroll along a well-traveled path, you observe water rushing from a broken water main. If you believe that nobody else will do so, you will certainly take the trouble to find a telephone and call the water department. But since the path is busy, many others will see the problem. If someone else calls, your effort will be wasted. But if everybody believes that someone else will call, the problem will go unreported.

1.1   The Volunteer's Dilemma

Andreas Diekmann (1985) modeled situations like this with a symmetric n-player, simultaneous-move game that he called the *Volunteer's Dilemma*. In the Volunteer's Dilemma game, each player can choose to take action or not. If at least one player acts, then all n players will receive a benefit b. Those who act must pay a cost c, where $0 < c < b$, and hence receive a net benefit of $b - c$. If no player acts, then all players receive a net benefit of 0.

1.1.1   Symmetric Nash Equilibrium
In the Volunteer's Dilemma with two or more players, there cannot be a symmetric Nash equilibrium in which all take action, since if everybody else acts, one's own best response is not to act. Nor can there be a symmetric Nash equilibrium in which none take action, since if nobody else acts, one's own best response is to act. In the only symmetric Nash equilibrium for this game, each player uses a mixed strategy; taking action with a positive probability less than 1. These results are stated formally in proposition 1.1, a proof of which is found in the appendix.

Proposition 1.1. (Diekmann) The n-player Volunteer's Dilemma has a unique symmetric Nash equilibrium. With n players, the Nash equilibrium probability that an individual player takes action is

$$p_N(n) = 1 - \left(\frac{c}{b}\right)^{\frac{1}{n-1}}, \tag{1.1}$$

which decreases as n increases and asymptotically approaches 0. The probability that at least one player takes action is

$$P_N(n) = 1 - \left(\frac{c}{b}\right)^{\frac{n}{n-1}}, \tag{1.2}$$

which also decreases with n and asymptotically approaches $1 - \frac{c}{b}$. The expected utility of each player is constant with respect to n and equal to $b - c$.

Proposition 1.1 leaves us with a vexing conundrum. The technology of the Volunteer's Dilemma game offers the potential for significant benefits from the formation of larger groups; an action taken by a single person is sufficient to benefit the entire group, no matter how large the group. Yet in the symmetric Nash equilibrium for this game, as the number of players increases, the probability that nobody takes action increases in such a way that none of these potential gains are realized. As group size grows, the expected payoff to each player remains constant at $b - c$.

1.1.2 Optimal Symmetric Mixed Strategies

In the Volunteer's Dilemma game, inefficiency of the symmetric Nash equilibrium arises from two sources. One is the standard problem of neglected externalities. Individuals do not account for the fact that an increase in their own probability of taking action benefits all other players. The second source of inefficiency is a coordination problem. Players do not know the actions that have been taken by others. Thus, in equilibrium, there is a positive probability that more than one player takes costly action, although the action of only one is needed to produce benefits for all.

Sometimes it is possible to coordinate the actions of players so that if more than one player volunteers, only a single volunteer will be selected to perform the task. For example, potential donors of stem cells from bone marrow or blood aphoresis join a registry of persons who have declared their willingness to donate if their contributions are needed. When a patient is in need of a transplant, if one or more potential donors of this patient's immunity type have volunteered, the registry selects exactly one of these volunteers to make the donation (Bergstrom, Garratt, and Sheehan-Connor 2009). Jeroen Weesie and Axel Franzen (1998) and Ted Bergstrom and Greg Leo (2012) analyze the comparative statics of Nash equilibria for versions of Volunteer's Dilemma in which at most one of the volunteers is required to pay.

Sometimes duplication of effort can be avoided, because potential volunteers can see immediately whether someone else has "beat them to it." Bergstrom (2017) studies the case of passersby on a more or less crowded highway, who are presented sequentially with the opportunity to help a distressed traveler. Christopher Bliss and Barry Nalebuff (1984), Marc Bilodeau and Al Slivinski (1996), and Weesie (1993) analyze a war-of-attrition game in which the first person to take action is observed by all and the benefits diminish as time passes. In deciding when to act, players face a trade-off between the costs of postponement and the possibility that if one waits a little longer, action will be unnecessary, because someone else will have done it.

This chapter studies situations where such coordination is technically infeasible. In the example at the beginning of this chapter, the cost of informing authorities would be minimized if only one passerby took action. But how can this be accomplished? It would not be cost-effective for everyone who has seen the problem to assemble and choose one of their number to contact the authorities.

1.1.3 An Appeal to Ethics

If players could be persuaded to abide by a self-enforced ethical rule that accounts for the well-being of others, they would all be better off than in symmetric Nash equilibrium. We will show that in the absence of coordination, there is an optimal symmetric ethical rule that mandates each player takes action with a probability that exceeds the Nash equilibrium probability but is less than 1. Notice that an ethic that demanded that all players take action would not be efficient. If all followed this rule, each would have an expected payoff of $b - c$, which is no better than the Nash equilibrium payoff.

An optimal symmetric ethical rule for the symmetric Volunteer's Dilemma game is a strategy that satisfies the *Kantian* principle: "Use the strategy that you would wish that everyone would use." This rule is characterized by proposition 1.2, which is proved in the appendix.

Proposition 1.2. In an n-player Volunteer's Dilemma, there is an optimal symmetric rule that requires each player to use a mixed strategy in which the probability of taking action is

$$p_O(n) = 1 - \left(\frac{c}{bn}\right)^{\frac{1}{n-1}}, \tag{1.3}$$

and the probability that at least one player takes action is

$$P_O(n) = 1 - \left(\frac{c}{bn}\right)^{\frac{n}{n-1}}. \tag{1.4}$$

Tables 1.1 and 1.2 illustrate the results of proposition 1.2 by showing the probabilities of taking action in Nash equilibrium and in the optimal ethical solution. This is done for two special cases, with cost-benefit ratios $c/b = .5$ and $c/b = .9$.

The tables show that when the number of players is small, the optimal ethical strategy requires players to take action with much higher probability than in Nash equilibrium. They also show (as predicted by proposition 1.1) that in Nash equilibrium, as the number of players increases, the probability that any individual acts declines asymptotically toward 0, while the probability that at least one player takes action declines asymptotically toward $1 - c/b$.

In these tables, it appears that if all players use the optimal ethical strategy, the probability that any individual takes action declines asymptotically toward 0, and the probability that at least one takes

Table 1.1
Symmetric Nash equilibrium and ethical optimum with $c/b = 0.5$.

n	Nash Equilibrium		Ethical Optimum	
	$p_N(n)$	$P_N(n)$	$p_O(n)$	$P_O(n)$
2	0.50	0.75	0.75	0.94
3	0.29	0.65	0.59	0.93
4	0.21	0.60	0.50	0.94
5	0.16	0.58	0.44	0.94
25	0.03	0.51	0.15	0.98
100	0.01	0.50	0.05	1.00
∞	0.00	0.50	0.00	1.00

Table 1.2
Symmetric Nash equilibrium and ethical optimum with $c/b = 0.9$.

n	Nash Equilibrium		Ethical Optimum	
	$p_N(n)$	$P_N(n)$	$p_O(n)$	$P_O(n)$
2	0.10	0.19	0.55	0.80
3	0.05	0.15	0.45	0.84
4	0.04	0.13	0.39	0.86
5	0.03	0.12	0.35	0.88
25	0.00	0.10	0.14	0.85
100	0.00	0.10	0.05	0.95
∞	0.00	0.10	0.00	1.00

action approaches 1. This result turns out to be true in general. We state this result formally in proposition 1.3, which is proved in the appendix.

Proposition 1.3. If all players use the optimal ethical rule, then in the limit as the number of players approaches infinity, the probability that any single individual takes action approaches 0, but the probability that at least one player takes action approaches 1.

If all players use the optimal ethical rule, they will all be better off than in Nash equilibrium, but in the absence of a coordinating device, there will still be some probability of duplicated effort. If a coordinating device were available to randomly select a single player to take action, then the expected payoff of each player would be $b - c/n$, which is higher than the expected payoffs in the uncoordinated optimal ethical outcome.

In table 1.3, we show the expected utility $\hat{u}(n)$ of each player in Nash equilibrium, expected utility $\bar{u}(n)$ when all players use the optimal ethical strategy, and expected utility $u_c(n)$ of each player in a coordinated equilibrium where one randomly selected player is assigned to take action. We show this for two special cases, where $c = .5$ and $b = 1$ and where $c = .9$ and $b = 1$.

1.2   Nash Equilibrium When Costs Differ

It is common practice to "simplify" game theoretic models like the Volunteer's Dilemma by assuming that all players have identical benefits and costs. While this simplification makes it easy to calculate a symmetric Nash equilibrium, the resulting mixed-strategy Nash

Table 1.3
Utility comparison: Nash equilibrium $\hat{u}(n)$, ethical optimum $u(n)$, and coordinated solution $u_C(n)$.

	$c = 0.5, b = 1$			$c = 0.9, b = 1$		
n	$\hat{u}(n)$	$u(n)$	$u_c(n)$	$\hat{u}(n)$	$u(n)$	$u_c(n)$
2	0.50	0.56	0.75	0.10	0.30	0.55
3	0.50	0.64	0.83	0.10	0.43	0.70
4	0.50	0.69	0.88	0.10	0.95	0.99
5	0.50	0.73	0.90	0.10	0.57	0.82
25	0.50	0.91	0.98	0.10	0.85	0.96
100	0.50	0.97	0.995	0.10	0.95	0.99

equilibrium has an air of implausibility. In the symmetric mixed-strategy equilibrium of the Volunteer's Dilemma game, all players are indifferent between the equilibrium mixed strategy and any other probability mix of the strategies "act" and "don't act." Given that this is the case, why should any player take the trouble to determine the equilibrium mixed-strategy proportions and act accordingly?[1] If we allow the realistic possibility that different players have different costs of taking action, we avoid this conundrum and can construct a manageable model in which players use pure strategies in a symmetric Nash equilibrium. In this case, we find that the optimal symmetric ethical rule recommends to each player a pure strategy that is determined by that player's realized cost of taking action.

Let us assume that the costs c of taking action differ among players and that if at least one player takes action, all players receive the same benefit b. Players cannot communicate before deciding whether to act. Individuals know their own costs but do not know the costs of the other players in the game.[2] Players' costs are chosen by independent draws from a distribution that is common knowledge. The distribution from which players' costs are drawn is assumed to satisfy the following assumption.

Assumption 1.1. Players' costs are drawn randomly from a population with a cumulative distribution of costs $F(\cdot)$ that is continuously differentiable on the interval $[\ell, h]$, where $0 \leq \ell < b \leq h$. We assume that $F(\ell) = 0$, $F(h) = 1$, and $F'(c) > 0$ for all $c \in [\ell, h]$.

If $F(b) < 1$, then with positive probability, a player's costs will exceed individual benefits. In Nash equilibrium, such a player would not act even if nobody else takes action.

The game that begins before individuals learn their costs can be modeled as a symmetric game. For each player, a strategy is a function that maps costs, once revealed, to actions. This game has a symmetric Nash equilibrium in which every player uses a *threshold strategy* of the form: "Act if and only if your costs c are no larger than the threshold level $\hat{c}$." The threshold strategy with threshold $\hat{c}$ will be a Nash equilibrium if and only if, when all other players follow this rule, a player with realized cost $c < \hat{c}$ will have a higher expected payoff from acting than from not acting, and a player with realized cost $c > \hat{c}$ will have a higher payoff from not acting.

Let us define $G(c) = 1 - F(c)$. If the $n - 1$ other players all use the threshold strategy with threshold $\hat{c}(n)$, then a player whose cost is $\hat{c}(n)$ must be indifferent between acting and not acting. For this player, the expected payoff from not acting is $b(1 - G(\hat{c}(n))^{n-1})$, and the expected payoff from acting is $b - \hat{c}(n)$. This result implies that

$$b(1 - G(\hat{c}(n))^{n-1}) = b - \hat{c}(n), \tag{1.5}$$

or equivalently,

$$bG(\hat{c}(n))^{n-1} = \hat{c}(n). \tag{1.6}$$

We have the following result, which is proved in the appendix.

Proposition 1.4. In an n-player Volunteer's Dilemma game, where the distribution of costs is common knowledge and satisfies assumption 1.1, there is a unique Nash equilibrium threshold strategy, with threshold $\hat{c}(n) \in (\ell, b)$ such that $\hat{c}(n)$ decreases as n increases and $\lim_{n \to \infty} \hat{c}(n) = \ell$.

The equilibrium probability that nobody takes action when there are n players is $G(\hat{c}(n))^n$. From equation 1.6, it follows that

$$G(\hat{c}(n))^n = G(\hat{c}(n))^{n-1}G(\hat{c}(n)) = \frac{1}{b}\hat{c}(n)G(\hat{c}(n)). \tag{1.7}$$

The function $G(\cdot)$ is assumed to be continuous, and $G(\ell) = 1$. According to proposition 1.4, $\lim_{n \to \infty} \hat{c}(n) = \ell$. It follows from equation 1.7 that

$$\lim_{n \to \infty} G(\hat{c}(n))^n = \lim_{n \to \infty} \frac{1}{b}\hat{c}(n)\lim_{n \to \infty} G(\hat{c}(n))$$

$$= \frac{\ell}{b}G(\ell) \tag{1.8}$$

$$= \frac{\ell}{b}.$$

Let us define $F^*(c, n)$ to be the the probability that at least one player takes action when there are n players, each of whom uses a threshold strategy with threshold c. Then

$$F^*(c,n) = 1 - G(c)^n. \tag{1.9}$$

Therefore equation 1.8 implies the following proposition.

Proposition 1.5. In a symmetric Nash equilibrium for an n-player Volunteer's Dilemma where the distribution of costs satisfies assumption 1.1, the limiting probability that at least one player takes action is

$$\lim_{n \to \infty} F^* (\hat{c}(n), n) = 1 - \frac{\ell}{b}. \tag{1.10}$$

Proposition 1.5 has the following corollary.

Corollary 1.1. If $\ell = 0$, then in symmetric Nash equilibrium, the probability that someone takes action approaches 1 as n gets large.

Where $\ell > 0$, the limiting value of the probability that someone takes action is less than 1. It is of some interest to explore whether this probability increases or decreases with the number of players.

Proposition 1.4 informs us that $\hat{c}(n)$ is a decreasing function of n. Therefore the probability that in equilibrium, nobody takes action increases (decreases) as n increases if $cG(c)$ is a decreasing (increasing) function of c over the interval (ℓ, h). Differentiating, we find that

$$\frac{d}{dc}(cG(c)) = G(c) + cG'(c) = G(c)\left(1 + \frac{cG'(c)}{G(c)}\right). \tag{1.11}$$

The ratio $cG'(c)/G(c)$ in equation 1.11 can be written as $\frac{c}{G}\frac{dG}{dc}$, which is recognizable as the elasticity of the function G with respect to c. It is useful to give this expression a name of its own.

Definition 1.1. The cost elasticity of refusals is the ratio $\eta_r(c) = \frac{cG'(c)}{G(c)}$. Refusals are cost-elastic at c if $\eta_r(c) < -1$ and cost-inelastic if $\eta_r(c) > -1$.

An immediate consequence of equation 1.11 and definition 1.1 is the following:

Lemma 1.1. The function $cG(c)$ is increasing in c over the interval (ℓ, h) if refusals are cost-inelastic and decreasing over this interval if refusals are cost-elastic.

According to proposition 1.4, $\hat{c}(n)$ is a decreasing function of n. With n players, the Nash equilibrium probability that nobody takes action is $\hat{c}(n)\, G(\hat{c}(n))$. It follows from lemma 1.1 that $\hat{c}(n)\, G(\hat{c}(n))$ increases with n if refusals are cost-elastic, and decreases with n if refusals are cost-inelastic. Since the probability that someone takes action is 1 minus the probability that nobody takes action, we have the following:

Proposition 1.6. If assumption 1.1 is satisfied, then in Nash equilibrium, the probability $F^*(\hat{c}(n),n)$ that at least one player takes action decreases with n if refusals are cost-elastic and increases with n if refusals are cost-inelastic. In either case, as n approaches infinity, this probability approaches $1 - \ell/b$.

1.3 Optimal Ethical Strategies When Costs Differ

To formulate an optimal ethical rule, we impose a "veil of ignorance" on differences in costs and benefits in such a way that before the veil is removed, all players seek to maximize the same objective function. We imagine an initial position in which players do not yet know their own costs but expect them to be drawn at random from a probability distribution that is common knowledge. In the initial position, players have identical prospects. We assume that it is common knowledge that the distribution $F(\cdot)$ from which individual costs are drawn satisfies assumption 1.1 of the previous section. We consider symmetric strategies that take the form of a threshold cost level $\bar{c}$ and a mandate that any player should take action if and only if this player has costs $c \leq \bar{c}$.

For every $n > 1$, there is an optimal ethical threshold strategy, with threshold $\bar{c}(n)$. Viewed from the initial position, this strategy, if followed by all players, yields a higher expected utility for each than would any other strategy used by all players.

Proposition 1.7. If the distribution of costs satisfies assumption 1.1, and if $nb > \ell$, then there is a unique optimal ethical strategy $\bar{c}(n)$. The threshold $\bar{c}(n)$ satisfies the equation

$$bG(\bar{c}(n))^{n-1} = \frac{\bar{c}(n)}{n}. \tag{1.12}$$

Not surprisingly, the optimal ethical threshold $\bar{c}(n)$ exceeds the Nash equilibrium threshold $\hat{c}(n)$. We show this as follows:

Corollary 1.2. For all $n > 1$, $\overline{c}(n) > \hat{c}(n)$, where $\hat{c}(n)$ is the symmetric Nash equilibrium threshold.

Proof. Where $\hat{c}(n)$ is the symmetric Nash equilibrium threshold, for n players, it follows from equations 1.6 and 1.12 that for all $n > 1$,

$$b\frac{G(\overline{c}(n))^{n-1}}{\overline{c}(n)} = \frac{1}{n} < 1 = b\frac{G(\hat{c}(n))^{n-1}}{\hat{c}(n)}. \tag{1.13}$$

Since $G(c) > 0$ and $G'(c) < 0$, it must be that that $\dfrac{G(c)^{n-1}}{c}$ is a strictly decreasing function of c for $c > 0$. Therefore the inequality in expression 1.13 implies that $\overline{c}(n) > \hat{c}(n)$. $\qquad\qquad\qquad\square$

Proposition 1.8 informs us that in the limit, for large n, the optimal ethical threshold $\overline{c}(n)$, like the Nash equilibrium threshold $\hat{c}(n)$, approaches ℓ, the lower bound of the support of the distribution of costs. However, $\overline{c}(n)$ approaches ℓ more slowly than does $\hat{c}(n)$, so that the limiting probability that at least one player takes action is 1 if all players use the optimal ethical threshold and is $1 - \ell/b$ in symmetric Nash equilibriium.

This result is stated formally in proposition 1.8, which is proved in the appendix.

Proposition 1.8. If the distribution of costs satisfies assumption 1.1, then $\lim_{n \to \infty} \overline{c}(n) = \ell$ and $\lim_{n \to \infty} F^*(\overline{c}(n), n) = 1$.

1.4   Examples

We illustrate our general results with examples from two special distribution families, the Pareto distributions and the uniform distributions.

1.4.1   Pareto Distribution
The Pareto distribution with parameters $\ell > 0$ and $\lambda > 0$ has a cumulative distribution function of the form

$$F(c) = 1 - \left(\frac{\ell}{c}\right)^{\lambda} \tag{1.14}$$

with support (ℓ, ∞). For the Pareto distribution,

$$G(c) = \left(\frac{\ell}{c}\right)^{\lambda},$$

(1.15)

and thus the cost elasticity of refusal is $\eta_r(c) = -\lambda$.

Nash equilibrium   From proposition 1.6, it is immediate that:

Remark 1.1.   If the distribution of costs is a Pareto distribution with parameters ℓ and λ, then the symmetric Nash equilibrium probability $F^*(\hat{c}(n),n)$ that at least one player takes action decreases with group size if $\lambda > 1$ and increases with group size if $\lambda < 1$.

If costs are Pareto distributed with parameters ℓ and λ, we can solve directly for $\hat{c}(n)$ and $\bar{c}(n)$. According to equation 1.6, it must be that $bG(\hat{c}(n))^{n-1} = \hat{c}(n)$. For the Pareto distribution, this implies that

$$b\left(\frac{\ell}{\hat{c}(n)}\right)^{\lambda(n-1)} = \hat{c}(n).$$

(1.16)

Rearranging the terms of equation 1.16, we have

$$\hat{c}(n) = b^{\frac{1}{1+\lambda(n-1)}} \ell^{\frac{\lambda(n-1)}{1+\lambda(n-1)}},$$

(1.17)

and hence the probability that any individual takes action is

$$1 - G(\hat{c}(n)) = 1 - \left(\frac{\ell}{\hat{c}(n)}\right)^{\lambda} = 1 - \left(\frac{\ell}{b}\right)^{\frac{\lambda}{1+\lambda(n-1)}}.$$

(1.18)

The probability that at least one player takes action is then

$$F^*(\hat{c}(n),n) = 1 - G(\hat{c}(n))^{n} = 1 - \left(\frac{\ell}{b}\right)^{\frac{\lambda n}{1+\lambda(n-1)}}.$$

(1.19)

Optimal Ethical strategies   From equation 1.12 of proposition 1.7 it follows that

$$b\left(\frac{\ell}{\bar{c}(n)}\right)^{\lambda(n-1)} = \frac{\bar{c}(n)}{n}.$$

(1.20)

From equations 1.16 and 1.20, it follows that

$$\frac{\bar{c}(n)}{\hat{c}(n)} = n^{\frac{1}{1+\lambda(n-1)}}. \tag{1.21}$$

Equations 1.15 and 1.21 imply that

$$\frac{G(\bar{c}(n))}{G(\hat{c}(n))} = \left(\frac{\hat{c}(n)}{\bar{c}(n)}\right)^{\lambda(n-1)} = n^{\frac{-\lambda(n-1)}{1+\lambda(n-1)}}. \tag{1.22}$$

Numerical examples Tables 1.4 and 1.5 show outcome probabilities for special cases where $b = 2$, $\ell = 1$ and with $\lambda = .5$ and $\lambda = 2$, respectively. Table 1.4 shows that if $\lambda = .5$, the Nash equilibrium probability $F^*(\hat{c}(n), n)$ that at least one player takes action increases as n increases. Table 1.5 shows that if $\lambda = 2$, this probability decreases with n. In both cases, $F^*(\hat{c}(n), n)$ approaches $\ell/b = .5$. The tables also show that for small n, the ethical optimum recommends a much higher probability of acting than does the Nash equilibrium probability.

Table 1.4
Pareto distribution with $\lambda = 0.5$, $\ell = 1$, and $b = 2$.

	Nash Equilibrium			Ethical Optimum		
n	$F(\hat{c}(n))$	$F^*(\hat{c}(n),n)$	$\hat{u}(n)$	$F(\bar{c}(n))$	$F^*(\bar{c}(n))$	$\bar{u}(n)$
2	0.21	0.37	0.48	0.37	0.60	0.62
3	0.16	0.41	0.62	0.36	0.74	0.91
4	0.13	0.43	0.70	0.34	0.81	1.11
5	0.11	0.44	0.76	0.32	0.85	1.24
25	0.03	0.49	0.95	0.14	0.98	1.79
100	0.01	0.50	0.99	0.05	0.99	1.94
∞	0.00	0.50	1.00	0.00	1.00	2.00

Table 1.5
Pareto distribution with $\lambda = 2$, $\ell = 1$, and $b = 2$.

	Nash Equilibrium			Ethical Optimum		
n	$F(\hat{c}(n))$	$F^*(\hat{c}(n),n)$	$\hat{u}(n)$	$F(\bar{c}(n))$	$F^*(\bar{c}(n),n),$	$\bar{u}(n)$
2	0.37	0.60	0.79	0.60	0.84	0.95
3	0.24	0.56	0.87	0.51	0.88	1.17
4	0.18	0.55	0.91	0.45	0.91	1.30
5	0.14	0.54	0.93	0.40	0.92	1.39
25	0.03	0.51	0.99	0.15	0.98	1.81
100	0.01	0.50	1.00	0.05	1.00	1.94
∞	0.00	0.50	1.00	0.00	1.00	2.00

1.4.2 Uniform Distribution

Consider the uniform distributed on an interval $[\ell, h]$, where $0 \le \ell < b \le h$. Then $F(c) = \dfrac{c - \ell}{h - \ell}$, and $G(c) = 1 - F(c) = \dfrac{h - c}{h - \ell}$.

With the uniform distribution, the cost elasticity of refusal is

$$\eta_r(c) = \frac{cG'(c)}{G(c)} = \frac{-c}{h - c}. \tag{1.23}$$

In this case, the cost elasticity of refusal is not constant but depends on c. From equation 1.23, it follows that if $c < h/2$, refusals are cost-inelastic with $\eta_r(c) > -1$; and if $c > h/2$, refusals are cost-elastic with $\eta_r(c) < -1$.

Although the cost-elasticity of refusals at the threshold $\hat{c}(n)$ depends on the value of $c(n)$, some simple conditions on the parameters of the distribution can confine $\hat{c}(n)$ to either the cost-inelastic or the cost-elastic region. According to proposition 1.4, it must be that $\ell < \hat{c}(n) < b$ for all $n \ge 2$. Therefore if $b < h/2$, it must be that $\hat{c}(n) < h/2$, and hence refusals are cost-inelastic at $\hat{c}(n)$. In contrast, if $h/2 < \ell$, then since $\hat{c}(n) > \ell$, it must be that if $\hat{c}(n) > h/2$, and therefore refusals are cost-elastic at $\hat{c}(n)$. From these facts and proposition 1.6, we conclude that

Remark 1.2. If the distribution of costs is uniform on the interval $[\ell, h]$ and if $b < h/2$, the Nash equilibrium probability that at least one player takes action decreases with the number of players. If $h/2 < \ell$, this probability increases with the number of players.

Tables 1.6 and 1.7 illustrate the general result of remark 1.2. In the example of table 1.6, $b < h/2$ and hence refusals are cost-inelastic at $\hat{c}(n)$ for $n \ge 2$. In the example of table 1.7, $h/2 < \ell$ and refusals are cost-elastic

Table 1.6
Uniform distribution on the interval $[1, 5]$ with $b = 2$.

n	Nash Equilibrium				Ethical Optimum		
	$\hat{c}(n)$	$\eta_r(\hat{c}(n))$	$F(\hat{c}(n))$	$F^*(\hat{c}(n),n)$	$\bar{c}(n)$	$F(\bar{c}(n))$	$F^*(\bar{c}(n),n)$
2	1.67	−0.50	0.17	0.31	2.50	0.38	0.61
3	1.52	−0.44	0.13	0.34	2.45	0.36	0.74
4	1.43	−0.40	0.11	0.36	2.34	0.34	0.81
5	1.36	−0.37	0.09	0.38	2.08	0.27	0.79
10	1.20	−0.31	0.05	0.43	1.92	0.23	0.93
25	1.10	−0.28	0.03	0.46	1.52	0.13	0.97
100	1.00	−0.25	0.00	0.50	1.20	0.05	0.99
∞	1.00	−0.25	0.00	0.50	1.00	0.00	1.00

Table 1.7
Uniform distribution on the interval [3, 5] with $b = 4$.

n	Nash Equilibrium				Ethical Optimum		
	$\hat{c}(n)$	$\eta_r(\hat{c}(n))$	$F(\hat{c}(n))$	$F^*(\hat{c}(n),n)$	$\bar{c}(n)$	$F(\bar{c}(n))$	$F^*(\bar{c}(n),n)$
2	3.33	−2.00	0.17	0.31	4.00	0.50	0.75
3	3.21	−1.79	0.10	0.28	3.86	0.43	0.82
4	3.15	−1.71	0.08	0.27	3.77	0.38	0.85
5	3.12	−1.66	0.06	0.27	3.69	0.34	0.90
10	3.00	−1.58	0.03	0.26	3.48	0.24	0.93
25	3.02	−1.53	0.01	0.25	3.25	0.13	0.96
100	3.01	−1.51	0.00	0.25	3.10	0.05	0.99
∞	3.00	−1.50	0.00	0.25	3.00	0.00	1.00

Table 1.8
Uniform distribution on the interval [2, 5] with $b = 4$.

n	Nash Equilibrium				Ethical Optimum		
	$\hat{c}(n)$	$\eta_r(\hat{c}(n))$	$F(\hat{c}(n))$	$F^*(\hat{c}(n),n)$	$\bar{c}(n)$	$F(\bar{c}(n))$	$F^*(\bar{c}(n),n)$
2	2.86	−1.33	0.29	0.4898	3.63	0.54	0.79
3	2.59	−1.07	0.20	0.4798	3.48	0.49	0.87
4	2.45	−0.96	0.15	0.4796	3.24	0.41	0.88
5	2.39	−0.90	0.12	0.4802	3.12	0.37	0.90
10	2.19	−0.78	0.07	0.4875	2.77	0.26	0.95
25	2.08	−0.71	0.03	0.4938	2.43	0.14	0.98
100	2.02	−0.68	0.01	0.4979	2.15	0.05	0.99
∞	2.00	−0.67	0.00	0.5000	2.00	0.00	1.00

at $\hat{c}(n)$ for $n \geq 2$. In the former case, the Nash equilibrium probability that at least one person acts increases, and in the latter case this probability decreases with n.

Remark 1.2 does not apply when $\ell < h/2 < b$. In this case, examples can be found in which refusals are cost-elastic for small n and cost-inelastic for large n. Hence the probability that at least one person acts decreases with n for small n and increases with n for large n. Table 1.8 shows an example in which $\ell < h/2 < b$. In this example, the Nash equilibrium probability that at least one player decreases with n for $n = 2$ and $n = 3$ and increases with n for $n > 3$.

Tables 1.6–1.8 illustrate the general result that in Nash equilibrium and also in the ethical optimum, the probability that any single individual takes action approaches 0 as n becomes large. However, as n becomes large, the Nash equilibrium probability that at least one takes action approaches ℓ/b, while if all players use the optimal ethical strategy, the probability that at least one takes action approaches unity.

1.5 Conclusion

Diekmann's model of a Volunteer's Dilemma with identical players yields a surprising and somewhat distressing conclusion. This game displays strong technical returns to scale for large groups—if at least one player takes a costly action, all will benefit. But the potential gains from group size are entirely dissipated by the "free-rider problem." As group size increases, the Nash equilibrium probability that at least one player takes action is reduced, and the equilibrium expected utility of each player remains constant.

In general, the dissipation of returns to scale is less severe in a Volunteer's Dilemma if benefits and/or costs of action differ among players. We consider a model in which if at least one player takes action, then all group members receive the same benefit, but the costs of acting differ between individuals. Nash equilibrium strategies take the form of threshold strategies, where players will take costly action if and only if their costs are below the threshold. In this model, although the equilibrium threshold and hence the probability that any individual takes action decreases, the probability that at least one player takes action may either increase or decrease, depending on the elasticity of the distribution of costs.

We show examples in which the probability that someone takes action increases with group size and decreases with group size. In the limit, as group size approaches infinity, the Nash equilibrium probability that any individual acts approaches 0, while the probability that at least one player takes action approaches $1 - \ell/b$, where b is the benefit received by all if someone takes action, and ℓ is the lower bound of the support of the distribution of costs.

Achieving efficient outcomes in the Volunteer's Dilemma game requires a balance between two competing forces, the externality that arises when the action of one player can benefit all, and the wasted resources that arise when more than one player takes costly action. If full coordination were possible, in an efficient outcome, only the player with lowest cost would take action. But in many situations it would be time consuming and expensive to coordinate the actions of all players. Furthermore, a player's costs of acting are often private information, known only by the potential actor.

In this environment, we explore the nature of an "optimal ethical strategy." Suppose that players have common priors about the distribution of costs. Before their own costs are revealed to them, they consider alternative cost thresholds, where players are mandated to take action if and only if their costs are below this threshold. Under our assumptions, there is some threshold $\bar{c}$ that gives all players the highest expected payoff before they learn their type. The threshold strategy with threshold $\bar{c}$ is the optimal ethical strategy for this group of players.

For any group of players, the optimal ethical strategy prescribes a higher threshold than the Nash-equilibrium threshold value and hence leads to a higher probability of acting. If all players use the optimal ethical strategy, then as n gets large, the probability that any individual acts approaches 0, while the probability that at least one acts approaches 1.

This discussion of optimal ethical strategies takes a fully Kantian approach, in which the chosen threshold strategy is the one that would be best for all if all were to use the same strategy. An alternative approach, taken by Bergstrom (1995, 2002) and by Alger and Weibull (2013, 2017) is to consider partially Kantian rules that ask players to use the strategy that would be best for them if they believed that each of the other group members would, with some probability between 0 and 1, use the same strategy that they use. It would be interesting to explore the implications of such rules for Volunteer's Dilemma games in which costs of helping differ between individuals.

In the Volunteer's Dilemma model, a costly effort by a single player results in a benefit b for every group member, regardless of the size of the group. In many realistic scenarios of mutual aid, as the group gets larger, there are likely to be more group members in need, so the cost of helping the needy increases with group size. In such situations it is often the case that the efforts of more than one donor can be pooled. There remains interesting work to be done in studying the effects of group size on Nash equilibrium and on ethical rules.

1.A   Appendix: Proofs of Propositions

1.A.1   Proof of Proposition 1.1
Proof. In a mixed-strategy equilibrium, each player is indifferent between taking action and not doing so. Anyone who takes action is certain to have a net payoff of $b - c$. In equilibrium, all players must be indifferent between taking action and not taking action. Therefore,

regardless of the number of players, the expected utility of each player in a symmetric Nash equilibrium must be $b - c$.

In a mixed-strategy equilibrium for n players who each take action with independent probability p, a player who chooses the strategy "do not act" will not pay any cost and will enjoy the benefit b if at least one other player takes action. Let $q = 1 - p$. If all other players take action with probability p then the probability that at least one of the others takes action is $1 - q^{n-1}$. Therefore the expected payoff from the strategy "do not act" is $b(1 - q^{n-1})$.

Let us define $p_N(n) = 1 - q_N(n)$ and $q_N(n)$ to be the probabilities respectively that a player acts and does not act in a symmetric mixed-strategy Nash equilibrium. In this mixed-strategy equilibrium, it must be that the expected payoff is the same from taking action and not taking action. Therefore it must be that

$$b(1 - q_N(n)^{n-1}) = b - c. \tag{1.24}$$

Rearranging terms in equation 1.24, we see that in symmetric equilibrium each player takes action with probability $p_N(n) = 1 - q_N(n)$, where

$$q_N(n) = \left(\frac{c}{b}\right)^{\frac{1}{n-1}}. \tag{1.25}$$

Let us define $Q_N(n) = q_N(n)$ to be the symmetric Nash equilibrium probability that no player takes action and $P_N(n) = 1 - Q_N(n)$ the probability that at least one player takes action. Equation 1.25 implies that

$$P_N(n) = 1 - Q_N(n) = 1 - q_N(n)^n = 1 - \left(\frac{c}{b}\right)^{\frac{n}{n-1}}. \tag{1.26}$$

A simple calculation shows that the equilibrium probability $P_N(n)$ that someone takes action is a decreasing function of n, which asymptotically approaches $1 - c/b$. □

1.A.2 Proof of Proposition 1.2

Proof. Where the mandated strategy is of the form "take action with probability $1 - x$," the probability that at least one player takes action is $1 - x^n$, and the expected cost to each player of following this strategy is $c(1 - x)$. The expected utility of every player is

$$b(1 - x^n) - c(1 - x). \tag{1.27}$$

Taking the derivative of expression 1.27 and arranging terms, we see that expected utility is maximized at $x = x_n$, when

$$x_n = n^{\frac{-1}{n-1}}\left(\frac{c}{b}\right)^{\frac{1}{n-1}}. \tag{1.28}$$

From equation 1.28, it follows that $x_n^{n-1} = \frac{1}{n}\frac{c}{b}$, which is a decreasing function of n. This implies that for $n \geq 2$, x_n is also a decreasing function of n.

From equations 1.28 and 1.25, it follows that

$$x_n = n^{\frac{-1}{n-1}}q_n. \tag{1.29}$$

Since $n^{\frac{-1}{n-1}} < 1$ for all $n > 1$, it must be that $0 < x_n < q_n$ and hence that $1 > 1 - x_n > 1 - q_n$, which means that the probability that an individual takes action under the optimal symmetric rule is less than 1, but greater than the probability of taking action in Nash equilibrium.   □

1.A.3   Proof of Proposition 1.3

Proof.   Equation 1.28 implies that

$$\begin{aligned}
\lim_{n\to\infty}\ln x_n &= \lim_{n\to\infty}\left(\frac{-1}{n-1}\right)\ln n + \lim_{n\to\infty}\left(\frac{1}{n-1}\right)\frac{c}{b} \\
&= \lim_{n\to\infty}\left(\frac{-\ln n}{n-1}\right) \\
&= 0.
\end{aligned} \tag{1.30}$$

It also follows from equation 1.28 that

$$\begin{aligned}
\lim_{n\to\infty}\ln x_n^n &= \lim_{n\to\infty}\left(\frac{-n}{n-1}\right)\ln n + \lim_{n\to\infty}\left(\frac{n}{n-1}\right)\frac{c}{b} \\
&= \lim_{n\to\infty}\left(\frac{-n\ln n}{n-1}\right) + \frac{c}{b} \\
&= -\infty,
\end{aligned} \tag{1.31}$$

where the final equalities in equations 1.30 and 1.31 are direct consequences of L'Hôpital's rule. Since $\lim_{n\to\infty}\ln x_n = 0$, it must be that $\lim_{n\to\infty}x_n = 1$, and since $\lim_{n\to\infty}\ln x_n^n = -\infty$, it must be that $\lim_{n\to\infty}x_n^n = 0$. Therefore as $n \to \infty$, the limiting probability that any single individual acts is $1 - \lim_{n\to\infty}x_n = 0$, and the probability that at least one individual acts is $1 - \lim_{n\to\infty}x_n^n = 1$.   □

1.A.4 Proof of Proposition 1.4

Proof. Assumption 1.1 implies that $G(\cdot) = 1 - F(\cdot)$ is a decreasing function and that $G(\ell) = 1$ and $G(b) < 1$. Let $H(c, n) = bG(c)^{n-1} - c$. Then H is a continuous, strictly decreasing function with $H(\ell, n) = b - \ell > 0$ and $H(b, n) = bG(b)^{n-1} - b < 0$. Therefore for any $n > 1$, there is exactly one solution $\hat{c}(n) \in (\ell, b)$ such that $H(\hat{c}(n), n) = 0$.

To show that $\hat{c}(n)$ decreases with n, take logs of both sides of equation 1.6 and differentiate with respect to n. This yields the equation

$$\ln G(\hat{c}(n)) + (n-1)\frac{\hat{c}(n)G'(\hat{c}(n))}{G(\hat{c}(n))}\left(\frac{\hat{c}'(n)}{\hat{c}(n)}\right) = \frac{\hat{c}'(n)}{\hat{c}(n)}, \tag{1.32}$$

and hence

$$\frac{\hat{c}'(n)}{\hat{c}(n)} = \frac{\ln G(\hat{c}(n))}{1 - (n-1)\dfrac{G'(\hat{c}(n))}{G(\hat{c}(n))}}. \tag{1.33}$$

Since $0 \le G(\hat{c}(n)) \le 1$ and $G'(\hat{c}(n)) \le 0$, the numerator of equation 1.33 must be negative and the denominator must be positive. It follows that $\hat{c}'(n) < 0$ and hence $\hat{c}(\cdot)$ is a decreasing function of n.

The sequence $\hat{c}(n)$ is a bounded monotone sequence. Hence, by the monotone convergence theorem, this sequence converges to a limit $\hat{c} \ge \ell$. Suppose that $\hat{c} > \ell \ge 0$. Then $G(\hat{c}) < 1$ and therefore for N sufficiently large, $G(\hat{c})^{N-1} < \hat{c}$. Since $\hat{c}$ is a lower bound for the sequence of $c(n)$s, it must be that $\hat{c}(N) > \hat{c}$. Since $G(\cdot)$ is a decreasing function, it must be that $G(\hat{c}(N))^{N-1} < G(\hat{c})^{N-1} < \hat{c} < \hat{c}(N)$. But this contradicts the requirement that $G(\hat{c}(N))^{N-1} = \hat{C}(N)$. Therefore it cannot be that $\hat{c} > \ell$. It follows that $\hat{c} = \ell$. □

1.A.5 Proof of Proposition 1.7

Proof. With threshold set at c, the probability that any single player will not take action is $G(c)$, and the probability that at least one player will take action is $1 - G(c)^n$. Individuals will take costly action if and only if their costs lie below the threshold level c. Before individuals learn their own costs, the expected value of the costs that each will have to pay is

$$\int_0^c xF'(x)dx = -\int_0^c xG'(x)dx.$$

Thus, if there are n players and if the threshold is set at c, then, before individual costs are revealed, the expected utility of every player must be

$$b(1-G(c)^n) + \int_0^c xG'(x)dx. \tag{1.34}$$

The first-order necessary condition for $c = \bar{c}(n)$ to maximize expression 1.34 is

$$bnG(\bar{c}(n))^{n-1}G'(\bar{c}(n)) - \bar{c}(n)G'(\bar{c}(n)) = 0. \tag{1.35}$$

Let us define

$$H(c,n) = bnG(\bar{c}(n))^{n-1} - \bar{c}(n) = 0. \tag{1.36}$$

Since $G'(c) > 0$ for all $c \in (\ell, h)$, equation 1.35 is equivalent to

$$H(c,n) = 0. \tag{1.37}$$

Since, by assumption, $nb > \ell$ and $G(\ell) = 1$, it must be that $H(\ell, n) = nb - \ell > 0$. Since $G(h) = 0$, it must be that $H(h, n) = -h < 0$. Since $H(c, n)$ is a decreasing function of c, it follows that there is exactly one solution $\bar{c}(n)$ to the equation $H(c, n) = 0$. This solution $\bar{c}(n)$ is the unique symmetric optimal threshold.   □

1.A.6   Proof of Proposition 1.8

Proof. Notice that $\lim_{n\to\infty} \bar{c}(n) = \ell$ if and only if for every $\epsilon > 0$, there exists $N(\epsilon)$ such that if $n > N(\epsilon)$, then $|\bar{c}(n) - \ell| < \epsilon$ for all $n > N(\epsilon)$. To show that $\lim_{n\to\infty} \bar{c}(n) = \ell$, let $\epsilon > 0$ and $c \in (\ell, h)$ with $|c - \ell| \geq \epsilon$. Then $c \geq \ell + \epsilon$, and since G is strictly decreasing in c, it must be that $G(c) \leq G(\ell + \epsilon) < 1$. Since $G(c) < 1$, it must be that $\lim_{n\to\infty} bnG(c)^{n-1} = 0$. It follows that there exists $N(\epsilon)$ such that $bnG(c)^{n-1} < \epsilon \leq \ell + \epsilon$ for all $n > N(\epsilon)$. Therefore if $|c - \ell| > \epsilon$, $bnG(c)^{n-1} > c$. This implies $|c(n) - \ell| < \epsilon$ for all $n > N(\epsilon)$. Therefore $\lim_{n\to\infty} \bar{c}(n) = \ell$.

If all players use the optimal ethical strategy then with n players, the probability that no player takes action is $G(\bar{c}(n))^n$. Since, according to Equation (1.12), $bG(\bar{c}(n))^{n-1} = \dfrac{\bar{c}(n)}{n}$, it follows that

$$G(\bar{c}(n))^n = \frac{1}{b}\frac{\bar{c}(n)}{n}G(\bar{c}(n)), \tag{1.38}$$

and hence

$$\lim_{n\to\infty} G(\bar{c}(n))^n = \lim_{n\to\infty} \frac{1}{b} \frac{\bar{c}(n)G(\bar{c}(n))}{n}$$
$$= \frac{1}{b} \lim_{n\to\infty} \frac{\ell G(\ell)}{n} \tag{1.39}$$
$$= 0.$$

The limiting probability that at least one player takes action is then

$$1 - \lim_{n\to\infty} G(\bar{c}(n))^n = 1. \tag{1.40}$$

Notes

1. Herbert Gintis (2009) describes this quandry as "the mixing problem."

2. The assumption of incomplete information seems appropriate for games in which players are thrown together by chance for a single interaction. Situations where the same players are engaged in repeated encounters and know one another well might better be treated as games of complete information. Weesie (1993) characterizes asymmetric equilibria for Volunteer's Dilemma games with differing payoffs but complete information in which players know one another's payoffs.

References

Alger, Ingela, and Jörgen Weibull. 2013. "Homo moralis—Preference Evolution under Incomplete Information and Assortative Matching." *Econometrica* 81 (6): 2269–2302.

Alger, Ingela, and Jörgen Weibull. 2017. "Strategic Behavior of Moralists and Altruists." *Games* 8 (3): 38.

Bergstrom, Ted. 2017. "The Good Samaritan and Traffic on the Road to Jericho." *American Economic Journal: Microeconomics* 9 (2): 33–52.

Bergstrom, Ted, Rodney Garratt, and Damien Sheehan-Connor. 2009. "One Chance in a Million: Altruism and the Bone Marrow Registry." *American Economic Review* 99 (4): 1309–1334.

Bergstrom, Ted, and Greg Leo. 2012. "Coordinated Volunteer's Dilemma." Working paper, Department of Economics, University of California–Santa Barbara.

Bergstrom, Theodore C. 1995. "On the Evolution of Altruistic Ethical Rules for Siblings." *American Economic Review* 85 (1): 58–81.

Bergstrom, Theodore C. 2002. "Evolution of Social Behavior: Individual and Group Selection." *Journal of Economic Perspectives* 16 (2): 67–88.

Bilodeau, Marc, and Al Slivinski. 1996. "Toilet Cleaning and Department Chairing: Volunteering a Public Service." *Journal of Public Economics* 59 (2): 299–308.

Bliss, Christopher, and Barry Nalebuff. 1984. "Dragon Slaying and Ballroom Dancing: The Private Supply of a Public Good." *Journal of Public Economics* 25 (1/2):1–12.

Diekmann, Andreas. 1985. "Volunteer's Dilemma." *Journal of Conflict Resolution* 29 (4): 605–610.

Gintis, Herbert. 2009. *The Bounds of Reason: Game Theory and the Unification of the Behavioral Sciences*. Princeton, NJ: Princeton University Press.

Weesie, Jeroen. 1993. "Asymmetry and Timing in the Volunteer's Dilemma." *Journal of Conflict Resolution* 37 (3): 569–590.

Weesie, Jeroen, and Axel Franzen. 1998. "Cost Sharing in a Volunteer's Dilemma." *Journal of Conflict Resolution* 42 (5): 600–618.

2 The Bright and Dark Sides of Altruism

Avner Ben-Ner and Fangtingyu Hu

2.1 Introduction

Altruism is defined as "disinterested and selfless concern for the well-being of others" (*Oxford Dictionary*) or the willingness to give away resources to benefit others without expectation of a return (Fehr and Schmidt 2006). Altruism is the sentiment of individual A toward a target B that leads to helpful actions. Target B is an individual or a group; the strength of A's altruistic feelings varies across different targets. Altruism is commonly viewed as being on a one-dimensional scale that ranges from extreme selfishness to extreme altruism. In the context of the dictator game, the scale is bounded by giving nothing to giving away the entire endowment.

Scholars and members of the public in general have recognized the essential role of altruism in supporting cooperation and reducing free-riding in the workplace, promoting social welfare through voluntary transfers of income and volunteering, and contributing to market efficiency through voluntary blood and organ donation, among other things. This bright side of altruism has stimulated much public and private support for altruistic sentiments and acts through education, tax policy, and other measures.[1]

However, altruism also has a dark side, although negative aspects of altruism have received less scholarly and public attention. Altruistic actions, especially if sustained over time, may cause dependence and inhibit self-improvement and initiative among recipients of unconditional gifts. Altruistic feelings are often directed at one's own group, however the group is defined, to the exclusion and sometimes at the expense of others, possibly fomenting conflicts between groups in the workplace, in communities, and among countries, to the detriment of the well-being of some and at the expense of economic efficiency. In terms of the dictator game, the degree of altruism not only varies in how much individuals give to different targets, but also in some cases, if they can, they take away others' endowments (List 2007).

This chapter reviews arguments concerning both sides of altruism; since the bright side is more familiar, we emphasize possible negative outcomes of altruism. By recognizing that altruism is not always desirable, we challenge the common wisdom that altruism should be unconditionally advocated and supported. We assess the effects of altruism on social welfare relative to the goals of poverty alleviation, reduction of polarization among groups, social stability and integration, and economic efficiency.

The chapter is organized as follows. Section 2.2 presents an overview of the bright side of altruism in different contexts. Section 2.3 reviews arguments and evidence illustrating the dark side of altruism. Section 2.4 discusses the implications of the two sides of altruism for policies that encourage or discourage altruistic attitudes and behaviors. Section 2.5 concludes the chapter.

2.2   The Bright Side of Altruism

Caring about others is good—this is a statement of what appears to reflect a broad consensus in social and behavioral sciences, among educators, politicians, and the broad citizenry. This section summarizes the principal arguments that support this statement.

2.2.1   Altruism in the Workplace

Altruism has been linked positively to cooperation in the workplace and therefore to better economic outcomes. First, altruism toward coworkers leads to reduced free-riding in teams. The free-rider problem arises because of the discrepancy between the cost of effort (which is borne by each employee alone) and the results of that effort (which are shared by all members of the team); however, the gains made by other team members are not valued by selfish employees. In contrast, altruistic employees who care about their coworkers value the benefits that accrue to the latter (even if less than those that accrue to themselves). Therefore, altruistic employees are less likely to free-ride, because their effort may generate (if they are altruistic enough) sufficient benefits to exceed their personal costs. Second, unconditional altruism may trigger favorable reactions by those who benefit from it and subsequently reciprocate, which contributes to organizational productivity (Akerlof 1982). Third, helping others in an altruistic fashion—not part of one's job duties or observable and compensated activities—by sharing expertise and experience and helping with work-related problems has been found to promote organizational productivity (O'Reilly and Pfeffer 1995). This is especially important for jobs that require high levels of coordination and cooperation.[2]

2.2.2 Altruism in Families

Families are vehicles for social stability and investments that enhance economic efficiency. Parents take care of, give gifts to, and leave bequests to their children out of altruism. Children rely on such altruistic gifts of time and money to accumulate financial and human capital. Economists recognize the role of altruism in intergenerational mobility. Becker (1991) suggests that the more altruistic parents are, the more they invest in their children's human capital accumulation. The "rotten parent theorem" argues that parents invest in children's human capital to change their preferences and make them more altruistic, so that they will be more likely to support their elderly parents in need (Becker, Murphy, and Spenkuch 2016).

More generally, evolution leans toward favorable treatment not only of one's own children but also of kin who are substantially genetically related. This is referred to as inclusive or kin altruism (Hamilton 1964). Altruism, in this respect, is essential for the reproduction and sustainability of humans (and other species).

2.2.3 Altruism in the Public Sphere

Charitable giving and volunteering motivated by altruism have positive impacts on many aspects of social welfare: aid for the poor, college scholarships for students in need, donations to medical institutions, donations for research, donations to organizations that work for social justice, and blood and organ donations, to name just a few examples. Reliance on altruism promotes efficiency and provides a corrective for market failures that arise from severe asymmetric information in favor of providers over consumers (e.g., Thorne 2006). Titmuss (1970) has famously shown that altruistically donated blood is better than blood sold for profit, a finding that influences legislation prohibiting blood and organ sales.

2.2.4   Benefits That Accrue to Altruistic Givers

The obvious beneficiaries of altruism are its targets. Altruistic acts also generate benefits for givers. Post (2005) shows that altruistic emotions and behaviors are positively associated with well-being, health, and longevity, as long as people are not overwhelmed by helping tasks. In addition, individuals who are in a negative mood are more likely to help others (Cialdini and Kenrick 1976) as a way to ease tension and stress and to experience feelings of satisfaction and gratitude (Glomb et al. 2011).

In a series of observational and experimental studies, Dunn, Aknin, and Norton (2008) found that giving money to others enhances happiness more than keeping the money to oneself; this finding holds also for young children (Aknin, Hamlin, and Dunn 2012). Research suggests that volunteers who donate their time, like those who give money, benefit in various psychological, physical health and social domains (Van Willigen 2000; Piliavin and Siegl 2007; Morrow-Howell 2010; Tang, Choi, and Morrow-Howell 2010). Andreoni (1990, 1995) suggests that the utility received by the giver from the act of giving—the "warm glow"—may in fact motivate donations more than the benefits that accrue to recipients. He thus contrasts impure with pure altruism.

2.3   The Dark Side of Altruism

The bright side of altruism is that it is good for recipients and givers. However, altruistic sentiments and acts can also have deleterious effects on both givers and recipients; in addition, they can generate negative externalities for others and the broader society. Frequently, the same altruistic act may have dual effects, positive for one group and negative for another, or even positive and negative for the same group.

2.3.1   Self-Serving Altruism and Oversupply of Donations

Giving may be motivated by the desire to help others or to satisfy the giver's needs. The motivation does not, in and of itself, make altruism good or bad, although as we argue below, in some instances self-serving altruism has a dark side.

Pure altruism, which leads to acts that are done only for the benefit of others, may be compared to impure or self-serving altruism, motivated by the enjoyment of acting good. This is the "warm glow" egoistic motivation for giving noted earlier (Andreoni 1990, 1995).

Self-serving altruism may also be motivated by donors' desire to gain social approval for their giving and improve their social status (Harbaugh 1998). Furthermore, as noted in section 2.2.4, people may act altruistically to relieve their own negative emotions.

From a libertarian perspective, no judgment can be passed on impure altruism, which may be regarded as a form of consumption. However, from a broader perspective that permits the passing of judgment on how people satisfy their social and psychological needs when the welfare of others is involved, impure altruism may result in the oversupply of donations. It also may result in socially inefficient allocation of donations due to insufficient consideration of the satisfaction of the recipients' needs from different sources. While giving to deserving causes seems to be always desirable, this is not so from a social welfare standpoint when the opportunity cost of giving to one deserving recipient implies giving less to another. If impure altruists tend to give more to some categories of deserving recipients, such as more visible ones—donations to whom may earn more social standing for the donors—then this shift of charitable resources is socially inefficient.

Altruism can go hand in hand with wrongdoing if it serves as a moral justification for unethical behaviors. Moral licensing theory (Miller and Effron 2010) offers two theoretical mechanisms that explain how engaging in altruistic acts can license people to subsequently engage in unethical acts, one operating through "moral credits" and the other through "moral credentials." According to this theory, moral credits are earned for doing good and may be used to purchase or license the right to behave unethically, and moral credentials enable individuals (in their own eyes) to construe questionable acts in favorable ways.

There is experimental evidence that is consistent with moral license theory. For instance, individuals who are given the opportunity to benefit another participant in addition to themselves cheat more than when they could not benefit others; people also feel less guilty about cheating when others benefit from their dishonesty (Wiltermuth 2011; Gino and Ariely 2012; Gino, Ayal, and Ariely 2013). Erat and Gneezy (2012) demonstrate in an experiment that although people are reluctant to tell lies that benefit both parties, they are willing to tell altruistic lies that help others but may hurt themselves. This can partially be attributed to the warm glow of altruism that conceals lying as a morally challenging behavior. Likewise, Gino and Pierce (2009) show in an experiment that wealth-based inequality can trigger dishonest helping via feelings of guilt and empathy. In other words, altruistic helping can alleviate the emotion of guilt. At the same time, helping behaviors obscure the moral content of dishonesty.

2.3.2 Giving May Limit Recipients' Social Preferences and Reduce Incentives to Work

Altruistic charitable giving may displace recipients' incentives to work, invest in their human capital, and insure themselves (Coate 1995). The risk is that recipients of such charitable giving, if the giving persists in the long run, will develop habits and attitudes that are not desirable for the individuals who possess them and for society at large.

Parental altruism, when exercised excessively because of parental insufficient self-control, may affect adversely children's well-being, similar to the idea of the Samaritan's dilemma (Buchanan 1975). When children begin to take parents' contributions for granted and do not hesitate to ask for more, they may become spoiled in the sense that they will tend to free-ride, shirk, and fail to value the importance of reciprocity, mutual respect, and gratification (Buchanan 1975; Lubatkin et al. 2005). Similar logic applies to giving to kin. For example, Di Falco and Bulte (2013) show that compulsory kinship sharing undermines people's incentive to adopt risk-mitigating farm management practices and encourages free-riding. Di Falco and Bulte (2011, 2015) show that kinship sharing norms may attenuate the incentive to accumulate income as well as to invest in human capital among poor households in South Africa, which may result in increased poverty.

Becker's rotten kid theorem (Becker 1991) suggests that with benevolent and altruistic parents, selfish children will behave in a family-efficient way that maximizes their own utility by maximizing family total income. However, relaxing the unrealistic assumptions of this theorem, such as the ignorance of leisure and omission of time, other scholars found that parental altruism may result in undesirable outcomes. For instance, Bergstrom (1989) suggests the case of the "lazy rotten kid"—children choose too much leisure and take advantage of parental transfers. Lindbeck and Weibull (1988) show that parental altruism can lead to inefficient choices by children between current and future consumption (early overconsumption and later underconsumption). Similarly, Bruce and Waldman (1990) investigate the two-period rotten kid theorem and show that if parents choose to transfer a large amount in the first period and make the second period transfer inoperative, the child will choose to maximize his own income instead of the family total income ("rotten kid inefficiency"); if parents only transfer a small amount in the first period, the child will realize that the second period transfer is operative and will choose to overconsume and undersave ("Samaritan dilemma"). Parental altruism leads to inefficiency in both cases.

In sum, "excessive" giving may induce a change in recipients' social preferences such that they will be less cooperative (more "spoiled") and less hard-working.[3]

2.3.3 Counterproductive Altruism in the Workplace

We argued earlier that altruistic behavior improves cooperation in the workplace. But altruism, in association with limited self-control, may manifest itself in being forgiving—too forgiving—of coworkers who shirk. Bernheim and Stark (1988) argue that altruists have difficulty enforcing agreements, because they may be reluctant to punish betrayals, and thus can be treated as "softies" whose actions are not intimidating enough to enforce agreements. Altruism thus encompasses exploitability that causes loss of efficiency and leaves both parties worse off.

Experimental evidence from a public goods game suggests that altruistic subjects are significantly less likely to punish low contributors than are other subjects (Carpenter et al. 2009). Building on this finding, Hwang and Bowles (2012) develop a theoretical argument that altruism attenuates the punishment motive and thus reduces efficient punishment of free riders and defectors, which eventually results in the discouragement of cooperation. In a similar vein, desirable mutual monitoring by members of a team may be limited by altruistic sentiments (Ben-Ner and Ellman 2013).

Altruism is hardly ever universalistic in the sense that an individual is equally generous to all others in general or even in a particular context. For example, manager altruism directed at a particular worker could endanger the fairness of performance evaluation and have negative effects on the performance of other workers (Podsakoff et al. 2000). Prendergast and Topel (1996) note that favoritism can lead to inefficiencies in various dimensions. First, organizations suffer from higher turnover costs and loss of specific human capital when employees quit due to unfair evaluation. Second, workers may engage in harmful activities, such as reduced work effort and increased ingratiating behaviors. Third, unfair evaluation can cause misallocation of workers to jobs. Similarly, worker altruism directed at a supervisor may result in counterproductive work behavior by other workers (Rotemberg 2006).

2.3.4 Particularistic, Parochial, and Discriminatory Altruism

Altruism is commonly analyzed as a general sentiment or disposition focused on "others," without specifying the others' identity or relationship to the individual altruist. This is a faulty conception of altruism. In general, it does not make sense to characterize an individual as a certain degree altruist on the selfish–altruist scale. The same individual may be simultaneously very altruistic toward target $B1$, much less so toward target $B2$, and a negative altruist toward $B3$ (wanting to take resources away).

In biological terms, altruism arises from genes' drive to reproduce; genes without it go extinct. Genes act through the individuals who carry them. Human behavior is guided by strategies, "traits," or behavior rules that overall promote the successful reproduction of genes. Individuals therefore possesses a selfishness trait, which implies that they will seek resources to survive and reproduce their genes through their offspring as well as through more distant kin. Thus, their selfish motives drive individuals to be altruistic toward those that help them reproduce their genes. Such kin altruism is a manifestation of "selfishness" of the genes (Dawkins 2016 [1974]), and it may be viewed as a strategy for global maximization of reproductive capability of an individual, given his or her resources. Thus one can reproduce one's genes by having children and by helping individuals with similar genes to raise their own children and to have their own children, and so on. Genetic relatedness declines from immediate family to extended family, followed by people who are increasingly more distant relations. Hence biologically driven altruism is inherently discriminatory in favor of offspring and other kin (for an evolutionary model of the emergence of behavioral traits, see Alger and Weibull 2012).

The degree of altruism depends not only on genetic relatedness but also on the resources that an individual possesses and the resources of his or her kin. When immediate family members have sufficient resources, generosity is extended to more distant relations and members of one's ethnic, linguistic, or other groups that may be genetically related to the individual. When people lived in small groups in ancestral environments, they were all related kin. As societies grew, natural distinctions between kin and non-kin became blurred, but the drive to distinguish between them for purposes of reproduction did not vanish. Individuals search for signals of relatedness: language, features, skin color, religion, culture, customs, and clothes, depending on historical and geographic contexts. Wealthier individuals with well-off immediate relations will maximize their genes' reproductive capacity by donating to more distant relations whose reproductive capacity can be enhanced by additional resources; in modern impersonal societies, such relations are identified by signals, such as those just mentioned. This calculus reflects maximization of reproductive capacity by equalizing the marginal returns from different investment opportunities (donations to targets who are related to the donor in varying degrees). This altruism may be termed particularistic or parochial altruism, which inclines the individual to favor some groups but not others.

What about individuals who do not contribute to the reproductive success of an individual's genes? These may be people who are essentially genetically unrelated and those who compete with the individual for resources. These competitors are not targets of positive altruism but instead are opposed. Biological altruistic favoritism is therefore ethnic, religious, cultural, and other favoritism and discrimination. Favoritism and discrimination are not restricted to degrees of positive altruism (giving different amounts of resources) but extend to negative altruism (taking away resources). This is the summary of the complementarity between selfishness and altruism, and between altruism and hatred directed at the "other" (for detailed analyses, see Shaw and Wong 1989, and Choi and Bowles 2007).

Altruism is therefore not universal but particularistic and parochial. Such altruism has been essential for the sustainability of living species, including the human species. But what had been essential in the ancestral environment of humankind has become excessive and damaging in the contemporary environment. The contemporary environment is far more complex, with individuals of very different backgrounds inhabiting common spaces. Members of different groups have to work together, share resources, and engage in common activities. Particularistic and discriminatory altruism manifests itself in favoritism toward related individuals and groups and discrimination against (or even hatred of) other individuals and groups, particularly those laying claim to the same resources.[4]

Horstmann, Scharf, and Slivinski (2007) suggest that charitable giving for public goods leads to voluntary segregation among individuals who differ only with respect to their preferences for public goods. Subsidies for charitable giving, such as tax benefits, exacerbate segregation. This result is obtained without explicit favoritism or discrimination; segregation is a consequence of different tastes for public goods (such as cultural activities, parks, and schools), which become lines of differentiation.

We have argued in this section that these different tastes, which define the boundaries among various groups of nearly homogenous individuals, arise from evolutionary forces that lead individuals to be altruistic toward those who are similar to them (e.g., by giving voluntarily to public goods that benefit their community) but not to those who are dissimilar.

Behaviors based on parochial altruism have obvious negative effects on those who are discriminated against. But most situations that involve discrimination also entail a loss of general social welfare and economic efficiency. Put differently, in some situations, the net effect of altruism on key outcomes is negative. In-group oriented altruism could lead to unfavorable outcomes: it negatively affects intergroup relations and exacerbates the tension among different groups, hinders cooperation in teams and organizations, enhances social segregation and polarization, and reduces cooperation and trust among people belonging to different groups (Ben-Ner 2016). Generally, the social and economic consequences of this behavior are negative—lowering economic output, bearing costs to protect resources from others and to abscond with others' resources, and so on. It is well to remember Edward Banfield's (1967) conclusions concerning excessive family-focused altruism, which leads to unwillingness to work cooperatively with members of other families to provide public goods and effective business organizations, resulting in "amoral familism." Banfield concluded that this leads to isolation, poverty, and social backwardness. Amoral familism is essentially parochial altruism, and Montegano, the fictional name of the place in Italy where he conducted his study, could be any place, in any country.[5]

2.4   Balancing the Bright and Dark Sides of Altruism: Policy Implications

The bifurcated consequences of altruism arise from the fact that it is not directed in equal measure toward all individuals and groups. The biologically driven altruism toward other people based on genetic relatedness has been both accentuated and moderated by culture and circumstances, so that in contemporary society, altruism has distinctly bright and dark sides.

For example, individuals may behave altruistically toward members of their in-group, which improves cooperation and productivity in the workplace and community. The same individuals may cooperate less effectively or even conflict with out-group members; this contributes to the emergence of factions, segregation, and a fractious workplace and community that operates less effectively. For another example, altruism toward one's children is clearly privately and socially beneficial, but excessive altruism may inculcate undesirable social preferences and attitudes to work that, if widespread, can stifle economic performance.

At the society level, particularistic altruism that supports beneficial pluralism and diversity under certain socioeconomic and political conditions, may, under different conditions, turn into undesirable discriminatory altruism that feeds factionalism, sectarianism, and polarization. For example, in the United States during the eighteenth and nineteenth centuries, particularistic or parochial in-group oriented altruism helped the emergence of useful institutions (as Alexis de Tocqueville famously argued). But in the early part of the twenty-first century, more universalistic altruism is needed to deal with issues that are central to society and require policy responses that are difficult to craft and carry out in a splintered or polarized society.[6]

Recognition of the two sides of altruism suggests that indiscriminate encouragement of altruistic behavior should be attenuated by concerns for the harm it can cause. Public policies that subsidize charitable giving of any kind, such as income tax exemption, may be undesirable at the present time, in line with the argument in the previous paragraph.[7] Tax and other policies should favor universalistic giving, which addresses neediness in general, without regard to affiliations to religious, ethnic, or other divisive identity groups. In a similar vein, to reduce the negative effects of excessive altruistic giving in families, progressive inheritance taxes should be considered, along with exemptions of taxes on bequests to universalistic causes.

More broadly, discriminatory, parochial, or particularistic altruism, along with pure selfishness, may be tempered through education, public discourse, and other institutions that emphasize the social, economic, and political benefits arising from universalistic altruism. In fractious and polarized societies, this argument has to be made not only by educators, politicians, and clergies (some of whom have contributed to the existing polarization) but also by scholars who are informed by research findings.

The literature in behavioral economics has tended to emphasize the benefits of altruism when countering the narrow view of classical economics focused on the self-interest of *Homo economicus*. The research findings concerning the dark side of altruism should be considered carefully to temper the assessment of altruism and to inform better public policies in contemporary society.

2.5 Conclusion

In this chapter, we have reviewed both the bright and dark sides of altruism. Altruism can be beneficial to organizations, families, and societies. Altruistic acts in the workplace encourage cooperation among coworkers and reduce free-riding, thus contributing to organizational effectiveness. Altruism can effectively promote social welfare, enhance market efficiency, and enforce social bonds in society. Altruistic givers acquire physical and mental health benefits. The literature in various disciplines, including behavioral economics, has tended to emphasize the bright side of altruism in contrast to pure selfishness.

However, the dark side of altruism should not be ignored. Altruistic behaviors can lead to negative economic, political, and social consequences. Altruism may act as a counterproductive force that inhibits self-improvement, creates conflicts, and obscures moral boundaries. Crucially for contemporary societies, discriminatory altruism has negative effects on those who are discriminated against and can increase social segregation and polarization, reduce trust and cooperation, and exacerbate intergroup conflicts.

Recognizing the dark side of altruism has implications for public policy. It adds a layer of complexity when evaluating policies that seek to promote altruistic acts, such as charitable donations. Should we continue tax exemption benefits for donations? Should we encourage an inheritance tax on bequests to children? Should we educate for selfishness or for altruism that is directed toward national, ethnic, religious, political, and other groups? When considering those policy questions, both the bright and the dark sides of altruism should be carefully taken into account to arrive at a comprehensive decision.

Future research should help us understand better the relationship between the two sides of altruism in individuals. There are important questions that have not been answered yet. For example, is a more altruistic attitude toward one's own kin, ethnic, or religious group associated with a diminished or negative altruistic attitude toward out-group members? Do altruistic preferences change in response to such variables as education, financial incentives, and other private or public interventions? Do particularistic and universalistic altruism respond similarly to such interventions?

Notes

Thanks to two referees for excellent comments.

1. Few have argued directly against altruism. Ayn Rand, a novelist and philosopher, has argued in favor of unbridled selfishness and against altruism (Rand 1964). Her work appears to have had only minor influence on economists (Hausman and McPherson 1993).

2. For example, at Southwest Airlines, employees are recruited carefully for what we term "altruistic inclinations" to help out one another routinely.

3. The term "excessive" is in quotation marks to indicate that it is defined relative to the consequences of giving: giving that has the effect of changing recipients' preferences as indicated in the text is excessive. As evidence of preference change, Becker, Murphy, and Spenkuch (2016) present a theoretical argument that parents invest in children to manipulate children's altruism toward parents. Ben-Ner, List, Putterman, and Samek (2017) find little experimental evidence that parents influence their children's generosity. Gaudeul and Kaczmarek (2017) present experimental evidence that nudges induce donations to charity, which eventually lead to attitude change (better attitude toward charity) based on cognitive dissonance theory (Festinger 1962). We make a similar argument; namely, that excessive giving makes children behave as "rotten kids," which may further induce attitude and preference changes, because people are prone to self-justify their attitudes to align with their behaviors in order to avoid cognitive dissonance. For a detailed discussion of changes in preferences and their impact in the workplace, see Ben-Ner and Ellman (2012).

4. Favoritism and discrimination are exercised on many attributes, some of which were noted above, and in many domains. In an experiment, Ben-Ner et al. (2009) found that individuals favor their in-group members over out-group members based on such characteristics as family and kin, political views, sports fanship, nationality, religion, dress preferences, body type, and culinary preferences. This preference is manifested when giving money in the dictator game, sharing an office, working on a team, and commuting. In the United States, the bulk of individual charitable giving is directed toward groups with which donors are affiliated: religious, social, or cultural (Ben-Ner 2016).

5. Competition among groups and cooperation in groups may have positive net economic benefits, but the literature on diversity in communities and countries tends to suggest otherwise (e.g., Alesina and La Ferrara 2005).

6. These issues include, for example, climate change, gay marriage, the threat of terrorism, income inequality, national budgets and debt, the role of religion in the public sphere, abortion rights, and immigration.

7. Horstmann, Scharf, and Slivinski (2007) suggest that elimination of such subsidies as tax exemption of charitable donations would be a Pareto-improving policy measure to reduce ethnic, political, and other forms of preferences-based segregation.

References

Akerlof, George A. 1982. "Labor Contracts as Partial Gift Exchange." *Quarterly Journal of Economics* 97 (4): 543–569.

Aknin, Lara B., J. Kiley Hamlin, and Elizabeth W. Dunn. 2012. "Giving Leads to Happiness in Young Children." *PLoS One* 7 (6): e39211.

Alesina, Alberto, and Eliana La Ferrara. 2005. "Ethnic Diversity and Economic Performance." *Journal of Economic Literature* 43 (3): 762–800.

Alger, Ingela, and Jörgen W. Weibull. 2012. "A Generalization of Hamilton's Rule—Love Others How Much?" *Journal of Theoretical Biology* 299: 42–54.

Andreoni, James. 1990. "Impure Altruism and Donations to Public Goods: A Theory of Warm-Glow Giving." *Economic Journal* 100 (401): 464–477.

Andreoni, James. 1995. "Warm-Glow Versus Cold-Prickle: The Effects of Positive and Negative Framing on Cooperation in Experiments." *Quarterly Journal of Economics* 110 (1): 1–21.

Banfield, Edward C. 1967. *The Moral Basis of a Backward Society*. New York: Free Press.

Becker, Gary S. 1991. *A Treatise on the Family*. Cambridge, MA: Harvard University Press.

Becker, Gary S., Kevin M. Murphy, and Jörg L. Spenkuch. 2016. "The Manipulation of Children's Preferences, Old-Age Support, and Investment in Children's Human Capital." *Journal of Labor Economics* 34 (S2): S3–S30.

Ben-Ner, Avner. 2016. "Is Altruism (Always) Good for Society? The Problem of Particularistic Giving in a Diverse Society." Working paper, Carlson School of Management, University of Minnesota, Minneapolis.

Ben-Ner, Avner, and Matthew Ellman. 2012. "The Effects of Organization Design on Employee Preferences." In *Towards a New Theory of the Firm: Humanizing the Firm and the Management Profession*, edited by Joan Enric Ricart Costa and Josep Maria Rosanas Marti, 401–420. Bilbao, Spain: Fundacion BBVA.

Ben-Ner, Avner, and Matthew Ellman. 2013. "The Contributions of Behavioural Economics to Understanding and Advancing the Sustainability of Worker Cooperatives." *Journal of Entrepreneurial and Organisational Diversity* 2 (1): 75–100.

Ben-Ner, Avner, John A. List, Louis Putterman, and Anya Samek. 2017. "Learned Generosity? An Artefactual Field Experiment with Parents and Their Children." *Journal of Economic Behavior & Organization* 143: 28–44.

Ben-Ner, Avner, Brian P. McCall, Massoud Stephane, and Hua Wang. 2009. "Identity and In-Group/Out-Group Differentiation in Work and Giving Behaviors: Experimental Evidence." *Journal of Economic Behavior & Organization* 72 (1): 153–170.

Bergstrom, Theodore C. 1989. "A Fresh Look at the Rotten Kid Theorem—And Other Household Mysteries." *Journal of Political Economy* 97 (5): 1138–1159.

Bernheim, B. Douglas, and Oded Stark. 1988. "Altruism within the Family Reconsidered: Do Nice Guys Finish Last?" *American Economic Review* 78 (5): 1034–1045.

Bruce, Neil, and Michael Waldman. 1990. "The Rotten-Kid Theorem Meets the Samaritan's Dilemma." *Quarterly Journal of Economics* 105 (1): 155–165.

Buchanan, James M. 1975. "The Samaritan's Dilemma." In *Altruism, Morality, and Economic Theory*, edited by E. S. Phelps, 71–86. New York: Russell Sage Foundation.

Carpenter, Jeffrey, Samuel Bowles, Herbert Gintis, and Sung-Ha Hwang. 2009. "Strong Reciprocity and Team Production: Theory and Evidence." *Journal of Economic Behavior & Organization* 71 (2): 221–232.

Choi, Jung-Kyoo, and Samuel Bowles. 2007. "The Coevolution of Parochial Altruism and War." *Science* 318 (5850): 636–640.

Cialdini, Robert B., and Douglas T. Kenrick. 1976. "Altruism as Hedonism: A Social Development Perspective on the Relationship of Negative Mood State and Helping." *Journal of Personality and Social Psychology* 34 (5): 907.

Coate, Stephen. 1995. "Altruism, the Samaritan's Dilemma, and Government Transfer Policy." *American Economic Review* 85 (1): 46–57.

Dawkins, Richard. 2016 [1974]. *The Selfish Gene*. Oxford: Oxford University Press.

Di Falco, Salvatore, and Erwin Bulte. 2011. "A Dark Side of Social Capital? Kinship, Consumption, and Savings." *Journal of Development Studies* 47 (8): 1128–1151.

Di Falco, Salvatore, and Erwin Bulte. 2013. "The Impact of Kinship Networks on the Adoption of Risk-Mitigating Strategies in Ethiopia." *World Development* 43: 100–110.

Di Falco, Salvatore, and Erwin Bulte. 2015. "Does Social Capital Affect Investment in Human Capital? Family Ties and Schooling Decisions." *Applied Economics* 47 (2): 195–205.

Dunn, Elizabeth W., Lara B. Aknin, and Michael I. Norton. 2008. "Spending Money on Others Promotes Happiness." *Science* 319 (5870): 1687–1688.

Erat, Sanjiv, and Uri Gneezy. 2012. "White Lies." *Management Science* 58 (4): 723–733.

Fehr, Ernst, and Klaus M. Schmidt. 2006. "The Economics of Fairness, Reciprocity and Altruism—Experimental Evidence and New Theories." *Handbook of the Economics of Giving, Altruism and Reciprocity* 1: 615–691.

Festinger, Leon. 1962. *A Theory of Cognitive Dissonance*, vol. 2. Stanford, CA: Stanford University Press.

Gaudeul, Alexia, and Magdalena Claudia Kaczmarek. 2017. "Does Nudging Intentions Translate into Action? Why Nudging Pledges to Charities Does Not Result in Increased Donations." Discussion Paper 318, Center for European Governance and Economic Development Research, Georg-August Universitat Gottingen.

Gino, Francesca, and Dan Ariely. 2012. "The Dark Side of Creativity: Original Thinkers Can Be More Dishonest." *Journal of Personality and Social Psychology* 102 (3): 445.

Gino, Francesca, Shahar Ayal, and Dan Ariely. 2013. "Self-Serving Altruism? The Lure of Unethical Actions That Benefit Others." *Journal of Economic Behavior & Organization* 93: 285–292.

Gino, Francesca, and Lamar Pierce. 2009. "Dishonesty in the Name of Equity." *Psychological Science* 20 (9): 1153–1160.

Glomb, Theresa M., Devasheesh P. Bhave, Andrew G. Miner, and Melanie Wall. 2011. "Doing Good, Feeling Good: Examining the Role of Organizational Citizenship Behaviors in Changing Mood." *Personnel Psychology* 64 (1): 191–223.

Hamilton, William D. 1964. "The Genetical Evolution of Social Behaviour. II." *Journal of Theoretical Biology* 7 (1): 17–52.

Harbaugh, William T. 1998. "What Do Donations Buy? A Model of Philanthropy Based on Prestige and Warm Glow." *Journal of Public Economics* 67 (2): 269–284.

Hausman, Daniel M., and Michael S. McPherson. 1993. "Taking Ethics Seriously: Economics and Contemporary Moral Philosophy." *Journal of Economic Literature* 31 (2): 671–731.

Horstmann, Ignatius J., Kimberley Scharf, and Al Slivinski. 2007. "Can Private Giving Promote Economic Segregation?" *Journal of Public Economics* 91 (5): 1095–1118.

Hwang, Sung-Ha, and Samuel Bowles. 2012. "Is Altruism Bad for Cooperation?" *Journal of Economic Behavior & Organization* 83 (3): 330–341.

Lindbeck, Assar, and Jörgen W. Weibull. 1988. "Altruism and Time Consistency: The Economics of Fait Accompli." *Journal of Political Economy* 96 (6): 1165–1182.

List, John A. 2007. "On the Interpretation of Giving in Dictator Games." *Journal of Political Economy* 115 (3): 482–493.

Lubatkin, Michael H., William S. Schulze, Yan Ling, and Richard N. Dino. 2005. "The Effects of Parental Altruism on the Governance of Family-Managed Firms." *Journal of Organizational Behavior* 26 (3): 313–330.

Miller, Dale T., and Daniel A. Effron. 2010. "Chapter Three—Psychological License: When It Is Needed and How It Functions." *Advances in Experimental Social Psychology* 43 (43): 115–155.

Morrow-Howell, Nancy. 2010. "Volunteering in Later Life: Research Frontiers." *Journals of Gerontology Series B: Psychological Sciences and Social Sciences* 65 (4): 461–469.

O'Reilly, Charles A., and Jeffrey Pfeffer. 1995. "Southwest Airlines: Using Human Resources for Competitive Advantage." Working paper, Graduate School of Business, Stanford University, Stanford, CA.

Piliavin, Jane Allyn, and Erica Siegl. 2007. "Health Benefits of Volunteering in the Wisconsin Longitudinal Study." *Journal of Health and Social Behavior* 48 (4): 450–464.

Podsakoff, Philip M., Scott B. MacKenzie, Julie Beth Paine, and Daniel G. Bachrach. 2000. "Organizational Citizenship Behaviors: A Critical Review of the Theoretical and Empirical Literature and Suggestions for Future Research." *Journal of Management* 26 (3): 513–563.

Post, Stephen G. 2005. "Altruism, Happiness, and Health: It's Good To Be Good." *International Journal of Behavioral Medicine* 12 (2): 66–77.

Prendergast, Canice, and Robert H. Topel. 1996. "Favoritism in Organizations." *Journal of Political Economy* 104 (5): 958–978.

Rand, Ayn. 1964. *The Virtue of Selfishness*. New York: Penguin.

Rotemberg, Julio J. 2006. "Altruism, Reciprocity and Cooperation in the Workplace." *Handbook of the Economics of Giving, Altruism and Reciprocity* 2: 1371–1407.

Shaw, R. Paul, and Yuwa Wong. 1989. *Genetic Seeds of Warfare: Evolution, Nationalism, and Patriotism*. Cambridge, MA: Routledge.

Tang, Fengyan, EunHee Choi, and Nancy Morrow-Howell. 2010. "Organizational Support and Volunteering Benefits for Older Adults." *Gerontologist* 50 (5): 603–612.

Thorne, Emanuel D. 2006. "The Economics of Organ Transplantation." *Handbook of the Economics of Giving, Altruism and Reciprocity* 2: 1335–1370.

Titmuss, Richard M. 1970. "The Gift Relationship." *London* 19: 70.

Van Willigen, Marieke. 2000. "Differential Benefits of Volunteering across the Life Course." *Journals of Gerontology Series B: Psychological Sciences and Social Sciences* 55 (5): S308–S318.

Wiltermuth, Scott S. 2011. "Cheating More When the Spoils Are Split." *Organizational Behavior and Human Decision Processes* 115 (2): 157–168.

3 Who Gives? The Roles of Empathy and Impulsiveness

James Andreoni, Ann-Kathrin Koessler, and Marta Serra-Garcia

3.1 Introduction

Over 390 billion US dollars, or about 2 percent of gross domestic product, are donated to charity in the United States every year (Giving USA 2017). A large body of literature has emerged examining what motivates people to give, ranging from reduced form models of warm-glow giving (Andreoni 1989) to detailed models of giving to manipulate social and self-image (Bénabou and Tirole 2006; Andreoni and Bernheim 2009; Ariely, Bracha, and Meier 2009).[1]

Recently, researchers have been examining the roles of two specific individual characteristics in determining the act of giving: empathy and impulsiveness. The large body of literature on empathic concerns argues that the ability of humans and a few other primates to feel what others feel is a fundamental link in the chain that leads to an altruistic act (see, e.g., Batson 1987; Batson 2011; and de Waal 2012, or research on the empathy-altruism hypothesis in nonhuman and human primates. For an application to economics, see Andreoni, Rao, and Trachtman 2017). However, empathy can require some attention to putting oneself in someone else's shoes (Andreoni and Rao 2011).

A second body of literature argues that giving is instead impulsive and nearly automatic, and that thoughtfulness could impede giving. This hypothesis has been strongly advocated by Rand and colleagues (Rand et al. 2012; Cone and Rand 2014; Rand and Kraft-Todd 2014; and in the meta-study Rand 2016). Some other researchers, however, do not find a significant relationship between giving and manipulations of cognitive load or time pressure (e.g., Tinghög et al. 2013; Verkoeijen and Bouwmeester 2014). Others have found the opposite result, that is, individuals who act more impulsively behave in more self-oriented ways (Curry, Price, and Price 2008; Piovesan and Wengström 2009; Fehr and Leibbrandt 2011; Martinsson, Myrseth, and Wollbrant 2012).[2] One evident difference between the mentioned studies is that Rand and colleagues examine the causal effect of impulsivity by manipulating external conditions, by, for example, limiting response time in hopes of triggering the use of intuitive responses instead of reasoning. The other studies, on the contrary, investigate correlations based on individual differences in disposition or endogenous reaction time. This may (partly) explain the differing results.[3] However, most studies focus on cooperation and not giving, and recipients are fellow students, expected to be financially well off.

In this chapter, we explore the impact of empathy and impulsiveness in a real donation study. We ask: Who gives? Is it those who are more empathic or those who are more impulsive, or both? In a real donation experiment, we elicit donation decisions and collect previously validated measures of empathic concern (Davis 1983) and impulsiveness (Barratt 1959; Frederick 2005). To the best of our knowledge, our study is the first to test the relationship between these psychological measures of empathy and impulsiveness and charitable giving.

We find that empathic individuals are significantly more likely to donate. A standard deviation increase in empathic concern increases the likelihood of a donation by eight percentage points. Hence, we can confirm the importance of empathy as a pillar of prosociality. But in contrast to Rand and coauthors, we find that impulsiveness is negatively related to giving. A one standard deviation increase in trait-impulsiveness (Barratt 1959) decreases the likelihood of a donation by eight percentage points. Interestingly, the negative relationship between impulsiveness and giving becomes stronger when financial resources are scarcer. Under such conditions more impulsive individuals are even less likely to donate.

3.2   Experimental Design

We designed a laboratory experiment in which actual donation decisions were elicited. The experiment took place over two days, one week apart. On the first day, the work of a charity, GiveDirectly, was described to the participants in the experiment in a carefully scripted five-minute presentation. They were then asked to donate $5 of their experimental payments to GiveDirectly. A week later, subjects returned to the lab and completed a follow-up survey, which elicited individuals' level of impulsiveness and empathy.

3.2.1 Measuring Empathy and Impulsiveness

The methodology used to elicit empathy and impulsiveness was based on widely used measurement scales of empathy and impulsiveness in the psychology literature. To measure the degree of empathy among the individuals in the experiment we used the Interpersonal Reactivity Index (IRI; Davis 1983). The IRI is a multidimensional tool used to assess individual differences in empathy. With help of 28 self-reported items, cognitive and emotional facets of empathy are assessed.[4] The index comprises four dimension of empathy in the following subscales: Fantasy, Perspective-Taking, Empathic Concern, and Personal Distress.[5] As our study is on prosocial behavior, we concentrate on the Empathic Concern subscale, which measures the emotional aspects of empathy, such as sympathy and concern for others.

To identify the degree of an individual's impulsiveness, we employ two measures, a measure of trait impulsiveness and a measure of behavioral impulsiveness, since previous research shows that trait impulsiveness does not necessarily correlate with behavioral measures of impulsiveness (Lane et al. 2003). As a trait measure, we use the Barrat Impulsiveness Scale (BIS; Barratt 1959), a 30-item instrument widely used to assess the varying dimensions of the impulsiveness of individuals.[6] As a behavioral measure of impulsiveness, we used the Cognitive Reflection Test (CRT; Frederick 2005). The CRT is a three-item measure designed to assess an individual's ability to control a first intuitive, but incorrect, response.

3.2.2 Experimental Procedures

The experiment was conducted at the University of California, San Diego, with a total of 175 participants. In the first four sessions, with a total of 81 subjects, each participant received a $6 show-up fee for the first part of the experiment. To incentivize students to return, the show-up fee for the second week of the experiment was $20. Since show-up fees may affect donation decisions, we conducted four additional sessions in which an equal show-up fee of $15 was paid each week. In total 94 subjects participated in this second set of experimental sessions. The structure of the show-up fees did not significantly affect average donation behavior (32.4 percent versus 29.3 percent in the first and second set of sessions; Z-stat $= 0.4276$, $p = 0.6690$).

Although the change in show-up fees does not affect the overall donation, we examine whether it influences the relationship among giving behavior and empathy and impulsiveness. The reason is that impulsive individuals may focus on the show-up fee paid out week 1, ignoring that of week 2, when making their donation decision. If impulsive behavior responds to scarcity, as has been suggested in psychology and now economics (Shah, Shafir, and Mullainathan 2015), impulsive individuals may be less likely to donate $5 from their show-up fee when the fee is $6 compared to $15.

At the beginning of the experiment, participants were randomly seated in separate computer cubicles and reminded of the longitudinal design of the study. Then the experimenter presented the work of Give-Directly in a slide presentation. At the end of this pitch, participants were asked whether they wanted to donate $5 of their show-up fee for the session. Participants indicated their donation decision via entries in their respective computer terminals and then completed a short questionnaire in which we elicited individual characteristics, including age, gender, study major, and fluency in English. Subjects were also asked to complete the CRT. Subsequently, participants were paid their corresponding show-up fee, minus the donation, if any. A week later participants returned to the laboratory to complete the experiment. During this session they completed the BIS and IRI measurement scales. Ten out of 175 subjects failed to complete the experiment,[7] and nine provided incomplete answers to the BIS and IRI measurement scales. The analysis that follows therefore focuses on 156 subjects, though conclusions remain qualitatively similar if subjects with incomplete answers are included.

3.3   Results

Thirty-one percent of the participants (48 out of 175) donated $5 to GiveDirectly. Importantly, measured empathy and impulsiveness varied between donors and nondonors. Table 3.1 shows the average values for the empathy and impulsiveness measures of subjects who decided to donate and those who decided against it. Empathy and impulsiveness predict donation behavior, controlling for other individual characteristics. Table 3.2 presents marginal effects of probit regressions on the likelihood of a donation. All specifications control for gender, study major, and English language skills.[8] To ease the interpretation of the coefficients, all empathy and impulsiveness measures are standardized. Column 1 of table 3.2 presents the estimation results pooling all sessions of the experiment. Consistent with the empathy-altruism hypothesis, we find that an individual is more likely to give the higher

Table 3.1
Empathy, impulsiveness, and donation behavior.

	Empathic Concern (IRI)		Trait Impulsiveness (BIS scale)		Behavioral Impulsiveness (CRT score)		
	Mean	SD	Mean	SD	Mean	SD	N
Panel A: $6 endowment							
No donation	25.2	3.5	75.1	7.0	1.3	1.0	50
Donation	25.7	2.6	72.1	6.5	1.6	1.1	24
Panel B: $15 endowment							
No donation	25.5	3.3	73.1	5.9	1.7	1.1	58
Donation	26.7	3.0	72.0	5.9	1.6	1.2	24

Notes: This table presents the raw data for the personality measures. The first row in each panel displays the average scores (and respective standard deviations) for subjects who decided not to donate. The second row in each panel displays the values for subjects who decided to donate to the charity. BIS, Barratt Impulsiveness Scale; CRT, Cognitive Reflective Test; IRI, Interpersonal Reactivity Index; SD, standard deviation.

the level of empathic concern he or she reports. A one standard deviation increase in the empathic concern score corresponds with an 8 percentage point increase in the likelihood of a donation ($p = 0.001$).

In contrast, impulsiveness has a negative relationship to charitable giving ($p = 0.001$). This finding is driven by behavior in the experimental sessions in which the donation constitutes a larger share of the subject's endowment ($5 out of $6, instead of $15), as shown in columns 2 and 3 of table 3.2. As shown in column 2, when subjects receive a $6 endowment, a higher degree of impulsiveness implies a significantly lower likelihood of donating. One standard deviation in the BIS measure corresponds to a likelihood of observing a donation that is 12 percentage points lower ($p < 0.001$). Furthermore, lower behavioral impulsiveness, as measured by a higher CRT score, has a weakly significant positive influence on donation behavior ($p = 0.08$). This result stands in contrast to some previous research that has found a negative relationship between CRT scores and dictator game giving (Ponti and Rodriguez-Lara 2015; Cueva et al. 2016). The reason for this may be found in the neediness of the recipient. The ability to suppress an intuitive response favors giving when the person is in need and resources are scarce, consistent with the framework of Shah, Shafir, and Mullainathan (2015). Then, when subjects receive a $15 endowment, as shown in column 3 of table 3.2, impulsiveness is no longer a significant negative predictor of donation decisions (BIS: $p = 0.456$, and CRT score: $p = 0.813$).[9]

Table 3.2
Probit regression on the likelihood of a donation.

Session	(1) $6 and $15 Endowment	(2) $6 Endowment	(3) $15 Endowment	(4) $6 and $15 Endowment
	Likelihood of Donation			
Empathy				
Empathic concern (IRI)	0.084*** (0.026)	0.059* (0.031)	0.107*** (0.037)	0.100*** (0.029)
IRI × $6 endowment				−0.031 (0.037)
Impulsiveness				
Trait (BIS)	−0.082*** (0.025)	−0.118*** (0.029)	−0.039 (0.052)	−0.027 (0.045)
BIS × $6 endowment				−0.093* (0.056)
Behavioral (CRT)	0.027 (0.042)	0.090* (0.052)	−0.015 (0.063)	−0.010 (0.071)
CRT × $6 endowment				0.071 (0.101)
$6 endowment	0.043 (0.044)			0.020 (0.050)
Number of observations	156	74	82	156

Notes: This table presents the average marginal effects (calculated at means of all variables) from probit regression on donations. Empathic concern is measured with the same titled subscale (EC) of the Interpersonal Reactivity Index (Davis 1983). The individual's level of Impulsiveness is elicited with two measures: the Barratt Impulsiveness Scale (BIS) and the Cognitive Reflection Test (CRT) (Frederick 2005). Column 1 presents the estimates of the likelihood of donation based on the entire sample. Estimations in column 2 are based on sessions where subjects received a $6 endowment. Estimations in column 3 include only sessions in which individuals received a $15 endowment. Standardized mean scores are taken as a basis for all personality measures (IRI-EC, BIS, and CRT). All specifications include the individual characteristics, gender, English-language skills, and whether an individual studied economics as control variables. Further, experimenter fixed effects are included in all specifications. Robust standard errors, clustered at the session level, are shown in parentheses. The symbols ***, **, and * indicate significance at the 1 percent, 5 percent, and 10 percent levels, respectively.

The difference in the relationship between trait impulsiveness and donations is significantly weaker when the endowment is $15, as shown in column 4 of table 3.2, where impulsiveness and endowment are interacted ($\chi^2 = 2.81$, $p = 0.094$).[10]

In sum, empathy is a consistently important factor in donation behavior. In contrast, impulsiveness is strongly related to altruistic actions only when immediate financial resources are scarce. Under such circumstances, an impulsive individual is less likely to donate, whereas a person who is able to suppress this first intuitive response and is capable of reflection might take future payments into account and may hence be more willing to donate.

3.4   Conclusion

Existing research has shown that charitable giving is driven by a wide array of motivations. Recently, economists have begun to consider two new motivations: empathy and impulsiveness. In this chapter we have examined the role of heterogeneity in these individual characteristics on giving. In a laboratory experiment we tested whether two important personality traits, empathy and impulsiveness, predict a real donation decision.

Our results confirm that empathy is a central factor in charitable giving. We also find support for a relationship between impulsiveness and donation behavior. Particularly, when financial means are limited, the individual's level of impulsiveness has a negative relation to the donation decision. Our results reaffirm the critical role of empathy in charitable giving. Our analysis also shows that the relationship between impulsivity and giving may not be consistent across contexts. We find a negative relationship that becomes increasingly negative when subjects see resources as more scarce. This finding is interesting for two reasons. First, it suggests that the relationship between giving and impulsiveness is complex and may be influenced by other contextual factors. Second, it suggests a topic for further exploration to understand the conflicting findings in this area: Does the relative degree of wealth or scarcity among the subjects in these studies differ in ways that may interact with impulsivity to create conflicting results?

3.A Appendix

3.A.1 Interpersonal Reactivity Index

The index consist of four subscales with seven items each. Each subscale targets a different aspect of empathy. First, the Fantasy scale measures the tendency that an individual imaginatively transposes himself or herself into the feelings and actions of fictional characters (*I really get involved with the feelings of a character in a novel*). The second scale, Perspective Taking, focuses on the cognitive aspect of empathy and assesses the tendency to take the psychological view of others into account (*I sometimes try to understand my friends better by imagining how things look from their perspective*). The third scale, Empathic Concerns, measures the emotional aspect of empathy, that is, sympathy and concern for others (*When I see someone being taken advantage of, I feel kind of protective toward them*). The last scale, Personal Distress, measures the kind of feelings (e.g., anxiety) that can get in the way of helping others (*In emergency situations, I feel apprehensive and ill-at-ease*).

3.A.2 Barrat Impulsiveness Scale

Based on factor analysis studies, the following subscales can be identified in the BIS that measure the varying subtraits of impulsiveness (Stanford et al. 2009, 392). (1) Attentional Impulsiveness: describing the diminished ability to focus on a task (Attentional:[11] *I don't "pay attention"*; and Cognitive Instability: *I have "racing" thoughts*). (2) Motor Impulsiveness: impulsiveness involved in acting without thinking (Motor: *I act "on impulse"*; and Perseverance: *I change jobs*). (3) Non-Planning Impulsiveness involved as a lack of forethought (Self-Control:[12] *I say things without thinking*; and Cognitive Complexity:[13] *I get easily bored when solving thought problems*).

3.A.3 Gender Differences

Below we present table 3.A.1, which analyzes the relationship between giving and empathy and impulsivity, by gender.

Table 3.A.1

Probit regression on the likelihood of a donation, by gender and including individual subscales.

	(1)	(2)	(3)	(4)	(5)	(6)
	All Subjects	Male Only	Female Only	All Subjects	Male Only	Female Only
Empathy						
Empathic concern (IRI)	0.084***	0.155***	0.078*	0.080***	0.060***	0.071*
	(0.026)	(0.058)	(0.047)	(0.030)	(0.014)	(0.041)
Other subscales in IRI						
Fantasy				0.055**	0.306*	-0.004
				(0.027)	(0.164)	(0.026)
Perspective-taking				0.034	0.058	0.039
				(0.034)	(0.049)	(0.047)
Personal distress				0.011	0.058	0.017
				(0.030)	(0.044)	(0.079)
Impulsiveness						
Trait (BIS)	-0.082***	0.036	-0.130**			
	(0.025)	(0.054)	(0.058)			
Subscales in Trait Impulsiveness (BIS)						
Lack of attention				-0.013	-0.183**	0.045
				(0.045)	(0.092)	(0.068)
Cognitive instability				-0.015	0.139*	0.001
				(0.045)	(0.081)	(0.096)

(continued)

Table 3.A.1 (continued)

	(1) All Subjects	(2) Male Only	(3) Female Only	(4) All Subjects	(5) Male Only	(6) Female Only
Motor impulsiveness				-0.018 (0.026)	0.077 (0.055)	-0.042 (0.078)
Perseverance				0.028* (0.015)	-0.037 (0.032)	0.024 (0.059)
Lack of self-control				-0.125*** (0.032)	-0.002 (0.026)	-0.171*** (0.039)
Low cognitive complexity				-0.053 (0.051)	0.020 (0.030)	-0.095 (0.067)
Cognitive reflection test	0.027 (0.042)	0.172*** (0.063)	-0.007 (0.043)	0.029 (0.051)	0.240** (0.121)	-0.020 (0.051)
Female	-0.072 (0.124)			-0.083 (0.123)		
$6 endowment	0.043 (0.044)	0.034 (0.086)	0.138 (0.127)	0.040 (0.057)	-0.032 (0.056)	0.095 (0.143)
Number of observations	156	60	96	156	60	96

Notes: This table presents the average marginal effects (calculated at means of all variables) from probit regression on the likelihood of donations. Column 1 replicates column 1 of table 3.2. Columns 2 and 3 show the same specification by gender. Columns 4–6 display the results when all scales of the Interpersonal Reactivity Index (IRI) (Davis 1983) and all subscales of the Barratt Impulsiveness Scale (BIS) (Barratt 1959) are included individually. The estimations are done on the basis of standardized mean scores for each subscale. All specifications also include the standardized mean scores from the Cognitive Reflection Test (Frederick 2005) and controls for gender, English language skills, and whether an individual had economics as a major. Experimenter and endowment fixed effects serve as additional controls. Robust standard errors, clustered at the session level, are shown in parentheses. The symbols ***, **, and * indicate significance at the 1 percent, 5 percent, and 10 percent levels, respectively.

Notes

1. For reviews, see Andreoni (2006) and Andreoni and Payne (2013).

2. An excellent review and discussion can be found in Riedl, Vesterlund, and Recalde (2014).

3. We thank an anonymous reviewer for valuable comments on this point.

4. Response options range from 0 (*does not describe me well*) to 4 (*describes me very well*).

5. A detailed description of these subscales, as well as example questions, can be found in the appendix.

6. We use the BIS for the analysis in its aggregate form; subscales are listed and explained in the appendix.

7. The rate at which students returned the second week was 98.8 percent for the first set of sessions and 90.3 percent for the second set. The difference is small in magnitude (8.5 percentage points) but statistically significant (Z-stat = -2.370, $p = 0.018$). Hence, we use the endowment amount as a control variable in all regressions.

8. Since variance in age was low in our sample, we refrain from adding age as another control variable. The results, however, do not change by doing so.

9. Interestingly, the relationship between behavioral and trait impulsiveness and dona-tion behavior is gender specific. For male subjects, behavioral impulsiveness is a strong predictor of donations. One unit of standard deviation in correct answers (more reflec-tion) increases the likelihood of donations by 17 percentage points in the male subsample ($p < 0.01$); see column 2 of table 3.A.1 in the appendix. For the female subsample, in contrast, the behavioral impulsiveness has almost no predictive power for the donation decision. Instead, donations made by females are strongly correlated with trait impulsive-ness. One unit of standard deviation in the BIS value decreases the donation likelihood by 13 percentage points ($p < 0.001$), as shown in column 3 of table 3.A.1 in the appendix.

10. There is no significant difference in the relationship between empathy and behavioral impulsiveness by endowment (IRI: $\chi^2 = 0.73$, $p = 0.393$; and CRT: $\chi^2 = 0.50$, $p = 0.482$).

11. We refer to this component as "Lack of Attention" in our regressions to avoid confusion.

12. This component corresponds with the variable "Lack of Self-Control" in our regressions.

13. We also renamed this variable to ease interpretation. This component can be found under "Low Cognitive Complexity."

References

Andreoni, James. 1989. "Giving with Impure Altruism: Applications to Charity and Ricardian Equivalence." *Journal of Political Economy* 97 (6): 1447–1458.

Andreoni, James. 2006. "Philanthropy." In *Handbook of the Economics of Giving, Altruism and Reciprocity 2*, edited by Serge-Christophe Kolm and Jean Mercier Ythier, 1202–1269. Oxford: Elsevier.

Andreoni, James, and B. Douglas Bernheim. 2009. "Social Image and the 50–50 Norm: A Theoretical and Experimental Analysis of Audience Effects." *Econometrica* 77 (5): 1607–1636.

Andreoni, James, and A. Abigail Payne. 2013. "Charitable giving." In *Handbook of Public Economics 5*, edited by Alan J. Auerbach, Raj Chetty, Martin Feldstein, and Emmanuel Saez, 1–50. Oxford: Elsevier.

Andreoni, James, and Justin M. Rao. 2011. "The Power of Asking: How Communication Affects Selfishness, Empathy, and Altruism." *Journal of Public Economics* 95 (7): 513–520.

Andreoni, James, Justin M. Rao, and Hannah Trachtman. 2017. "Avoiding the Ask: A Field Experiment on Altruism, Empathy, and Charitable Giving." *Journal of Political Economy* 125 (3): 625–653.

Ariely, Dan, Anat Bracha, and Stephan Meier. 2009. "Doing Good or Doing Well? Image Motivation and Monetary Incentives in Behaving Prosocially." *American Economic Review* 99 (1): 544–555.

Barratt, Ernest S. 1959. "Anxiety and Impulsiveness Related to *Psychomotor* Efficiency." *Perceptual and Motor Skills* 9 (3): 191–198.

Batson, Charles Daniel. 1987. "Prosocial Motivation: Is It Ever Truly Altruistic?" *Advances in Experimental Social Psychology* 20: 65–122.

Batson, Charles Daniel. 2011. *Altruism in Humans*. New York: Oxford University Press.

Bénabou, Roland, and Jean Tirole. 2006. "Incentives and Prosocial Behavior." *American Economic Review* 96 (5): 1652–1678.

Cone, Jeremy, and David G. Rand. 2014. "Time Pressure Increases Cooperation in Competitively Framed Social Dilemmas." *PLoS One* 9 (12): e115756.

Cueva, Carlos, Inigo Iturbe-Ormaetxe, Esther Mata-Pérez, Giovanni Ponti, Marcello Sartarelli, Haihan Yu, and Vita Zhukova. 2016. "Cognitive (Ir)Reflection: New Experimental Evidence." *Journal of Behavioral and Experimental Economics* 64 (C): 81–93.

Curry, Oliver S., Michael E. Price, and Jade G. Price. 2008. "Patience Is a Virtue: Cooperative People Have Lower Discount Rates." *Personality and Individual Differences* 44 (3): 780–785.

Davis, Mark H. 1983. "Measuring Individual Differences in Empathy: Evidence for a Multidimensional Approach." *Journal of Personality and Social Psychology* 44 (1): 113–126.

De Waal, Frans B. M. 2012. "The Antiquity of Empathy." *Science* 336 (6083): 874–876.

Fehr, Ernst, and Andreas Leibbrandt. 2011. "A Field Study on Cooperativeness and Impatience in the Tragedy of the Commons." *Journal of Public Economics* 95 (9): 1144–1155.

Frederick, Shane. 2005. "Cognitive Reflection and Decision Making." *Journal of Economic Perspectives* 19 (4): 25–42.

Giving USA. 2017. "Giving USA 2017: Total Charitable Donations Rise to New High of $390.05 Billion." https://givingusa.org/giving-usa-2017-total-charitable-donations-rise -to-new-high-of-390-05-billion/ (accessed August 3, 2017).

Lane, Scott D., Don R. Cherek, Howard M. Rhoades, Cynthia J. Pietras, and Oleg V. Tcheremissine. 2003. "Relationships among Laboratory and Psychometric Measures of

Impulsivity: Implications in Substance Abuse and Dependence." *Addictive Disorders & Their Treatment* 2 (2): 33–40.

Martinsson, Peter, Kristian Ove R. Myrseth, and Conny Wollbrant. 2012. "Reconciling Pro-social vs. Selfish Behavior: On the Role of Self-Control." *Judgment and Decision Making* 7 (3): 304–315.

Piovesan, Marco, and Erik Wengström. 2009. "Fast or Fair? A Study of Response Times." *Economics Letters* 105 (2): 193–196.

Ponti, Giovanni, and Ismael Rodriguez-Lara. 2015. "Social Preferences and Cognitive Reflection: Evidence from a Dictator Game Experiment." *Frontiers in Behavioral Neuroscience* 9 (146). http://doi.org/10.3389/fnbeh.2015.00146.

Rand, David G. 2016. "Cooperation, Fast and Slow: Meta-analytic Evidence for a Theory of Social Heuristics and Self-Interested Deliberation." *Psychological Science* 27 (9): 1192–1206.

Rand, David G., Joshua D. Greene, and Martin A. Nowak. 2012. "Spontaneous Giving and Calculated Greed." *Nature* 489 (7416): 427–430.

Rand, David G., and Gordon T. Kraft-Todd. 2014. "Reflection Does Not Undermine Self-Interested Prosociality." *Frontiers in Behavioral Neuroscience* 8 (300). http://doi.org/10.3389/fnbeh.2014.00300.

Riedl, Arno, Lise Vesterlund, and P. María Recalde. 2014. "Error Prone Inference from Response Time: The Case of Intuitive Generosity." CESifo working paper, Center for Economic Studies, Munich.

Shah, Anuj K., Eldar Shafir, and Sendhil Mullainathan. 2015. "Scarcity Frames Value." *Psychological Science* 26 (4): 402–412.

Stanford, Matthew S., Charles W. Mathias, Donald M. Dougherty, Sarah L. Lake, Nathaniel E. Anderson, and Jim H. Patton. 2009. "Fifty Years of the Barratt Impulsiveness Scale: An Update and Review." *Personality and Individual Differences* 47 (5): 385–395.

Tinghög, Gustav, David Andersson, Caroline Bonn, and Harald Böttiger. 2013. "Intuition and Cooperation Reconsidered." *Nature* 498 (7452): E1–E2.

Verkoeijen, Peter P. J. L., and Samantha Bouwmeester. 2014. "Does Intuition Cause Cooperation?" *PloS One* 9 (5): e96654.

4   Charitable Giving in the Laboratory: Advantages of the Piecewise Linear Public Goods Game

Michael Menietti, María P. Recalde, and Lise Vesterlund

4.1   Introduction

The vast majority of US households make significant charitable contributions. When examining the effectiveness of the mechanisms fundraisers use to solicit such funds, it is often essential that researchers elicit or control the donor's return from giving. While much can be gained from examining data on actual donations, insights on giving increasingly result from laboratory studies. An advantage of the laboratory is that it permits control of the donor's return from giving and thus facilitates the identification of donor motives as well as their responses to different fundraising or solicitation strategies (see Vesterlund 2016 for a review).

Economists have traditionally modeled charitable giving as a voluntary contribution to a public good. The reason for this modeling choice is that charitable donations benefit everyone who cares about the charity's mission and output. Thus, the benefit from the sum of donations is nonrival and nonexcludable and can be treated as a public good. To introduce similar incentives in the laboratory, past studies have primarily examined giving in the classic linear public goods game, also known as the voluntary contribution mechanism (VCM). Participants in the VCM are paired in groups and are each given an amount of money to individually allocate between a private and a public account. Money in the private account benefits only the individual, while money in the public account benefits all members of the group. Using a linear payoff structure, the returns from the private and public accounts are held constant and are set to ensure that it is a dominant strategy for the individual to allocate all money to the private account (i.e., give nothing), but group-payoffs are maximized by allocating all money to the public account (i.e., give everything). Although the linear structure makes the game simple and easy to explain to participants, the VCM has the important drawback that all deviations from equilibrium are consistent with other-regarding behavior. While clever experimental manipulations have made clear that some contributions in the VCM are made in error (see, e.g., Andreoni 1995; Anderson, Goeree, and Holt 1998; and Houser and Kurzban 2002), the linear structure of the VCM does not make it possible, in the game, to determine whether a contribution is intentional or a mistake. Thus, it is not possible to determine whether overcontributions in the VCM result from other-regarding behavior.

If instead the equilibrium and the group-payoff-maximizing outcome were moved away from the two boundaries and into the interior of the strategy set, then it would be easier to identify choices that are dominated from both an individual and a group perspective, and one could potentially evaluate whether overcontributions in the VCM result from errors being truncated in the VCM. Initial studies of pubic goods games with an interior equilibrium, however, reveal behavior that is not too different from that observed in the classic VCM (e.g., Keser 1996; Sefton and Steinberg 1996; Isaac and Walker 1998; Laury, Walker, and Williams 1999; and Willinger and Ziegelmeyer 1999, 2001). Contributions in excess of equilibrium are also observed in public goods games with an interior equilibrium. Of concern, however, is that, consistent with a high degree of subject confusion, these studies document a low frequency of equilibrium play, typically ranging between 0 and 33 percent. In addition, average contributions are rather insensitive to the location of the equilibrium and often fall in the middle of the strategy set. A possible explanation for the limited sensitivity to the location of the equilibrium may be that standard nonlinear functions were used to secure the necessary concave payoff function. Drawbacks of using standard nonlinear functions are that the incentive for equilibrium play decreases as play approaches the equilibrium and that it results in a less transparent payoff structure.

We examine instead a piecewise linear public goods game (henceforth PL-PG game), where an interior equilibrium is secured through a transparent and easier to understand piecewise linear payoff structure. We describe the properties of the PL-PG game, showcase its flexibility, and analyze data from a number of different implementations of the game. Behavior in the PL-PG game demonstrates high rates of equilibrium play; a limited number of mistakes; and importantly, that the mean, median, and modal contributions all track the equilibrium with repeated play. While the contributions by some participants can be characterized as other-regarding, most choices are consistent with maximizing own payoffs.

Section 4.2 describes the standard voluntary contribution game and outlines how the classic linear VCM captures the incentives of this model. Section 4.3 provides an overview of previous public goods games with an interior equilibrium, and section 4.4 presents the PL-PG game and examines behavior in several different implementations of the game. Section 4.5 provides examples of charitable-giving applications of the framework, and section 4.6 concludes.

4.2 Voluntary Contribution and the Linear VCM

We first review how economists traditionally model charitable giving and demonstrate how the classic VCM maps onto that model. The motive for donating to a charity is thought to be a concern for the well-being of those who receive services from the charity. That is, the motive for giving is one of altruism, with the donor's return from giving arising from the effect donations have on the well-being of the recipients. With the benefit from giving resulting from the impact of the gift, an individual's donation benefits the recipient and the donor, as well as anyone else who is concerned for the recipient's well-being. Thus, when donors are altruistically inclined, the recipient's well-being is a public good (Becker 1974).

To model voluntary contribution to a public good, assume that n individuals care about private consumption x_i and the total provision of a public good G. Let individual i's contribution to the public good be g_i and the provision of the public good be the sum of these contributions: $G = \Sigma_{i=1}^{n} g_i$. With consumption of the public good being nonrival and nonexclusive, everyone benefits from the total provision of the public good. Denoting income by w and normalizing prices such that $p_G = p_x = 1$, i's budget constraint is given by $g_i + x_i \leq w$. Representing preferences by a continuous and strictly quasiconcave function $U_i(x_i, G)$, i's preferred provision level is given by the continuous demand function $G^* = q_i(w + G_{-i})$, where $G_{-i} = \Sigma_{i \neq j} g_j$ is the amount given by others to the public good. As shown by Bergstrom, Blume, and Varian (1986), there exists a unique equilibrium $(g_1^*, g_2^*, \ldots, g_n^*)$ of this game when both the public and the private goods are normal goods, where i's gift is given by $g_i^* = max\{0, -G_{-i} + q_i(w + G_{-i})\}$. As an illustration, consider the two-person example in figure 4.1. Contributions by individuals 1 and

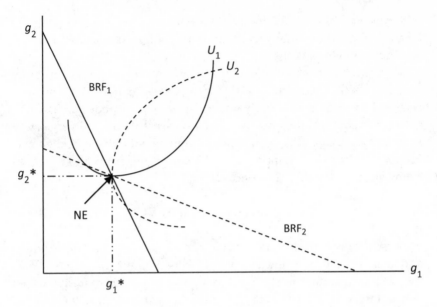

Figure 4.1
Voluntary contribution equilibrium. *Source*: Vesterlund (2016), figure 1.

2 are measured on the horizontal and vertical axis, respectively, and the intersection of the two downward sloping best response functions, BRF_1 and BRF_2, demonstrates the resulting Nash equilibrium (g_1^*, g_2^*). Looking at the individuals' indifference curves through (g_1^*, g_2^*) and recalling that utility is strictly increasing with the contributions of others, it is apparent that there exist contributions that are preferred by both contributors and result in greater overall provision of the public good. Thus, the classic free-rider problem results, and the voluntary provision of the public good $(G^* = g_1^* + g_2^*)$ is inefficiently low.

To capture the incentive to free ride, numerous studies have used the linear public goods game (i.e., VCM) to study giving in the laboratory. The classic VCM, by Isaac, Walker, and Thomas (1984), examines giving in an environment where participants are paired in groups of n people and each is given an endowment w, which they must distribute between a private and a public account.[1] Payoffs are linear, with the private account generating an individual return of r and the public account generating a return of m to every member of the group. Thus, an allocation to the public account, g_i, constitutes a contribution to a public good. The individual return from giving, m/r, is referred to as the marginal per capita return (MPCR), and the individual's payoff from contributing g_i equals

$$\pi_i = r(w - g_i) + m\Sigma_{i=1}^{n} g_i.$$

The individual's return from the public good is $m\Sigma_{i=1}^{n} g_i$. The conflict between self and others arises in the social dilemma setting where $\frac{1}{n} < \frac{m}{r} < 1$, when it is socially optimal to give yet costly for the individual to do so. Placing the VCM in the context of the voluntary contribution game in figure 4.1, note that deviations from equilibrium always improve group payoffs. The dominant strategy and the group-payoff-maximizing outcome are at opposite boundaries of the strategy set. With a dominant strategy equilibrium that predicts that the entire endowment is placed in the private account, nothing is placed in the public account and there is zero provision ($G = \Sigma_{i=1}^{n} g_i^* = 0$). In contrast to the group-payoff-maximizing outcome is one where everything is placed in the public account and there is full provision ($G = \Sigma_{i=1}^{n} g_i^* = nw$).

In contrast to the equilibrium prediction of zero giving, experimental investigations of the public goods game demonstrate substantial contributions. In the VCM, average contributions typically start off at around 50 percent of endowment, then decrease with repetition (see, e.g., Ledyard 1995 and Chaudhuri 2011 for reviews). To illustrate the contributions typically observed in the VCM, we present data from a VCM treatment conducted by Recalde, Riedl, and Vesterlund (forthcoming) (henceforth, RRV) in figures 4.2 and 4.3. For 11 rounds, 40 participants made contribution decisions in groups of 4.[2] In each round, they decided how much of an $8 endowment to contribute, in $1 increments, to a group account in which the money contributed was doubled and was split equally among group members. Money not placed in the group account was kept in a private account, with a dollar for dollar return. That is, the marginal per capita return ($MPCR = \frac{m}{r}$) was 0.5. Participants were randomly rematched after every round and received feedback after every decision round. Specifically, they learned the total and average contributions made by other group members as well as their earnings and the average earnings of other group members. One choice made by participants was randomly selected to be paid at the end of the experiment.

Figure 4.2 presents a histogram of the contribution decisions observed across all rounds of play. The solid vertical line indicates the location of the dominant strategy equilibrium prediction, and the dashed vertical

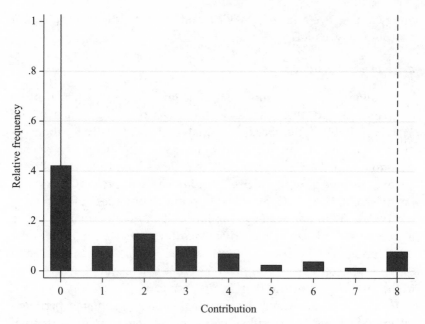

Figure 4.2
Histogram of contributions, VCM RRV. *Source*: Recalde, Riedl, and Vesterlund (forthcoming). *Notes*: The solid vertical reference line indicates the location of the dominant strategy. The dashed vertical reference line indicates the location of the group-payoff-maximizing choice. RRV, Recalde, Riedl, and Vesterlund (forthcoming); VCM, voluntary contribution mechanism.

line indicates the location of the group-payoff-maximizing contribution. Figure 4.2 shows that the modal contribution choice is the dominant strategy equilibrium prediction of 0 contribution to the group account. The rate of equilibrium play is 42.3 percent across all decisions and rounds. This aggregate rate of equilibrium play, however, masks the learning that occurs across rounds. Figure 4.3 demonstrates how play progresses with repetition by showing the mean and median contributions in every round. As is standard in the literature, the mean and median contributions start close to 50 percent of the endowment in the first decision round and decrease with experience. While the mean contribution remains positive in the last round of play, the median reaches the equilibrium prediction by round 9. The rate of equilibrium play increases from 20 percent in the first decision round to 70 percent in the last decision round.

While the VCM presents a transparent conflict between the individual and the group, the game fails to capture important aspects of the voluntary contribution game demonstrated in figure 4.1. In

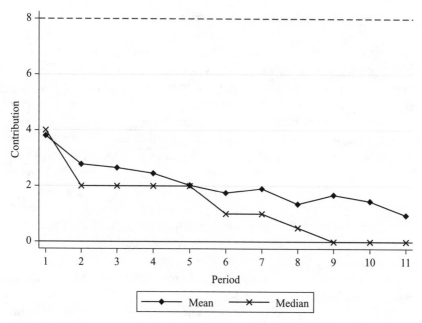

Figure 4.3
Mean and median contribution by round, VCM RRV. *Source*: Recalde, Riedl, and Vesterlund (forthcoming). *Notes*: The solid horizontal line indicates the location of the dominant strategy. The dashed horizontal line indicates the location of the group-payoff-maximizing contribution. RRV, Recalde, Riedl, and Vesterlund (forthcoming); VCM, voluntary contribution mechanism.

particular, it is not possible for participants to make choices that are dominated from both an individual and a group perspective. Clever experimental manipulations, however, make clear that some contributions are made in error (e.g., Andreoni 1995; Anderson, Goeree, and Holt 1998; and Houser and Kurzban 2002), and that the payoff structure of the VCM does not make it possible to identify such mistakes. An additional drawback of the VCM framework is that it is not sufficiently flexible to capture the incentives individuals face when presented with more complex fundraising mechanisms.

To better identify mistakes and to mirror the model of voluntary contributions, scholars have begun to study environments where, as in figure 4.1, there is instead an interior equilibrium. As noted below, these studies have found behavior that largely mirrors the overcontributions revealed in the VCM. While consistent with other-regarding behavior, the pattern of contributions suggests that confusion contributes to this finding.

4.3 Public Goods Games with Interior Equilibria

An interior equilibrium of the public goods game is predicted to arise when participants are given a strictly concave payoff function. This has been secured by introducing either a strictly convex cost of contributing or a strictly concave return to the public good. More precisely, assume a separable payoff function $U(x_i, G) = u(x_i) + v(G)$ with the constraint $x_i + c_2(g_i) \le w$, where $c_2(\cdot)$ is the cost of contributing. Then the participant's objective when choosing a contribution g_i is to maximize $U(g_i, G_{-i} + g_i) = u(w - c(g_i)) + v(G_{-i} + g_i)$, where $G_{-i} = G - g_i$.[3] As made clear in the review of interior public goods games by Laury and Holt (2008), the introduction of strictly convex costs $c(g_i)$ secures the equilibrium in dominant strategies, while an interior Nash equilibrium in total contributions (nondominant strategies) is secured when instead $v(G_{-i} + g_i)$ is made strictly concave.[4] When including strict concavity of either $u(\cdot)$ or $v(\cdot)$, scholars have relied on standard nonlinear functions, with the majority using a quadratic payoff function.

Often the studies conducted reveal a low frequency of equilibrium play. Mirroring the VCM, there have been several implementations in dominant strategies. Keeping $v(G_{-i} + g_i)$ linear while using quadratic payoffs for $u(w - c(g_i))$, Keser (1996) studies a public goods game with an individual-payoff-maximizing dominant strategy contribution rate of 35 percent of the individual's endowment. In 25 consecutive rounds, she studies the choices made in fixed groups of 4, and she finds an overall frequency of equilibrium play of only 27 percent. Willinger and Ziegelmeyer (2001) extend this design by varying the individual-payoff-maximizing dominant strategy equilibrium contribution rate across 35, 50, 65, and 80 percent of the endowment. The corresponding frequency of equilibrium play remains low at 17, 24, and 30 percent for the first three treatments, respectively, and reaches 40 percent in the last treatment, where the equilibrium is close to the group-payoff-maximizing outcome. Other studies have used the dominant strategy equilibrium payoff structure to study more complex public good environments, but nonetheless report on the frequency of equilibrium play in a comparable baseline treatment. These studies also find that the frequency of equilibrium play ranges between 10 and 33 percent (Falkinger et al. 2000; van Dijk, Sonnemans, and van Winden 2002; Gronberg et al. 2012; Maurice, Rouaix, and Willinger 2013; Rouaix, Figuières, and Willinger 2015).

Several studies examine instead behavior in games where the return from the public good is concave and the interior equilibrium is not in dominant strategies. Guttman (1986) uses a root function to secure strict concavity of $v(G_{-i} + g_i)$. Varying group size and whether there is heterogeneity in preferences, in comparable homogeneous treatments he finds substantial overcontribution.[5] Andreoni (1993) uses a public goods game with an interior equilibrium to study crowd-out. Participants are rematched in groups of 3 after a sequence of 4 rounds of repeated play, for a total of 20 decision rounds. Payoffs are given by a Cobb-Douglass function and presented in a payoff table. The frequency of equilibrium play across two different treatments is 24 percent (tax treatment) and 34 percent (no-tax treatment). Isaac and Walker (1998) use a quadratic function to make $v(\cdot)$ concave and vary across treatments the location of the symmetric Nash equilibrium in nondominant strategies. Examining treatments with symmetric equilibria at 19.4, 50, and 80 percent of the endowment, the corresponding frequency of symmetric equilibrium play is merely 12, 14, and 20 percent for the three respective treatments. Other papers using similar nonlinear public goods games with an interior symetric equilibrium in nondominant strategies include Chan et al. (1996, 1999, 2002), Laury, Walker, and Williams (1999), and Sutter and Weck-Hannemann (2004). These studies also report baseline treatments with homogeneous agents, perfect information, and no taxes or subsidies; they reveal a frequency of equilibrium play that typically ranges between 0 and 33 percent.[6]

Sefton and Steinberg (1996) compare behavior in public goods games in which the interior symetric equilibrium is or is not in dominant strategies. Keeping the equilibrium fixed at 25 percent of the endowment, they find with random rematching of groups of 4, over 10 consecutive rounds, that the frequency of equilibrium play is quite similar: 18 percent (dominant strategies) and 12 percent (nondominant strategies).

When using standard nonlinear functions to secure public goods games with an interior equilibrium, we have found low rates of equilibrium play across studies that vary both the location and the type of equilibrium. What raises concern is the low frequency of equilibrium play along with the fact that, similar to the classic VCM, we find for many of these games average contribution rates close to 50 percent of the endowment. What is particularly striking is that this average contribution pattern appears to be relatively insensitive to the location of the equilibrium. For example, as seen in the review by Laury and Holt (2008), the average contribution rate remains around 50 percent of the endowment when the equilibrium prediction is a contribution rate of 35 percent (Keser 1996), 25 percent (Sefton and Steinberg 1996), or 20 and 50 percent (Isaac and Walker 1998).

Below we report on data revealing that greater sensitivity to the location of the equilibrium and a higher frequency of equilibrium play is secured when instead a piecewise linear payoff structure is used to secure an interior equilibrium.

4.4   The Piecewise Linear Public Goods (PL-PG) Game

Instead of using standard nonlinear functions to secure an interior equilibrium of the public goods game one can instead use a simple piecewise linear approximation of a concave payoff function. The class of piecewise linear public goods games, PL-PG games, secures very flexible concave payoffs $(U(g_i, G) = u(w - c(g_i)) + v(G))$, wherein the researcher easily controls the complexity of the payoff structure, the marginal incentives, the location of the equilibrium, and the group-payoff-maximizing contribution, as well as the payoffs associated with different contribution levels. For example, Menietti, Morelli, and Vesterlund (2012) (MMV) and Bracha, Menietti, and Vesterlund (2011) (BMV) examine contributions in two-person PL-PG games, where an interior equilibrium is implemented in dominant strategies by maintaining a linear return from the public good, $v(G) = mG$, and introducing a piecewise linear convex cost function $c(g_i)$, such that $u(g_i) = w - c(g_i)$ is concave. Placing both the equilibrium and the group-payoff-maximizing contribution in the interior, they include two kinks in the piecewise linear cost function $c(g_i)$:

$$c(g_i) = \begin{cases} k_1 g_i & \text{if} \quad 0 \le g_i \le g^* \\ k_1 g^N + k_2(g_i - g^*) & \text{if} \quad g^N < g_i \le g^{GM} \\ kg^N + k_2(g^{GM} - g^*) + k_3(g_i - g^{GM}) & \text{if} \quad g^{GM} \le g_i \end{cases} \quad (4.1)$$

Let $k_1 < k_2 < k_3$ be constants, and g^* and g^{GM} denote the dominant strategy equilibrium and group-payoff-maximizing contribution level, respectively. Then the monetary payoffs individuals receive is given by

$$U(g_i, G_{-i} + g_i) = \begin{cases} w + \alpha g_i + mG_{-i} \\ w + \alpha g^* + \beta(g_i - g^*) + mG_{-i} \\ w + \alpha g^* + \beta(g^{GM} - g^*) + \gamma(g_i - g^{GM}) + mG_{-i} \end{cases}$$

$$\begin{matrix} \text{if} \quad 0 \le g_i \le g^* \\ \text{if} \quad g^N < g_i \le g^{GM}, \\ \text{if} \quad g^{GM} \le g_i \end{matrix} \quad (4.2)$$

where $\alpha = m - k_1$, $\beta = m - k_2$, and $\gamma = m - k_3$. To secure an interior unique dominant-strategy equilibrium contribution g^* and an interior group-payoff-maximizing contribution g^{GM}, it must be that $\alpha > 0 > \beta > \gamma$ and $\beta + m(n - 1) > 0$ and $\gamma + m(n - 1) < 0$. With two kinks in the cost function, both g^* and g^{GM} are placed in the interior. Cason and Gangadharan (2015) extend this setting to groups of four people, while Robbett (2016) uses the PL-PG game with only one kink to generate either an interior dominant strategy or an interior group-payoff-maximizing contribution in a three-person setting with heterogeneous agents. RRV construct instead a PL-PG game with three kinks to hold features constant across treatments. Specifically, RRV vary the location of the equilibrium while keeping constant the group-payoff-maximizing choice, the payoffs associated with corner solutions and equilibrium play, as well as the costs of deviating from equilibrium toward the middle of the strategy set. In a robustness check, RRV introduce an additional kink in the payoff function on $v(\cdot)$ rather than $u(\cdot)$ to make contributions in excess of g^{GM} dominated from an individual and a group perspective. Finally, Menietti (2012) studies the PL-PG case where instead $v(\cdot)$ is concave, to secure an interior equilibrium provision level in nondominant strategies. Thus, the PL-PG game is flexible in providing the researcher precise control over the payoff structure while permitting a relatively simple payoff structure. While it is straightforward to summarize the participant's marginal return from actions, these can also be presented using transparent payoff tables or by presenting both the marginal returns and the associated payoff table.[7]

To examine behavior in the PL-PG game, we use data from all treatments we have conducted in which decisions are made simultaneously without a time limit, preferences are constant across group members, and where there is no uncertainty in payoffs. To make it clear how the treatments and studies included in this analysis differ, we summarize in table 4.1 the characteristics of each of the examined PL-PG game environments.

As table 4.1 shows, there is variation in the characteristics of the treatments included in this analysis. In two of the studies (three treatments) subjects interact in groups of two, and in one study (four treatments) they interact in groups of four. The equilibrium is in dominant strategies in all studies, and at least one treatment in each study examines contributions in a scenario where the equilibrium contribution is located below the midpoint of the strategy set, specifically, at $g_i^* = 3$. All treatments randomly rematch subjects after every round

Table 4.1
PL-PG games included in the analysis.

Study	Treatment	Label	w	g^*	g^{GM}	N	T
BMV	Simultaneous move, no threshold	BMV	10	3	7	2	14
MMV	No threshold	MMV12	12	3	7	2	14
MMV	Rerun, no threshold	MMV10	10	3	7	2	14
RRV	Low	RRV Low	10	3	9	4	11
RRV	High	RRV High	10	7	9	4	11
RRV	Modified-Low	RRV Modified-Low	10	3	9	4	11
RRV	Modified-High	RRV Modified-High	10	7	9	4	11

Notes: w denotes the endowment; g^* and g^{GM} denote the dominant and group-payoff-maximizing contributions, respectively; n denotes group size; and T is the number of one-shot replications (rounds). All studies randomly rematch participants into new groups after every round. BMV, Bracha, Menietti, and Vesterlund (2011); MMV, Menietti, Morelli, and Vesterlund (2012); RRV, Recalde, Riedl, and Vesterlund (forthcoming).

and have subjects make choices simultaneously. We exclude treatments with a threshold or sequential moves to limit attention to the most basic scenario, making the treatments directly comparable to the classic VCM as well as to previous studies on interior equilibria.[8]

Figure 4.4 presents histograms of the contributions made by subjects in the pooled sample of PL-PG games. The left panel shows the contributions made by subjects in MMV and BMV. The middle and right panels show behavior in RRV, distinguishing among contributions by the location of dominant strategy Nash prediction. The support of the distribution ranges between 0 and 10 in all panels, even though the endowment of subjects in one treatment of MMV (MMV12) was 12, because no subject ever made a choice above 10 in MMV12. The solid vertical line in each panel represents the location of the dominant strategy. The dashed vertical line indicates the location of the group-payoff-maximizing contribution. Choices below the dominant strategy are dominated from both an individual and other-regarding perspective and can thus be classified as mistakes, as alternative contributions simultaneously secure higher payoffs for the individual and all other group members. Contributions in excess of the group-payoff-maximizing choice are dominated from a group perspective.[9]

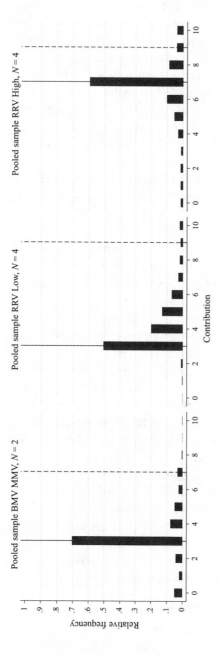

Figure 4.4
Histogram of contribution choices, by group size, PL-PG game. *Notes:* The solid vertical reference line in each panel indicates the location of the dominant strategy. The dashed vertical reference line in each panel indicates the location of the group-payoff-maximizing choice. Due to the difference in number of rounds and sessions in each of the studies, 2,156 decisions are included in the pooled sample of BMV and MMV, while 1,320 decisions are included in each of the pooled RRV samples (Low and High). BMV, Bracha, Menietti, and Vesterlund (2011); MMV, Menietti, Morelli, and Vesterlund (2012); PL-PG, piecewise linear public goods; RRV, Recalde, Riedl, and Vesterlund (forthcoming).

Across all panels, we can see that behavior responds to incentives. The modal choice is always the dominant strategy equilibrium prediction in the pooled sample of studies depicted in figure 4.4 and when differentiating the analysis by treatment (see figure 4.A.1). The rate of equilibrium play is 70.4 percent in the two-person PL-PG games we analyze, 50.5 in the pooled sample of four-person PL-PG games with a low dominant strategy, and 59.3 percent in the pooled sample of four-person PL-PG games with a high dominant strategy. The high rates of equilibrium play documented in the four-person groups suggest that the high frequency of equilibrium play documented in the two-person PL-PG games are not an artifact of the small group size.[10]

We also find a low frequency of choices that can be characterized as dominated from an individual and a group perspective. In games with two-person groups, we find that 11 percent of choices fall below the dominant strategy and that less than 1 percent exceed the group-payoff-maximizing contribution. In RRV Low, these numbers are 1 and 2 percent, respectively, and in RRV High, we find 24 percent of contributions being below the dominant-strategy and 4 percent being in excess of the group-payoff-maximizing contribution.

The histograms presented in figure 4.4 mask the learning that takes place as subjects make repeated decisions in the experiment. To illustrate what happens with repetition, figure 4.5 presents graphs of the mean and median contribution choices by group size and the location of the dominant-strategy-equilibrium prediction. The horizontal solid line in each panel indicates the location of the dominant strategy, and the horizontal dashed line indicates the location of the group-payoff-maximizing contribution. See figure 4.A.2 in appendix 4.A for the mean and median contributions by treatment.

The first thing that becomes evident when looking at the two-person PL-PG games panel of figure 4.5 is that, unlike the standard linear VCM scenario, there is little deviation from the dominant strategy over the course of the experiment. The median contribution coincides exactly with the dominant-strategy-equilibrium prediction in every round of play. This is true for the pooled sample (figure 4.5) and when analyzing data for each of the studies separately (figure 4.A.2). Average contributions start slightly above the equilibrium prediction but converge very quickly to the dominant strategy. Session-level tests in fact fail to reject the null hypothesis that average contributions coincide with the equilibrium prediction once we reach the fourth round of play. We also fail

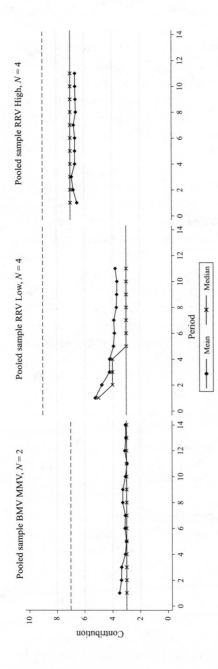

Figure 4.5
Mean and median contribution, by group size, PL-PG game. *Notes*: The solid horizontal reference line in each panel indicates the location of the dominant strategy. The dashed horizontal reference line in each panel indicates the location of the group-payoff-maximizing contribution. There are 154 participants (11 sessions) in the pooled sample of BMV and MMV, and 120 participants (6 sessions) in each of the pooled RRV samples (Low and High). BMV, Bracha, Menietti, and Vesterlund (2011); MMV, Menietti, Morelli, and Vesterlund (2012); PL-PG, piecewise linear public goods; RRV, Recalde, Riedl, and Vesterlund (forthcoming).

to reject that average play in the pooled sample of all rounds equals the predicted equilibrium (mean contribution = 3.18, two-sided t-test $p = 0.163$).[11]

In four-person groups, the mean and median also converge to the equilibrium prediction, but the story is slightly different. When the dominant strategy is to contribute below the midpoint of the strategy set, mean and median contributions start at approximately 50 percent of the endowment and decline over rounds. This is similar to the result typically documented in the standard linear VCM. The median converges to and reaches the equilibrium prediction by round 5 of the pooled sample of games with a low dominant strategy. Average contributions initially exceed the equilibrium by a substantial amount, and although over contribution decreases over time, it persists across rounds. In fact we can reject that mean contributions equal the equilibrium prediction (mean contribution = 4.08, two-sided t-test $p < 0.01$ both across and within rounds).

Stronger convergence is seen when looking at behavior in the pooled sample of PL-PG games in which the dominant strategy is to contribute an amount above the midpoint of the strategy set. The median contribution level coincides with the dominant strategy in all rounds of play, and we find that average contributions across rounds only differ slightly from the dominant strategy (mean contribution = 6.67, two-sided t-test $p < 0.10$ across all rounds of play).[12] Thus, in four-person PL-PG games, we find that average contributions converge to equilibrium, but while close, fail to reach it by the end of the repeated play.[13]

The rate of equilibrium play increases with repetition in all treatments. It starts at 66.1 in round 1 of the pooled sample of two-person PL-PG games and increases to 75.9 in round 14 (the last round of MMV and BMV). The rate of equilibrium play in the four-person games starts lower (at 30 and 33 percent, respectively, in the Low and High designs), but it increases quickly with repetition to levels similar to those seen in the two-person environment by the end of the experiment. In round 11 of RRV (the last round), the rate of equilibrium play is 64.2 and 74.2 percent, respectively, in the four-person Low and High designs. Figure 4.A.3 shows the rate of equilibrium play documented in each treatment by round.

Examining participant behavior in various implementations of the PL-PG game, we find that play is very sensitive to the location of the equilibrium. Across studies we find a high and increasing frequency of equilibrium play; a low rate of mistakes; and importantly, that mean, median, and modal contributions track the equilibrium. Relative to previous studies, we find evidence consistent with incentives being well understood, which is essential when studying giving in the laboratory, and in particular when the goal is to study more complex contribution environments. Below we provide examples of using the PL-PG framework to study charitable giving.

4.5   Using the PL-PG Game to Study Charitable Giving

The PL-PG game was used by MMV to study questions in the context of philanthropy. They asked theoretically and experimentally how a goal for a charitable campaign could affect overall giving. Specifically, they examined an environment where donors can pledge funds but where contributions are collected only when a goal or threshold is reached. Of central concern was how a fundraiser would wish to set his or her goal. Using a simple model, they show that the fundraiser will set the goal or threshold at an inefficiently high level. This raises the question of whether inefficiently high provision indeed can result in the context of the environment presented. By mere design, the VCM is not suited for examining this question in the laboratory. MMV conduct instead a laboratory experiment with two treatments that varied in a two-person simultaneous-move PL-PG game whether or not there existed an inefficiently large threshold, under which the public good would not be provided and contributions would be refunded. Consistent with the theoretical prediction, they show that a threshold can raise contributions to an inefficiently high level. In contrast to our standard understanding of charitable giving, it need not be the case that underprovision results. If the fundraiser is able to commit to a sufficiently high goal, then contributions to the public good may instead be inefficiently large.

BMV instead use the PL-PG game to examine why nonprofit organizations announce seed donations in fundraising campaigns. Andreoni (1998) showed theoretically that seed donations, and thus sequential contributions, can increase public good provision in environments where fixed costs give rise to multiple contribution equilibria. In a game with multiple equilibria (zero and positive provisions), sequential moves permit coordination on a positive provision outcome. BMV tested this predicted comparative static by conducting a laboratory experiment using a two-person PL-PG game in a 3×2 between-subject design that varied the size of a fixed cost in the payoff function (none, small, or large), and the timing of decisions (sequential versus simultaneous). Consistent with the theory put forward by Andreoni (1998), they find that sequential giving secures provision in environments where sufficiently high fixed costs gives rise to a coordination problem and contribution failure in the simultaneous game. When the fixed costs are instead low, participants overcontribute relative to the Nash prediction in the simultaneous move environment, and this overcontribution disappears with sequential moves.

Menietti (2012) relies on the PL-PG game to study how fundraising goal announcements can reduce the uncertainty about public good provision and generate a threshold that increases donations relative to an environment without goal announcements. He used a two-person PL-PG game to conduct a laboratory experiment with three treatments, varying the presence of a goal in an environment with uncertainty and whether or not the goal reduced such uncertainty. Results show that goal announcement increases donations relative to a no-announcement treatment, but that the reduction in uncertainty generated by the goal announcement does not increase contributions relative to an environment with goal announcement but no reduction in uncertainty. The reduction in uncertainty, however, does facilitate coordination on the symmetric equilibrium and thus increases the average earnings of participants relative to the treatment with goal announcement and no reduction in uncertainty.

RRV use a series of four-person PL-PG games to determine whether response time (how fast individuals make choices) in the public goods game can be used to identify whether the act of giving is intuitive or deliberate. Past studies have examined contributions in the VCM and have found that individuals with fast decision times are more generous than those with slow decision times, and these studies argue that the intuitive response is to be other-regarding. RRV explore this claim by examining contributions in two PL-PG treatments that vary the location of the dominant-strategy-equilibrium prediction, with one lying below the midpoint and the other above the midpoint of the strategy set. RRV's results show that fast decisions are not associated with selfish or generous choices but rather with mistakes, which fall on average in the middle of the strategy set.[14] With deliberation, contributions move on average in the direction of the dominant strategy equilibrium prediction. Thus, when the equilibrium prediction is at the bottom of the strategy set, RRV find that fast decision makers are more generous than slow decision makers, and when the equilibrium prediction is toward the top of the strategy set, they find instead that fast decision makers are less generous than slow decision makers. This study clearly demonstrates the false inference that may be drawn in the classic VCM, where mistakes cannot be identified. The inference on the extent to which giving is intuitive or deliberative has natural consequences for the manner in which fundraisers best solicit donations.

4.6 Conclusion

This chapter has described the advantages of a recently introduced payoff structure for studying charitable giving in the laboratory. Using piecewise linear payoffs, the PL-PG games allow the researcher to move both the equilibrium and group-payoff-maximizing contribution off the boundary and into the interior of the strategy set, while also presenting participants with an easy to understand payoff function. Not only do these payoffs make it easy to identify clearly dominated choices, they also generate behavior that suggests limited confusion with repeated play. Reviewing behavior in these games, we find that play is very sensitive to the location of the equilibrium. We find a high frequency of equilibrium play across implementations. In fact, with the frequency of equilibrium play ranging between 51 and 70 percent, such play dominates that seen in the VCM as well as in other types of public goods games with an interior equilibrium. We also document a low rate of mistakes; and that mean, median, and modal contributions track the equilibrium. As scholars begin to examine increasingly complex fundraising mechanisms in the laboratory, they may benefit from considering the flexible and transparent PL-PG games.

4.A Appendix A

This appendix presents supporting material that disaggregates the data presented in section 4.4 by study and treatment.

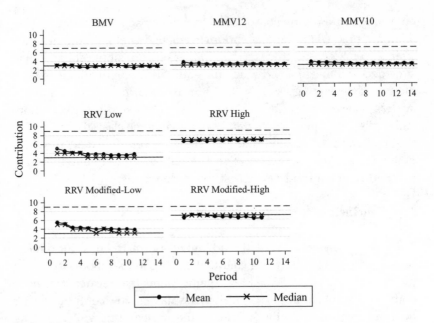

Figure 4.A.1
Mean and median contribution, by round and treatment. *Notes:* The solid horizontal reference line in each panel indicates the location of the dominant strategy. The dashed horizontal reference line in each panel indicates the location of the group-payoff-maximizing choice. The number of participants (sessions) in each treatment is: 42 (three) in BMV and MMV12, 28 (two) in MMV10, 80 (four) in RRV Low and High, and 40 (two) in RRV Modified-Low and Modified-High. BMV, Bracha, Menietti, and Vesterlund (2011); MMV, Menietti, Morelli, and Vesterlund (2012); MMV10, MMV with endowment of 10; MMV12, MMV with endowment of 12; RRV, Recalde, Riedl, and Vesterlund (forthcoming).

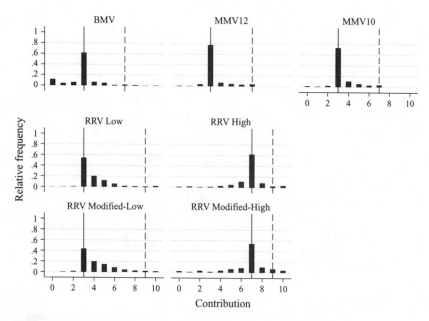

Figure 4.A.2
Histogram of contributions, by treatment. *Notes*: The solid reference line indicates the location of the dominant strategy. The dashed reference line indicates the location of the group-payoff-maximizing choice. Due to the difference in number of rounds and sessions the number of decisions included in each of the treatments is: 588 in BMV and MMV12, 392 in MMV10, 880 in RRV Low and RRV High, and 440 in RRV Modified-Low and RRV Modified-High. BMV, Bracha, Menietti, and Vesterlund (2011); MMV, Menietti, Morelli, and Vesterlund (2012); MMV10, MMV with endowment of 10; MMV12, MMV with endowment of 12; RRV, Recalde, Riedl, and Vesterlund (forthcoming).

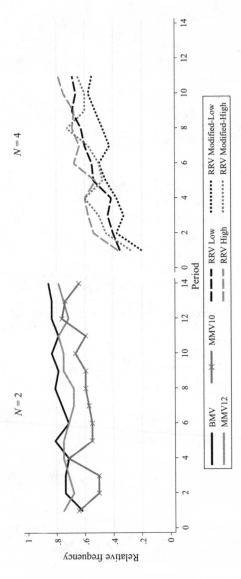

Figure 4.A.3

Equilibrium play, by round and treatment. *Notes:* The number of decisions per round observed in each treatment is: 42 in BMV and MMV12, 28 in MMV10, 80 in RRV Low and RRV High, and 40 in RRV Modified-Low and RRV Modified-High. BMV, Bracha, Menietti, and Vesterlund (2011); MMV, Menietti, Morelli, and Vesterlund (2012); MMV10, MMV with endowment of 10; MMV12, MMV with endowment of 12; RRV, Recalde, Riedl, and Vesterlund (forthcoming).

4.B   Appendix B

This appendix presents the instructions used by RRV in the treatments with PL-PG games and no time pressure or time delay.

4.B.1   Instructions

This is an experiment on decision making. The earnings you receive today will depend on the decisions made by you and by other participants in this room. Please do not talk or communicate with others in any way. If you have a question, please raise your hand and an experimenter will come to where you are sitting to answer you in private.

4.B.2   Earnings

There will be two parts of the experiment. Only one of the two parts will count for payment. Once part 1 and 2 are completed we will flip a coin to determine which part counts for payment. Your earnings in the experiment will be the sum of a $6 payment for showing up on time and your earnings from either part 1 or part 2. We will first explain how earnings are determined in part 1. Once part 1 is completed we will explain how earnings in part 2 are determined. Decisions in part 1 only

Decision Screen

Dollars to invest in group account [   ]   [Finalize Decision]

Average investment made by the other group members

Your investment	0	1	2	3	4	5	6	7	8	9	10
0	$A00 / $B00	$A01 / $B01	$A02 / $B02	$A03 / $B03	$A04 / $B04	$A05 / $B05	$A06 / $B06	$A07 / $B07	$A08 / $B08	$A09 / $B09	$A010 / $B010
1	$A10 / $B10	$A11 / $B11	$A12 / $B12	$A13 / $B13	$A14 / $B14	$A15 / $B15	$A16 / $B16	$A17 / $B17	$A18 / $B18	$A19 / $B19	$A110 / $B110
2	$A20 / $B20	$A21 / $B21	$A22 / $B22	$A23 / $B23	$A24 / $B24	$A25 / $B25	$A26 / $B26	$A27 / $B27	$A28 / $B28	$A29 / $B29	$A210 / $B210
3	$A30 / $B30	$A31 / $B31	$A32 / $B32	$A33 / $B33	$A34 / $B34	$A35 / $B35	$A36 / $B36	$A37 / $B37	$A38 / $B38	$A39 / $B39	$A310 / $B310
4	$A40 / $B40	$A41 / $B41	$A42 / $B42	$A43 / $B43	$A44 / $B44	$A45 / $B45	$A46 / $B46	$A47 / $B47	$A48 / $B48	$A49 / $B49	$A410 / $B410
5	$A50 / $B50	$A51 / $B51	$A52 / $B52	$A53 / $B53	$A54 / $B54	$A55 / $B55	$A56 / $B56	$A57 / $B57	$A58 / $B58	$A59 / $B59	$A510 / $B510
6	$A60 / $B60	$A61 / $B61	$A62 / $B62	$A63 / $B63	$A64 / $B64	$A65 / $B65	$A66 / $B66	$A67 / $B67	$A68 / $B68	$A69 / $B69	$A610 / $B610
7	$A70 / $B70	$A71 / $B71	$A72 / $B72	$A73 / $B73	$A74 / $B74	$A75 / $B75	$A76 / $B76	$A77 / $B77	$A78 / $B78	$A79 / $B79	$A710 / $B710
8	$A80 / $B80	$A81 / $B81	$A82 / $B82	$A83 / $B83	$A84 / $B84	$A85 / $B85	$A86 / $B86	$A87 / $B87	$A88 / $B88	$A89 / $B89	$A810 / $B810
9	$A90 / $B90	$A91 / $B91	$A92 / $B92	$A93 / $B93	$A94 / $B94	$A95 / $B95	$A96 / $B96	$A97 / $B97	$A98 / $B98	$A99 / $B99	$A910 / $B910
10	$A100 / $B100	$A101 / $B101	$A102 / $B102	$A103 / $B103	$A104 / $B104	$A105 / $B105	$A106 / $B106	$A107 / $B107	$A108 / $B108	$A109 / $B109	$A1010 / $B1010

The BLUE number on the left is your payoff. The BLACK number on the right is the payoff of each of the other group members when they each invest the amount listed.

Figure 4.B.1
Decision Screen. *Source*: Recalde, Riedl, and Vesterlund (forthcoming).

affect possible earnings in part 1, and decisions in part 2 only affect possible earnings in part 2. Your total earnings will be paid to you in cash and in private at the end of the experiment.

4.B.3 Part 1

In part 1 you will be matched in groups of four. That is the computer will randomly match you with three other participants.

You will each have to make one decision, and earnings will depend on the decision made by you and the decisions made by other members of your group. Neither during nor after the experiment will you get to know who the other members of your group are or what decisions they make. Likewise, no one in your group will know who you are and what decision you make.

You and each of the other group members will be given $10 and asked to make an investment decision. You may select to invest any dollar amount between $0 and $10 in a group account. Investments in the group account affect both your earnings and those of the other members of the group. That is, individual earnings depend on the individual investment in the group account and the investment by the other group members.

Decision Screen

Your investment decision will be made using a decision screen. You make a decision by entering the number of dollars you wish to invest in the group account in the area labeled: *Dollars to invest in group account*. Once you have made your investment decision, please click the red *Finalize Decision* button. You will not be able to modify your decision once your choice is finalized.

A decision screen is shown below. The actual decision screen will include a payoff table with the earnings that result from the investments made by you and the three other group members. We will use the screenshot below to demonstrate how to read the table. The first column shows all possible investments by you. The first row shows all possible average investments by the other group members. If the average investment by the other group members is say $2, then it may result from each investing $2, or from one member investing $0, another investing $2, and a third investing $4.

Each cell reports the payoff you and the other group members receive given your investment and the average investment by the other group members. Your payoff will be depicted in blue and located in the upper left corner of each cell. The average payoff of the other group members will be depicted in black and located in the bottom right corner of each cell. To determine the payoffs from a specific combination of investments you look at the cell where the row of your investment crosses the column of the average investment by the other group members. In this cell you will see your payoff on the left (in blue) and the average payoff of the other group members on the right (in black). The average payoff for the other group members refers to the payoff they each get when they invest the same amount in the group account.

Consider an example where you invest $1 and the average investment by the other group members is $4. Your earnings from this investment decision will be $A14, where the first number refers to your $1 investment and the second to the $4 average investment by the other group members. Similarly the earnings of each of the three other group members will be $B14. If you were to increase your investment to $2 you move down one row to see that your earnings would become $A24 and the average earnings of the other group members would become $B24. Likewise if the average investment of the other group members increased by $1, such that you invest $2 and the other group members on average invest $5, you move over one column to see that your earnings would become $A25 and the average payoff to the other group members would be $B25. Before we begin we will give you a tutorial on how to read the payoff table.

Results Screen
After everyone has made an investment decision you will see a results screen. The results screen will indicate the investments made by you and the other group members and will summarize the earnings you and the other group members receive if part 1 counts for payment. The average earnings for the other group members reported in the payoff table refer to the earnings that result when the three other group members make the same investment decision. In the event that they do not invest the same amount their actual average earnings may differ slightly from that reported in the table. Your own payoff from the listed investment combination will be precisely that listed in the payoff table.

4.B.4   Instructions Part 2
[Distributed after Part 1 is completed]

Part 2 is very similar to part 1. The only difference is that you now must make investment decisions over a sequence of ten rounds. At the beginning of each round you will be randomly matched with three other people to form a new group of four. You will never be matched with the same three people twice in a row. It is also unlikely that you will meet the same set of three other group members twice. You will not get to know who the other members of your group are nor will you be informed of their past investment. Likewise, no one will know who you are and what investments you made in the past.

Just as for part 1 you will be presented with a decision screen which reports the earnings that you and the other group members get from the different investments. The decision screen will be the same in each round. That is, the earnings are the same for each of the ten rounds and are identical to those seen in part 1.

After each round is complete you will be shown a result screen which reports the investments made by you and the other group members in that round, as well as the earnings you and the other group members made in that round.

If part 2 is selected for payment we will randomly select a number between one and ten. The earnings for the corresponding round will be paid to the participants along with the $6 show up fee. The part that counts for payment will be determined by the flip of a coin. The round that counts in part 2 will be determined by having a participant draw a number between 1 and 10.

Notes

1. See also Dawes, McTavish, and Shaklee (1977); Marwell and Ames (1979, 1980, 1981), and Isaac, McCue, and Plott (1985).

2. Decisions made in period 1 were made without the knowledge that another ten periods would follow of the same game. After period 1 was completed, participants were informed that there would be an additional ten periods of the same game.

3. In the VCM, $u(w - c(g_i)) = r(w - g_i)$ and $v(G) = mG$, where r and m are constants.

4. Making both $u(\cdot)$ and $v(\cdot)$ concave is, of course, possible. We illustrate the simplest approach taken by the literature, which makes utility separable, keeps one function linear, and makes the other one strictly concave.

5. The paper does not report the rate of equilibrium play. The symmetric Nash equilibrium in nondominant strategies in the environment with homogeneous preferences is for subjects to contribute 42.9 percent of their endowment when group size is 3, and 21.4 percent of the endowment when it is 6. Guttman finds in these treatments overcontribution relative to the symmetric Nash prediction of 67 to 100 percent.

6. Harrison and Hirshleifer (1989), Cason, Saijo, and Yamato (2002), and Croson, Fatas, and Neugebauer (2005) also examine contributions in a nonlinear public goods games

with interior solutions in nondominant strategies, but they do so in different environments. Harrison and Hirshleifer (1989) vary across three treatments the public goods production function technology $v(\cdot)$, making it either linear, weakest link, or best shot. The weakest link function generates multiple symmetric Nash equilibria consistent with all possible contribution choices, while the best shot technology generates multiple asymmetric Nash equilibria and no symmetric interior solution. Croson, Fatas, and Neugebauer (2005) compare contributions in a linear and weakest link public goods game. Cason, Saijo, and Yamato (2002) use instead a Cobb-Douglass production function to generate a unique interior symmetric Nash equilibrium in nondominant strategies, but they implement a two-stage game that has subjects first decide whether they want to contribute and then how much to contribute, with feedback after the first stage.

7. See appendix 4.B for sample instructions from RRV.

8. Treatments with sequential decisions, fixed costs or thresholds, and exogenous manipulations of available decision time (RRV) are not included.

9. Full contribution choices also constitute mistakes in RRV Modified-Low and Modified-High.

10. Another difference between groups with two and four participants is whether payoffs only were presented in payoff tables (groups with four) or whether they were accompanied by a description of the payoff function (groups with two). When describing the payoff function, one might be concerned that the cutoffs were made focal to the participants. However, the consistently high frequency of equilibrium play across games suggests that equilibrium play is high even when only a payoff table is used to present payoffs. Subjects in RRV completed a tutorial on how to read payoff tables and were only presented with payoff information via payoff tables displayed on the screen that subjects used to make choices. That is, payoff functions, kinks, and cost cutoffs were never mentioned to subjects in RRV.

11. All tests, unless otherwise noted, are two-sided session-level one-sample t-tests of the null hypothesis that average contributions equal the Nash prediction.

12. Within rounds, the null hypotheses that mean contributions equal the dominant strategy Nash prediction ($g_i = 7$) can be rejected in rounds 1, 8, and 11, where the two-sided t-test $p = 0.021$, 0.077, and 0.079, respectively. In 3 additional rounds, deviations are marginally insignificant. Two-sided one-sample t-tests provide $p < 0.15$ in a total of 6 rounds.

13. If the average deviation from the Nash prediction on RRV High is entirely due to error, then extrapolating across treatments suggests that only 30 percent of the average overcontribution in RRV Low can be explained by error.

14. Neither a selfish nor a generous person would select actions that decrease both the earnings of the individual and the earnings of other groups' members. RRV therefore classify such actions as mistakes.

References

Anderson, Simon P., Jacob K. Goeree, and Charles A. Holt. 1998. "A Theoretical Analysis of Altruism and Decision Error in Public Goods Games." *Journal of Public Economics* 70 (2): 297–323.

Andreoni, James. 1993. "An Experimental Test of the Public-Goods Crowding-Out Hypothesis." *American Economic Review* 83 (5): 1317–1327.

Andreoni, James. 1995. "Cooperation in Public-Goods Experiments: Kindness or Confusion?" *American Economic Review* 85 (4): 891–904.

Andreoni, James. 1998. "Toward a Theory of Charitable Fund-Raising." *Journal of Political Economy* 106 (6): 1186–1213.

Becker, Gary S. 1974. "A Theory of Social Interactions." *Journal of Political Economy* 82 (6): 1063–1093. http://www.jstor.org/stable/1830662.

Bergstrom, Theodore, Lawrence Blume, and Hal Varian. 1986. "On the Private Provision of Public Goods." *Journal of Public Economics* 29 (1): 25–49.

Bracha, Anat, Michael Menietti, and Lise Vesterlund. 2011. "Seeds to Succeed? Sequential Giving to Public Projects." *Journal of Public Economics* 95 (5–6): 416–427. doi: 10.1016/j .jpubeco.2010.10.007.

Cason, Timothy N., and Lata Gangadharan. 2015. "Promoting Cooperation in Nonlinear Social Dilemmas through Peer Punishment." *Experimental Economics* 18 (1): 66–88. doi: 10.1007/s10683-014-9393-0.

Cason, Timothy N., Tatsuyoshi Saijo, and Takehiko Yamato. 2002. "Voluntary Participation and Spite in Public Good Provision Experiments: An International Comparison." *Experimental Economics* 5 (2): 133–153. doi: 10.1023/A:1020317321607.

Chan, Kenneth S., Rob Godby, Stuart Mestelman, and R. Andrew Muller. 2002. "Crowding-Out Voluntary Contributions to Public Goods." *Journal of Economic Behavior & Organization* 48 (3): 305–317. doi: 10.1016/S0167-2681(01)00232-3.

Chan, Kenneth S., Stuart Mestelman, Rob Moir, and R. Andrew Muller. 1996. "The Voluntary Provision of Public Goods under Varying Income Distributions." *Canadian Journal of Economics* 29 (1): 54–69.

Chan, Kenneth S., Stuart Mestelman, Robert Moir, and R. Andrew Muller. 1999. "Heterogeneity and the Voluntary Provision of Public Goods." Experimental Economics 2 (1): 5–30.

Chaudhuri, Ananish. 2011. "Sustaining Cooperation in Laboratory Public Goods Experiments: A Selective Survey of the Literature." *Experimental Economics* 14 (1): 47–83. doi: 10.1007/s10683-010-9257-1.

Croson, Rachel, Enrique Fatas, and Tibor Neugebauer. 2005. "Reciprocity, Matching and Conditional Cooperation in Two Public Goods Games." *Economics Letters* 87 (1): 95–101. doi: 10.1016/j.econlet.2004.10.007.

Dawes, Robyn M., Jeanne McTavish, and Harriet Shaklee. 1977. "Behavior, Communication, and Assumptions about Other Peoples' Behavior in a Commons Dilemma Situation." *Journal of Personality and Social Psychology* 35 (1): 1–11.

Falkinger, Josef, Ernst Fehr, Simon Gächter, and Rudolf Winter-Ember. 2000. "A Simple Mechanism for the Efficient Provision of Public Goods: Experimental Evidence." *American Economic Review* 90 (1): 247–264. doi: 10.1257/aer.90.1.247.

Gronberg, Timothy J., I. I. I. R. Andrew Luccasen, Theodore L. Turocy, and John B. Van Huyck. 2012. "Are Tax-Financed Contributions to a Public Good Completely Crowded-Out? Experimental Evidence." *Journal of Public Economics* 96 (7-8): 596–603. doi:10.1016/j .jpubeco.2012.04.001.

Guttman, Joel M. 1986. "Matching Behavior and Collective Action: Some Experimental Evidence." *Journal of Economic Behavior & Organization* 7 (2): 171–198. doi: 10.1016 /0167-2681(86)90004-1.

Harrison, Glenn W., and Jack Hirshleifer. 1989. "An Experimental Evaluation of Weakest Link/Best Shot Models of Public Goods." *Journal of Political Economy* 97 (1): 201–225. http://www.jstor.org/stable/1831060.

Houser, Daniel, and Robert Kurzban. 2002. "Revisiting Kindness and Confusion in Public Goods Experiments." *American Economic Review* 92 (4): 1062–1069. doi:10.1257 /00028280260344605.

Isaac, R. Mark, Kenneth F. McCue, and Charles R. Plott. 1985. "Public Goods Provision in an Experimental Environment." *Journal of Public Economics* 26 (1): 51–74. doi: 10.1016 /0047-2727(85)90038-6.

Isaac, R. Marc, and James M. Walker. 1998. "Nash as an Organizing Principle in the Voluntary Provision of Public Goods: Experimental Evidence." *Experimental Economics* 1 (3): 191–206.

Isaac, R. Mark, James M. Walker, and Susan H. Thomas. 1984. "Divergent Evidence on Free Riding: An Experimental Examination of Possible Explanations." *Public Choice* 43 (2): 113–149.

Keser, Claudia. 1996. "Voluntary Contributions to a Public Good When Partial Contribution Is a Dominant Strategy." *Economics Letters* 50 (3): 359–366. http://www.jstor.org /stable/30023863.

Laury, Susan K., and Charles A. Holt. 2008. "Voluntary Provision of Public Goods: Experimental Results with Interior Nash Equilibria." In *Handbook of Experimental Economics Results*, vol. 1, edited by Charles R. Plott and Vernon L. Smith, 792–801. Amsterdam: North-Holland. doi: 10.1016/S1574-0722(07)00084-4.

Laury, Susan K., James M. Walker, and Arlington W. Williams. 1999. "The Voluntary Provision of a Pure Public Good with Diminishing Marginal Returns." *Public Choice* 99 (1/2): 139–160. doi: 10.1023/A:1018302432659.

Ledyard, John. 1995. "A Survey of Experimental Research." In *The Handbook of Experimental Economics*, edited by John H. Kagel and Alvin E. Roth, 111–194. Princeton, NJ: Princeton University Press.

Marwell, Gerald, and Ruth E. Ames. 1979. "Experiments on the Provision of Public Goods. I. Resources, Interest, Group Size, and the Free-Rider Problem." *American Journal of Sociology* 84 (6): 1335–1360. http://www.jstor.org/stable/2777895.

Marwell, Gerald, and Ruth E. Ames. 1980. "Experiments on the Provision of Public Goods. II. Provision Points, Stakes, Experience, and the Free-Rider Problem." *American Journal of Sociology* 85 (4): 926–937. http://www.jstor.org/stable/2778712.

Marwell, Gerald, and Ruth E. Ames. 1981. "Economists Free Ride, Does Anyone Else?" *Journal of Public Economics* 15 (3): 295–310. doi: 10.1016/0047-2727(81)90013-X.

Maurice, Jonathan, Agathe Rouaix, and Marc Willinger. 2013. "Income Redistribution and Public Good Provision: An Experiment." *International Economic Review* 54 (3): 957–975. doi: 10.1111/iere.12024.

Menietti, Michael. 2012. "Fundraising Goals." Working paper, Social Science Research Network. doi: 10.2139/ssrn.2142765.

Menietti, Michael, Massimo Morelli, and Lise Vesterlund. 2012. "Provision Point Mechanisms and the Over-provision of Public Goods." Working paper, University of Pittsburgh, Pittsburgh, PA.

Recalde, María P., Arno Riedl, and Lise Vesterlund. Forthcoming. "Error-Prone Inference from Response Time: The Case of Intuitive Generosity in Public-Good Games." *Journal of Public Economics*.

Robbett, Andrea. 2016. "Sustaining Cooperation in Heterogeneous Groups." *Journal of Economic Behavior & Organization* 132 (Part A): 121–138. doi: 10.1016/j.jebo.2016.09.012.

Rouaix, Agathe, Charles Figuières, and Marc Willinger. 2015. "The Trade-Off between Welfare and Equality in a Public Good Experiment." *Social Choice and Welfare* 45 (3): 601–623. doi: 10.1007/s00355-015-0893-4.

Sefton, Martin, and Richard Steinberg. 1996. "Reward Structures in Public Good Experiments." *Journal of Public Economics* 61 (2): 263–287.

Sutter, Matthias, and Hannelore Weck-Hannemann. 2004. "An Experimental Test of the Public Goods Crowding Out Hypothesis When Taxation Is Endogenous." *FinanzArchiv/ Public Finance Analysis* 60 (1): 94–110. http://www.jstor.org/stable/40913030.

van Dijk, Frans, Joep Sonnemans, and Frans van Winden. 2002. "Social Ties in a Public Good Experiment." *Journal of Public Economics* 85 (2): 275–299. doi: 10.1016/S0047 -2727(01)00090-1.

Vesterlund, Lise. 2016. "Using Experimental Methods to Understand Why and How We Give to Charity." In *The Handbook of Experimental Economics*, vol. 2, edited by John H. Kagel and Alvin E. Roth, 91–151. Princeton, NJ: Princeton University Press.

Willinger, Marc, and Anthony Ziegelmeyer. 1999. "Framing and Cooperation in Public Good Games: An Experiment with an Interior Solution." *Economics Letters* 65 (3): 323–328.

Willinger, Marc, and Anthony Ziegelmeyer. 2001. "Strength of the Social Dilemma in a Public Goods Experiment: An Exploration of the Error Hypothesis." *Experimental Economics* 4 (2): 131–144. doi: 10.1007/BF01670009.

5 Increasing the Social Impact of Giving: An Experiment at Six Universities

Claudia Schwirplies, Jon Behar, and Greg Bose

5.1 Introduction

In 2015, more than 1.5 million charitable organizations were registered in the United States, and the number continues to grow,[1] which makes the choice among charities and charitable projects increasingly complex for (potential) donors. Charitable organizations, however, may differ in effectiveness or productivity in two important ways. First, from a conventional economic perspective, a charity might be more effective than another if both provide the same public good but one is able to produce more units per donation dollar. Second, from the perspective of the global effective altruism movement and philosophy, a charity is more effective than another if it provides different public goods and ensures a higher social welfare. Accordingly, a charity that addresses basic needs like health, housing, education, or human development is considered to be more effective than another charity that, for example, provides luxury (e.g., a new tennis court for an elite school or other amenities for students). In this chapter, the term "effectiveness" refers to the latter understanding.

Given that donors have a limited budget of time and money, it becomes increasingly important to help them direct their resources to more effective charities and charitable projects in order to maximize the social impact of their gifts. This is particularly important if donations are mainly driven by warm-glow motives, where donors derive considerable utility from the pure act of giving but little from the public good itself (Andreoni 1990). Consequently, the social impact of charitable organizations or purposes might play a minor role for the warm-glow givers (for a theoretical framework on this argument, see Null 2011), which requires greater attention focused on their choices of charities.

The purpose of this study is to identify strategies to influence donation decisions toward choices of charitable organizations and purposes that have enhanced social impact. In this respect, we let participants at six universities decide whether to donate $1 to their university's student aid program or to an organization that fights extreme poverty. While findings from the existing literature suggest that participants are more willing to give (or give a larger piece of the pie) to their in-group members due to their geographical and social proximity (e.g., Buchan, Johnson, and Croson 2006, and Charness and Gneezy 2008) or simply for self-interested reasons (if the participant is a student who receives student aid herself), in our experiment we try to shift the distribution of donations toward fighting extreme poverty in order to maximize global welfare benefits per dollar donated.

So far, the effectiveness of giving has received little attention in the economic literature, and the existing experiments all refer to the economic perspective discussed above. Most similar to our experiment is the study by Null (2011). She lets 200 participants divide a fund between a set of charities in a modified dictator game and finds that, even if matching grants make one charity most effective, remarkable amounts of money are still given to other charities. In contrast, Karlan and Wood (2014) vary the information about a charity's social impact in a fundraising campaign. They identify two important target groups in their observations: warm-glow givers (who usually donate smaller amounts and respond negatively) and altruists (who usually give higher amounts and respond positively to information on the effectiveness of the organization).

Existing experiments (in the lab and the field), however, mainly address the question of how to boost donations (by increasing the number of donors or the average donation) for one single charitable organization or purpose and thereby evaluate established or novel fundraising strategies. This involves the impact of matching grants or rebates (e.g., Frey and Meier 2004; Karlan and List 2007; Anik, Norton, and Ariely 2014; Karlan and McConnell 2014), the effectiveness of seed money (e.g., Eckel and Grossman 2003) and challenge gifts (e.g., List and Lucking-Reiley 2002; Rondeau and List 2008; Huck and Rasul 2011), the effects of social information (e.g., Frey and Meier 2004; Shang and Croson 2009) and defaults or recommendations on the donation amount (e.g., Edwards and List 2014), the role of small gifts for (potential) donors (e.g., Landry et al. 2006, 2010; Falk 2007), as well as the visibility of the donation (e.g., Vesterlund 2003; Soetevent 2005, 2011; Karlan and

McConnell 2014). Jasper and Samek (2014) provide an excellent and comprehensive summary of this literature.

For our experiment, we take up some ideas from this literature and use interventions that have been shown to significantly influence giving to one recipient. We test whether these interventions are able to redistribute donations from a charity with a lower social impact to one with a higher social impact. Specifically, we run a modified dictator game where participants (mostly students) at six universities in the United States and Canada are asked to decide where to donate $1 of a fund provided by the nonprofit organization The Life You Can Save for this experiment. Students choose between their school's student aid program and GiveDirectly, a nonprofit that transfers unrestricted cash grants to families living in extreme poverty. We employ social information about the decisions made by other participants, ask participants for a justification of their donation decision or both. We test whether these treatments increase donations for GiveDirectly and lead to more subscriptions to the mailing lists of the effective altruism groups. Our findings are highly heterogeneous across the six universities. Both treatments justification and social information seem to have the potential to change the distribution of donations toward fighting extreme poverty at certain schools, but reactions patterns are very different at the six universities. Most promising are the high- and low-anchor social information treatments in influencing decisions of students with a stronger self-interest in giving to their university's student aid fund toward making less self-interested donation decisions.

The chapter proceeds as follows. In section 5.2 we describe our experimental design and derive the hypotheses for our analysis. Section 5.3 presents the experimental results, and section 5.4 summarizes and draws some conclusions.

5.2   Experimental Design and Procedure

5.2.1   Experimental Design

We employ a modified version of the dictator game. In the original game, participants divide a certain amount of money between themselves and another participant. In our game, participants were asked to decide where to donate $1 from a fund provided by the nonprofit organization The Life You Can Save for this experiment.[2] Participants could choose between the student aid program of their school and GiveDirectly, an organization that engages in fighting extreme poverty by transferring cash to the poorest in the world. In contrast to the original dictator game, participants were not allowed to keep the dollar for themselves.

The experiment was carried out between September 2015 and January 2016 by the local effective altruism student groups at six universities in the United States and Canada: Cornell University, McGill University, University of British Columbia (UBC), University of California at Berkeley, University of Pennsylvania (Penn), and Yale University. The members of each effective altruism student group set up tables in a busy area on the campus of their university and solicited passersby to stop and take part in the game. Participants made their decisions on laptops and tablets by filling in an online form. For the implementation, the chapter members received comprehensive general instructions on how to run the experiment (see the instructions in the appendix) and were asked to precisely follow the script in order to minimize experimenter effects and biases.

The experiment started with a button on a web page that randomly directed each participant to one of the treatment surveys. These surveys were created in LimeSurvey and involved four screens.[3] At the beginning, participants were given a brief introduction to the game, including an explanation that they help determine where to donate to a real fund. This screen also provided the description of the two charities the participants were choosing between (i.e., their university's student aid program and GiveDirectly).[4] On the second screen, participants indicated their decisions.[5] The two final screens contained questions on the participants' characteristics (e.g., age, gender, and major) and provided the option to sign up to the mailing lists for The Life You Can Save and their school's effective altruism group.[6]

The experiment was implemented in two stages. In stage 1, we employed a 2×2 design (1) asking participants to justify their choice, (2) telling them that we simultaneously run this game at other universities and will show decision outcomes at their school to students at other schools before they will make the same decision, or (3) both. Specifically, in the justification treatments, the starting screen contained the following additional note: "You will be asked to provide a justification why exactly you chose one charity instead of the other." Participants provided the reasons for their decision on the second screen after they made their decision. In the stage 1 social information treatments, participants found another note on the second screen: "We are simultaneously running this game at other universities, and will show decision outcomes from your school to students at other universities before they make the same decision."

In stage 2, we only employ two social information treatments. The collected decisions from stage 1 served to provide a high and a low anchor. That is, at this stage of the experiment we included either of the following two social information statements on screen 2:

1. "Over the past few months, we have been running these Giving Games at other elite universities and so far found that almost 90% of people vote for GiveDirectly" (a result taken from the decisions at Berkeley at that point of the experiment).

2. "Over the past few months, we have been running these Giving Games at other elite universities and so far found that slightly more than 40% of people vote for GiveDirectly" (a result taken from the decisions at Cornell at that point of the experiment).

Stage 1 ran from September to December 2015, and we implemented four treatments: the control treatment without justification and social information (C), a treatment with justification but without social information (J), a treatment with social information but without justification (SI1), and a treatment involving justification and social information (J&SI). Stage 2 was then implemented in January 2016 and contained three treatments: the control treatment (C), social information with the high anchor (SI2) and social information with a low anchor (SI3). Table 5.1 summarizes the treatments (panel A) and descriptive statistics of our sample (panel C).

Overall, we collected 707 observations from the six universities, but McGill is the only university where we collected observations for all treatments. Most participants were undergraduates and graduate students with a major in economics, mathematics and information technology, engineering, natural sciences, or political science. Average age was about 22, the share of male and female participants was nearly balanced, and 40 percent of the participants received student aid. More than half of the observations are from Penn and McGill University.

Major differences arise in treatments SI2 and SI3, because these two treatments were only implemented at McGill University and UBC. Participants in these treatments were mostly undergraduates,[7] and only about 30 percent of them received student aid (differences from the control treatment are not statistically significant). The share of female participants is higher in SI2 (differences from the control treatment are

Table 5.1
Summary of treatments, outcomes, and descriptive statistics.

	Treatment Option													
Panel A	**All**		**C**		**J**		**SI1**		**J&SI**		**SI2**		**SI3**	
Social information			no		no		(b)		(b)		(c)		(d)	
Justification			no		(a)		no		(a)		no		no	
Panel B **Outcome variables**	Obs	Mean	Obs	Mean	Obs	Mean	Obs	Mean	Obs	Mean	Obs	Mean	Obs	Mean
GiveDirectly	707	0.67	196	0.68	147	0.69	134	0.69	139	0.67	34	0.62	57	0.60
Newsletter	707	0.20	196	0.21	147	0.11	134	0.16	139	0.27	34	0.32	57	0.18
Panel C **Characteristics**	Obs	Mean	Obs	Mean	Obs	Mean	Obs	Mean	Obs	Mean	Obs	Mean	Obs	Mean
Female	683	0.52	189	0.53	145	0.55	130	0.45	132	0.55	33	0.61	54	0.39
Age	697	21.52	194	22.17	146	20.64	131	21.73	136	21.62	34	22.76	56	20.04
Receive student aid	650	0.42	182	0.41	133	0.46	120	0.42	128	0.48	34	0.29	53	0.30
Major														
Economics	688	0.11	189	0.08	143	0.14	132	0.14	134	0.13	34	0.06	56	0.09
Math&IT	688	0.12	189	0.13	143	0.11	132	0.13	134	0.10	34	0.12	56	0.11
Engineering	688	0.10	189	0.12	143	0.12	132	0.05	134	0.12	34	0.06	56	0.13
NatScience	688	0.15	189	0.13	143	0.17	132	0.12	134	0.13	34	0.21	56	0.20
PolScience	688	0.03	189	0.04	143	0.03	132	0.02	134	0.03	34	0.03	56	0.05
Role														
Administrator	682	0.00	192	0.00	143	0.00	127	0.02	132	0.00	32	0.00	56	0.00
Faculty	682	0.01	192	0.01	143	0.01	127	0.02	132	0.02	32	0.03	56	0.00
Graduate student	682	0.17	192	0.19	143	0.17	127	0.19	132	0.23	32	0.00	56	0.04
Staff member	682	0.01	192	0.02	143	0.01	127	0.02	132	0.02	32	0.00	56	0.00
Undergraduate	682	0.78	192	0.75	143	0.79	127	0.76	132	0.72	32	0.94	56	0.95

University	ALL	C	J&SI	J	SI1	SI2	SI3
Berkeley	0.08	0.08	0.10	0.11	0.09	0.00	0.00
Penn	0.27	0.26	0.29	0.28	0.42	0.00	0.00
Yale	0.15	0.15	0.18	0.20	0.18	0.00	0.00
Cornell	0.11	0.10	0.18	0.15	0.11	0.00	0.00
McGill	0.30	0.31	0.24	0.25	0.20	0.56	0.56
UBC	0.08	0.10	0.00	0.00	0.00	0.44	0.44
Obs	707	196	147	134	139	34	57

Notes: ALL, total of all observations; C, control treatment without justification and social information; J&SI, treatment involving justification and social information; J, treatment with justification but without social information (stage 1); SI1, treatment with social information but without justification (stage 1); SI2, social information with a high anchor (stage 2); SI3, social information with a low anchor (stage 2); Obs, number of observations; Penn, University of Pennsylvania; UBC, University of British Columbia.

(a) Note on screen 1: "You will be asked to provide a justification why exactly you chose one charity instead of the other."

(b) Note on screen 2: "We are simultaneously running this game at other universities, and will show decision outcomes from your school to students at other universities before they make the same decision."

(c) Note on screen 2: "Over the past few months, we have been running the game at other universities and so far found that almost 90 percent of people vote for GiveDirectly."

(d) Note on screen 2: "Over the past few months, we have been running the game at other elite universities and so far found that slightly more than 40 percent of people vote for GiveDirectly."

not statistically significant) and lower in SI3.[8] To control for these differences, we also ran a regression analysis and discuss the results in Section 5.3.2.

In August 2016, The Life You Can Save implemented all the donations: $475 to GiveDirectly and $232 to the universities' student aid funds ($16 to Berkeley's, $32 to Cornell's, $93 to McGill's, $47 to Penn's, $20 to UBC's, and $24 to Yale's). Altogether, 138 participants subscribed to the mailing lists.

5.2.2   Hypotheses

Social information has been identified as a powerful tool influencing contributions to public goods if the information provides a sufficiently strong incentive. Andreoni and Petrie (2004) use a 2×2 design in a public goods game by providing information about other players' contributions, a picture of these players, or both, and they show that only information plus photo significantly increase giving to the public account. Shang and Croson (2009) revealed previous gifts of other donors in a radio station fundraiser, but only the announcement of the highest donation given previously (a $300 gift) had a significant effect. Frey and Meier (2004) provided information about the share of alumni who previously gave to funds supporting foreign students or students in financial difficulties. In their field experiment, informing participants about a relatively high percentage contributing to these charitable purposes induced norm-compliant behavior. Social information may, however, not only affect donations but also contributions to other public goods like water conservation (Ferraro and Price 2013) or movie ratings (Chen et al. 2010).

Our social information treatment is carried out in two stages. In stage 1 we tell participants that we will show decision outcomes from their school to students at other universities before they make the same decision. This might arouse the participants' desire to lead by example or signal the right decision (see also Andreoni and Petrie 2004), so that we expect participants in the stage 1 social information treatment to be more likely to donate to GiveDirectly compared to the control treatment (Hypothesis 1).

In stage 2, we use decision outcomes from stage 1 to provide social information either with a high (90 percent of decisions for GiveDirectly) or with a low (40 percent decisions for GiveDirectly) anchor, which might trigger feelings of social comparison and competition and induce norm-compliant donations. In line with the previous research, we expect the high-anchor social information to increase donations to GiveDirectly (Hypothesis 2), whereas the low-anchor social information might reduce the share of those donations if participants follow the norm (Hypothesis 3).

The reasoning behind our justification treatment is that the decision between giving to student aid or the extremely poor might release an inner conflict or tension—the so-called cognitive dissonance (see Konow 2000)—between the self-interested choice of increasing the student aid fund and the more effective choice of fighting extreme poverty. This might particularly be true for students who receive student aid themselves and thus are more inclined to make the self-interested decision to give to the student aid program. On the one hand, justification (i.e., finding appropriate reasons for the decision) might help participants reflect on the pros and cons of both charities more thoroughly and reduce self-interested choices. On the other hand, justification may also serve to reduce the tension associated with this decision by finding arguments for the self-interested behavior (in Konow 2000, this behavior is referred to as self-deception). Thus, the direction of the effect of our justification treatment is not clear in the first place, but we expect the former mechanism to be dominant and thus expect higher donation rates for GiveDirectly in these treatments (Hypothesis 4).

5.3   Experimental Results

5.3.1   Main Treatment Effects

Figure 5.1 shows the main results of our experiment. We focus on two outcome variables: (1) a binary variable equal to 1 if the participant voted for GiveDirectly and (2) a binary variable equal to 1 if the participant subscribed to the mailing lists. Figure 5.1 and panel B in table 5.1 indicate that between 60 and 69 percent of the participants decided that the dollar should go to GiveDirectly. Apparently, there is virtually no difference in decisions between the treatments in stage 1, but a slightly lower share of students give to GiveDirectly in both stage 2 social information treatments. The latter observation could potentially be attributed to special features of the two universities where these two treatments were implemented (McGill and UBC). Section 5.3.2. takes a closer look at the heterogeneity among the six universities. However, the differences in donations to GiveDirectly in the treatment and control groups are statistically not significant on the basis of Mann-Whitney U tests.

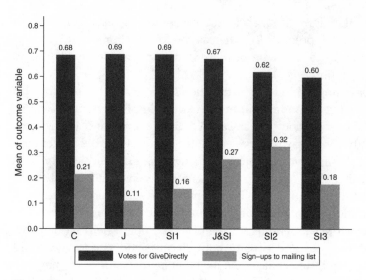

Figure 5.1
Main treatment effects. *Note*: See text for definitions of treatment options.

In the justification treatments, reasons given for the donation decisions are very similar. Participants who gave to GiveDirectly mainly argued that this donation is more effective, that it is more important to give to the poor, or that there is already plenty of money for student aid such that the additional dollar would have little impact. In contrast, participants who picked student aid argued that they picked financial aid because they knew exactly where the money is going and how it will benefit the recipient, that they benefited from the program themselves, or that they felt it is important to financially support the next generation of potential donors.

The newsletter subscriptions seem to be more reactive to our treatments. In stage 1, subscription rates tended to decrease in the justification and social information treatment, but increased with justification plus social information. We also collected more subscriptions to the mailing lists with the stage 2 high-anchor social information, which potentially goes in the same direction as the findings in the literature discussed in section 5.2.2, in which outcome variables take higher values only if the social information is strong enough. Statistically, however, only the difference between the control and the justification treatment is significant ($z = 2.574$, $p = 0.01$). This finding might suggest that justification did not reduce the tension associated with the choice between the two charities but potentially even reinforced this disutility, making those participants less willing to receive more information about effective giving, the issue that "caused" this cognitive dissonance.

Overall, none of our four hypotheses can be confirmed. Because we ran the experiment in very different universities and parts of North America, it is possible that the observed treatment effects are heterogeneous across universities and different environments. The next section investigates these heterogeneities.

5.3.2 Heterogeneity in Treatments

First, we look at differences between the six universities. Figure 5.2 displays the shares of participants who gave the dollar to GiveDirectly and who subscribed to the mailing lists for each university separately. In the control treatment, participants from Cornell and McGill University give significantly less to GiveDirectly compared to participants from Penn (Cornell: $z = -1.771$ and $p = 0.08$, McGill: $z = -1.947$ and $p = 0.05$) and Yale University (Cornell: $z = -2.164$ and $p = 0.03$, McGill: $z = -2.307$ and $p = 0.02$). At Berkeley and Cornell, justification and social information alone seem to increase donations for GiveDirectly (in line with our hypotheses 1 and 4), while the combined treatment tends to have a negative effect at Berkeley and a positive effect at Cornell. At McGill and Yale, participants decrease their donations to GiveDirectly in any of the stage 1 treatments (which somewhat contradicts our hypotheses 1 and 4). At Penn, reactions to the treatments are almost negligible, again not in line with our hypotheses.

The social information in stage 2 has opposing effects at McGill University and UBC. While the high-anchor social information increases donations for GiveDirectly at McGill, it decreases those donations at UBC. The contrary is true for the low anchor. All the differences between treatments in both stage 1 and stage 2 are, however, again not statistically significant. With 57 to 210 observations per university,[9] we apparently did not have enough power to detect significant differences, but our experimental design made it technically impossible to further increase the sample sizes.

When we look at the subscription rates for the mailing lists, we find a few statistically significant effects. Stage 1 social information reduces newsletter subscriptions at Berkeley ($z = 1.795$, $p = 0.07$); justification in combination with social information significantly increases subscriptions at Cornell ($z = -2.169$, $p = 0.03$); the high-anchor social information

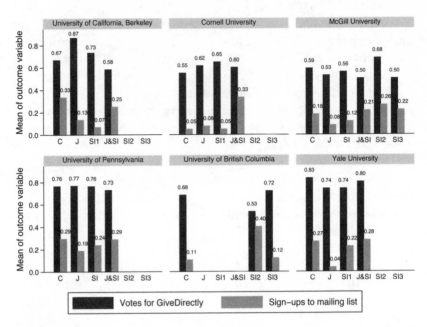

Figure 5.2
Treatment effects by university. *Note*: See text for definitions of treatment options.

increases sign-up rates at UBC ($z = -1.982$, $p = 0.05$); and justification decreases sign-up rates at Yale ($z = 2.353$, $p = 0.02$). Overall, we also cannot detect a clear tendency for the subscription rates, and the two outcome variables do not seem to follow a clear response pattern in the sense that a higher share of decisions in favor of GiveDirectly is accompanied by lower subscription rates or vice versa. We find a highly nuanced picture across the different universities, which does not allow for comprehensive conclusions.

Another source of heterogeneity is the strength of self-interest that participants might have in giving to their university's student aid fund. This self-interest clearly increases if students profit from the student aid program themselves. Figure 5.3 presents the differences in shares of participants who give the dollar to GiveDirectly for participants who receive and those who do not receive student aid. What becomes clear from this graph is that the two groups react differently to the social information in stage 2. Students who receive student aid (i.e., the group with the stronger self-interest in giving to the student aid fund) are more likely to give to GiveDirectly compared to participants who do not profit from these funds, regardless of the type of social information (high or low anchor) that we provide. Newsletter subscriptions are

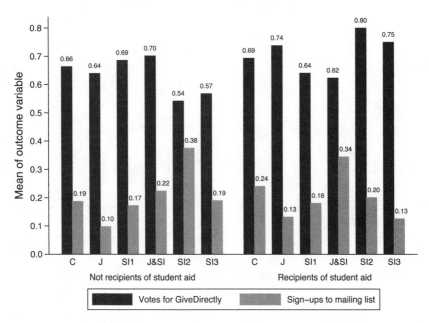

Figure 5.3
Treatment effects by recipient of student aid. *Note*: See text for definitions of treatment options.

highest with the high-anchor social information in the group of non-recipients of student aid and with justification and social information in the group of recipients of student aid. Again, the differences are statistically not significant on the basis of Mann-Whitney U tests.

Finally, we ran a regression analysis that controls for the detected heterogeneity among participants in the treatments (as discussed in section 5.2.1). We conducted this analysis for all participants as well as for the recipients and nonrecipients of student aid separately.[10] Using logit models, we estimated the following specification:

$$Y_i = \beta_0 + \beta_1 T_i + \beta_2 X_i + \varepsilon_i,$$

where Y_i is a vector of our binary outcome variables, T_i is a vector of binary variables for the treatments, and X_i is a vector of the further control variables for age, gender, recipient of student aid, and binary variables for the participant's major (if the participant is an undergraduate) and for the schools. Standard errors are robust to heteroscedasticity, and the error terms are clustered at the university level (i.e., we allow for correlations between the errors of all participants from one university). Results are reported in table 5.2.

Table 5.2
Parameter estimates in logit regression models.

Variable	Donation for GiveDirectly			Newsletter Subscription		
	All	Recipient of Student Aid	Not Recipient of Student Aid	All	Recipient of Student Aid	Not Recipient of Student Aid
Treatment						
J	0.05	0.29	−0.11	−0.83***	−0.82***	−0.86**
	(0.18)	(0.32)	(0.26)	(0.26)	(0.27)	(0.40)
SI1	−0.17	−0.46	0.00	−0.29**	−0.36	−0.14
	(0.14)	(0.49)	(0.15)	(0.15)	(0.35)	(0.19)
J&SI	−0.16	−0.44**	0.10	0.21	0.40	0.02
	(0.12)	(0.22)	(0.21)	(0.21)	(0.26)	(0.38)
SI2	−0.18	1.11***	−0.60	1.14***	0.56	1.43***
	(0.37)	(0.34)	(0.46)	(0.35)	(0.54)	(0.22)
SI3	0.18***	0.99	−0.11	0.23	−0.30	0.42
	(0.05)	(0.85)	(0.13)	(0.25)	(0.49)	(0.56)
Further controls						
Female	−0.09	−0.41	0.16	0.01	−0.19	0.27
	(0.19)	(0.32)	(0.16)	(0.16)	(0.33)	(0.28)
Age	0.03**	0.10**	0.03	0.01	0.07**	−0.03
	(0.02)	(0.05)	(0.02)	(0.03)	(0.03)	(0.04)
Recipient of student aid	−0.04			0.16		
	(0.13)			(0.14)		
Major (*base: all other*)						
Economics	−0.14	−0.25	0.05	0.07	−0.04	0.07
	(0.24)	(0.37)	(0.27)	(0.34)	(0.40)	(0.43)
Math&IT	0.16	0.39	0.09	0.14	0.44	−0.18
	(0.16)	(0.38)	(0.22)	(0.18)	(0.38)	(0.38)

	(1)	(2)	(3)	(4)	(5)	(6)
Engineering	-0.38**	-0.63	-0.27	0.23	0.22	0.08
	(0.18)	(0.59)	(0.22)	(0.46)	(1.07)	(0.36)
NatScience	0.14	0.33	0.06	-0.24	0.04	-0.68
	(0.31)	(0.41)	(0.32)	(0.21)	(0.27)	(0.45)
PolScience	-0.22	1.48	-0.67*	-0.94**		-0.56
	(0.45)	(1.82)	(0.35)	(0.48)		(0.67)
Role (*base: graduates and non-students*)						
Undergraduate	0.53*	0.76	0.63**	-0.11	0.92**	-1.06***
	(0.28)	(0.53)	(0.26)	(0.18)	(0.43)	(0.21)
School (*base: Yale*)						
Berkeley	-0.45***	-0.41***	-0.87***	-0.17***	-0.18*	-0.14*
	(0.03)	(0.05)	(0.05)	(0.02)	(0.10)	(0.07)
Cornell	-0.96***	-1.28***	-0.71***	-0.72***	-0.68***	-0.77***
	(0.03)	(0.06)	(0.03)	(0.04)	(0.06)	(0.13)
McGill	-1.12***	-1.85***	-0.78***	-0.34***	-0.37***	-0.32***
	(0.06)	(0.24)	(0.05)	(0.04)	(0.13)	(0.12)
Penn	-0.11	-0.44***	0.19	0.19**	0.36	0.04
	(0.13)	(0.12)	(0.18)	(0.07)	(0.23)	(0.14)
UBC	-0.86***	-1.68**	-0.47***	-0.88***	-1.36***	-0.49**
	(0.15)	(0.68)	(0.11)	(0.13)	(0.52)	(0.22)
Constant	0.30	-0.83	0.02	-1.27**	-3.08***	0.15
	(0.44)	(1.20)	(0.47)	(0.60)	(0.89)	(0.96)
Number of observations	624	264	360	624	258	360

Notes: Robust estimated standard errors are listed in parentheses. Error terms are clustered at the university level. The first three columns refer to the binary dependent variable, which is 1 if the participant donated the dollar to GiveDirectly; the forth to sixth columns refer to the binary dependent variable, which is 1 if the participant subscribed to the mailing lists. J, treatment with justification but without social information; J&SI, treatment involving justification and social information (stage 1); SI1, treatment with social information but without justification (stage 1); SI2, social information with a high anchor (stage 2); SI3, social information with a low anchor (stage 2); Penn, University of Pennsylvania; UBC, University of British Columbia. The symbols ***, **, and * indicate significance at the 1 percent, 5 percent, and 10 percent levels, respectively.

Regarding our treatments, the regression results indicate that the stage 2 low-anchor social information increases donations for Give-Directly. This effect seems to be driven by students who receive student aid. For this group, the high-anchor social information increases the probability of giving to GiveDirectly as well, while the stage 1 social information plus justification significantly decreases donations for Give-Directly compared to the control. In addition, the high-anchor social information significantly increases subscriptions to the mailing lists. This time the effect is particularly driven by participants who do not receive student aid. Thus, as already seen in figure 5.3, providing social information seems to be a promising approach for shifting donations of participants with the stronger self-interest in giving to the university's student aid fund toward a cause with a higher social impact.

We further find that participants who receive student aid and are older are more likely to give to GiveDirectly and subscribe to the mailing lists. Engineers are less likely to donate to GiveDirectly. Undergraduates, especially those who do not receive student aid, have a higher probability of donating to GiveDirectly but are less likely to subscribe to the mailing lists. Participants from Yale (the baseline in table 5.2) and Penn exhibit the highest probability of donating to GiveDirectly and signing up to the mailing lists compared to the other universities, but student aid recipients from Penn fall behind participants from Yale in terms of donations.

5.4 Conclusion

The constantly increasing number of nonprofit organizations makes it more and more important that research not only evaluates fundraising strategies of a single charity in isolation but also assesses the decisions on where to donate time and money. In this chapter, we report the results from an experiment at six universities in the United States and Canada that tests interventions from the existing donation literature and their effects on the participants' choice between a charity that fights extreme poverty and the university student aid program.

Although we do not find strong treatment effects due to the tests' lack of power, our results are highly promising that both justification of the donation decision and social information have the potential to shift donations toward the charity with the higher social impact, at least at some universities. The high- and low-anchor social information treatments seem to be especially suitable for influencing decisions of participants with a stronger self-interest to give to their university's student aid fund. Our experimental results are, however, highly heterogeneous across universities, such that they hardly indicate a "one size fits all" solution. Even when we form clusters that we expected to show some similarities—such as Canadian schools (McGill, UBC), public universities (Berkeley, UBC), "elite" schools (Yale, Penn, Cornell, Berkeley, McGill), or private "elite" US schools (Yale, Penn, Cornell)—we cannot draw a general conclusion for any of these clusters.

Our experiment should be seen as a starting point in a field that certainly needs more attention and further research. Future studies might particularly address some shortcomings of our experimental design. On one hand, a future experiment should involve a sufficiently large number of participants from the population of interest in order to have enough power to detect significant differences. On the other hand, attention should be paid to potential endowment effects. In our experiment, participants were asked to donate a dollar endowment but were not allowed to keep the money. In a recent study, Lange and Schwirplies (2017) look at such endowment effects in an online donation experiment in Germany. This experiment also finds hardly any treatment effect in the group that was asked to distribute a third party fund that they were not allowed to keep for themselves. In contrast, other groups that were asked to donate their own earnings, an endowment, or a lottery prize that they could alternatively keep for themselves showed strong reactions to the treatments. That is, the zero overall treatment effects in our experiment might only be the consequence of the specific design.

5.A Appendix

5.A.1 General Instructions for the Giving Game for Effective Altruism Student Groups

Thank you for making this field experiment possible!

Please read these instructions carefully before starting the Giving Game!

It is very important that you strictly follow the instructions; this is the only way we will produce reliable results and learn more about individuals' donation decisions!

5.A.2 Instructions for Preparation

Set up a table in a busy area on the campus of your university. Decisions and data collection take place online. You will need devices like laptops or tablets to run the Game.

Links to the button that starts the experiment: [*link deleted*]

This link will guarantee randomization across treatments. Please, always use this link to start the Giving Game.

If you do not see a link for your school, please contact Claudia Schwirplies.

5.A.3 Procedures for Conducting the Game

The first step in a Giving Game is to solicit passersby to stop and engage with you. Please approach people by asking: "Would you like to donate someone else's money to charity?" This is an opening line a lot of groups have had success with.

Once you have the attention of a participant, please read the following *script*. We think this is a good script for everyone to read because (a) it's quite short and (b) it concisely explains to participants what they will be doing in the Giving Game. That said, please let us know if you have any suggestions based on your experience.

Please try to generally memorize this script, so you can read "naturally" rather than reading it directly from a piece of paper.

"I'm from the <Campus Group Name> student group, and today we are running a charitable giving game on behalf of the nonprofit organization The Life You Can Save. Basically, we are giving you the opportunity to donate $1 of someone else's money, to one of two charities right now. The whole process should only take a couple of minutes.

We'll introduce you to the two charities, and then you'll decide where to donate $1 of real money. After your decision, you'll respond to a short questionnaire. Your decision is absolutely anonymous and your answers will be treated strictly confidential."

Start by pressing "Start Giving Game," and then leave the student alone to complete the game. (Please do not press "Start Giving Game" until the participant is about to begin, so that (a) we can at least roughly time how long the survey takes and (b) the survey doesn't time out.)

Participant completes Giving Game

"Thank you for participating!"

Make sure that the survey is completed by pressing the "submit" button, if the participant has not already done so. You should see the "Thank you" screen.

Once the Game is over, you can chat with the participant. **To the extent possible, please try to keep a bit of distance between the people you talk to after voting and the people who haven't voted yet so that the latter don't overhear the former.**

5.A.4   Screens

The first screen provides the brief introduction to the Game and the description of the two charities the participant will be choosing between.

The two charities in the Giving Game will be *GiveDirectly* and *your school's student aid fund*.

Welcome to our Giving Game!

Help us decide which charity receives $1 from a fund provided by the non-profit organization The Life You Can Save.

Please read the following charity descriptions, and indicate your decision on the next page.

You will later be asked to provide a justification why exactly you chose one charity instead of the other.

Here is a brief introduction to the two charities you'll be choosing between:

Harvard Financial Aid

The Harvard Financial Aid Office operates a need-based financial aid program that seeks to make Harvard accessible to any student who is admitted. Because of a commitment to seeking the best possible students, Harvard is committed to helping exceptional students of all financial circumstances enroll. This program allows Harvard to maintain its place as an elite educational institution by attracting exceptional students of all financial circumstances, and maintain a more diverse student body.

What is the problem?

The cost of attending college has risen dramatically as tuition increases have significantly outpaced overall inflation for decades. Most undergraduate students enrolled at Harvard each year require some form of financial assistance to attend.

How is Harvard helping?

Harvard is able to provide substantial financial aid packages to at least 45-55% of students. These packages have a total annual cost of $200-400 million, which equates to less than a small percentage of Harvard's multi-billion dollar endowment.

How much would $1,000 help?

A yearly grant for a student on financial aid is approximately 40,000, so $1,000 would contribute about 4% of an average grant for one student. This would roughly cover tuition for five days of school, or one year's worth of textbooks.

GiveDirectly

GiveDirectly provides cash transfers to some of the poorest families in Kenya using a mobile payment system, and the recipients are free to use the money however they need.

What is the problem?

There are approximately 1 billion people in the world living in extreme poverty—defined as living on less than $1.25 per day. People living in extreme poverty routinely suffer from hunger and malnutrition, easily preventable diseases, and lack of access to clean water.

How is GiveDirectly helping?

GiveDirectly has transferred $6.4 million to families in extreme poverty and has plans in place to distribute another $8.6 million. GiveDirectly's programs are growing at a fast rate and over time they hope to expand to other countries.

How much would $1,000 help?

GiveDirectly's sends each recipient household roughly $1,000 over the course of the year, or about $200 per household member on average.   A rigorous study of GiveDirectly's programs found that families who received a cash transfers had 34% more earnings, 58% more assets, and reported 42% less hunger relative to a randomized control group.

Exit and clear survey   Next ›

Figure 5.A.1
First screen: brief introduction to the game and description of the charities.

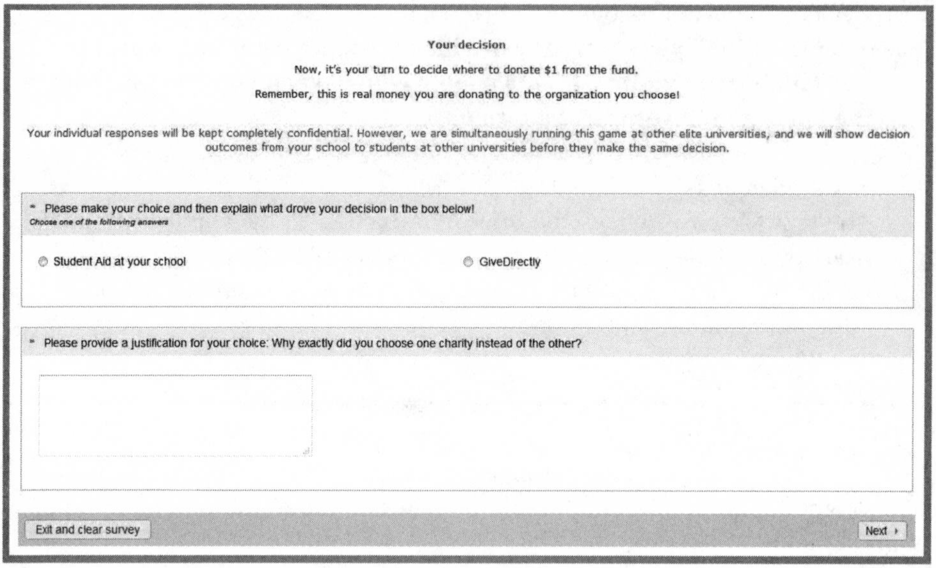

Figure 5.A.2
Second screen: Decision screen.

There are **two versions** of this screen: one with and one without a note that the participants will be asked to give reasons for his/her decision.

The second screen is the decision screen:

The third screen asks the person to indicate some personal information. This information is absolutely anonymous and will help us understand and interpret the results.

The fourth screen asks the person whether he/she wants to subscribe for the newsletter of the campus group and The Life You Can Save.

Please note that we embedded a separate form for newsletter subscriptions and will not be able to pair the answers to the preceding questions with the student's email address. Email addresses will be collected in a separate data file. Claudia and the University of Hamburg will have no access to this data base.

Important: Notice that on this final page, there are *two* submit buttons. Participants must click the first submit button to subscribe to the newsletter, and click the second submit button to submit the survey itself. We have had some issues with participants not clicking the second submit button.

Personal information

This information is absolutely anonymous and will help us understand and interpret the results.

Are you male or female?

Female Male No answer

How old are you?
Only numbers may be entered in this field.

What is your major? If you have not declared your major yet, what is your expected major?
Choose one of the following answers

Please choose...

What best describes your role in the [School Name] community?
Choose one of the following answers

Please choose...

Do you receive student aid?

Yes No No answer

Exit and clear survey

Next

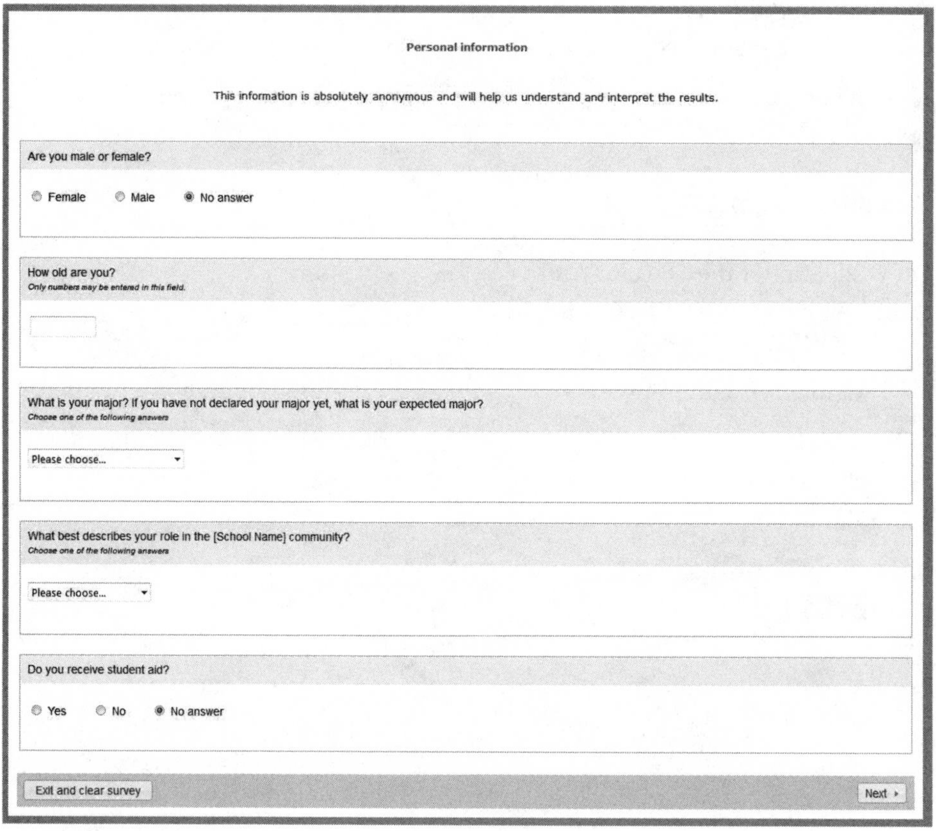

Figure 5.A.3
Third screen: questionnaire.

So, when you reset the survey for the next participant, you may have to click the second "submit" if the previous participant has not already done so. If you simply refresh the page without formally submitting the form, we lose their data.

The game ends with "thank you" page that provides a link ("Home") back to the "Start Giving Game" button. Just click "Home" to start a new game with the next participant:

Figure 5.A.4
Forth screen: newsletter subscription.

Figure 5.A.5
Fifth screen: last page.

Notes

We thank John List and his whole team for organizing the Summer Institute on Field Experiments that made this partnership possible. We are grateful for the engagement of the student campus groups at the University of California at Berkeley, Cornell University, McGill University, University of British Columbia, University of Pennsylvania, and Yale University. We thank Luigi Butera, Christina Gravert, Jan Schmitz, and Jonathan Meer for helpful comments on the experimental design. Funding of the project by the Life You Can Save is gratefully acknowledged.

1. See National Center for Charitable Statistics, www.nccs.urban.org/statistics/quickfacts .cfm.

2. The money used in our experiment was an undirected fund raised by the nonprofit organization The Life You Can Save.

3. http\\:www.limesurvey.org.

4. The descriptions can be found in figure 5.A.1 in the appendix, which is a screenshot of the first screen. For GiveDirectly, we used the same text at all universities. For the student aid program, we only changed the school name and the figures if necessary.

5. On this screen, the two organizations were displayed in a random order.

6. The newsletter sign-up form was embedded via iframe such that email addresses were exclusively collected by The Life You Can Save, and researchers had no access to these data.

7. The share of undergraduates significantly differs from control on the basis of Mann-Whitney U tests with $z = -2.353$, $p = 0.0186$ for SI2 and $z = -3.194$, $p = 0.00$ for SI3.

8. The share of female participants in the SI3 treatment is significantly different from the control treatment on the basis of Mann-Whitney U tests with $z = 1.882$ and $p = 0.06$.

9. That is, 57 from Berkeley, 81 from Cornell, 210 from McGill, 191 from Penn, 59 from UBC, and 109 from Yale.

10. We also ran the regressions for each school separately but could not detect significant effects. Again, this result must be attributed to the small sample sizes. We do not report these results for reasons of brevity, but they are available on request.

References

Andreoni, James. 1990. "Impure Altruism and Donations to Public Goods: A Theory of Warm-Glow Giving." *Economic Journal* 100 (401): 464–477.

Andreoni, James, and Ragan Petrie. 2004. "Public Goods Experiments without Confidentiality: A Glimpse into Fund-Raising." *Journal of Public Economics* 88 (7–8): 1605–1623.

Anik, Lalin, Michael I. Norton, and Dan Ariely. 2014. "Contingent Match Incentives Increase Donations." *Journal of Marketing Research* 51 (6): 790–801.

Buchan, Nancy R., Eric J. Johnson, and Rachel T. A. Croson. 2006. "Let's Get Personal: An International Examination of the Influence of Communication, Culture and Social

Distance on Other Regarding Preferences." *Journal of Economic Behavior & Organization* 60 (3): 373–398.

Charness, Gary, and Uri Gneezy. 2008. "What's in a Name? Anonymity and Social Distance in Dictator and Ultimatum Games." *Journal of Economic Behavior & Organization* 68 (1): 29–35.

Chen, Yan, F. Maxwell Harper, Joseph Konstan, and Sherry X. Li. 2010. "Social Comparisons and Contributions to Online Communities: A Field Experiment on MovieLens." *American Economic Review* 100 (4): 1358–1398.

Eckel, Catherine C., and Philip J. Grossman. 2003. "Rebate Versus Matching: Does How We Subsidize Charitable Contributions Matter?" *Journal of Public Economics* 87 (3–4): 681–701.

Edwards, James T., and John A. List. 2014. "Toward an Understanding of Why Suggestions Work in Charitable Fundraising: Theory and Evidence from a Natural Field Experiment." *Journal of Public Economics* 114: 1–13.

Falk, Armin. 2007. "Gift Exchange in the Field." *Econometrica* 75 (5): 1501–1511.

Ferraro, Paul J., and Michael K. Price. 2013. "Using Nonpecuniary Strategies to Influence Behavior: Evidence from a Large-Scale Field Experiment." *Review of Economics and Statistics* 95 (1): 64–73.

Frey, Bruno S., and Stephan Meier. 2004. "Social Comparisons and Pro-social Behavior: Testing 'Conditional Cooperation' in a Field Experiment." *American Economic Review* 94 (5): 1717–1722.

Huck, Steffen, and Imran Rasul. 2011. "Matched Fundraising: Evidence from a Natural Field Experiment." *Charitable Giving and Fundraising Special Issue* 95 (5–6): 351–362.

Jasper, Cynthia R., and Anya Samek. 2014. "Increasing Charitable Giving in the Developed World." *Oxford Review of Economic Policy* 30 (4): 680–696.

Karlan, Dean, and John A. List. 2007. "Does Price Matter in Charitable Giving? Evidence from a Large-Scale Natural Field Experiment." *American Economic Review* 97 (5): 1774–1793.

Karlan, Dean, and Margaret A. McConnell. 2014. "Hey Look at Me: The Effect of Giving Circles on Giving." *Journal of Economic Behavior & Organization* 106: 402–412. http://www.sciencedirect.com/science/article/pii/S0167268114002017.

Karlan, Dean, and Daniel H. Wood. 2014. "The Effect of Effectiveness: Donor Response to Aid Effectiveness in a Direct Mail Fundraising Experiment." NBER working paper 20047, National Bureau of Economic Research, Cambridge, MA.

Konow, James. 2000. "Fair Shares: Accountability and Cognitive Dissonance in Allocation Decisions." *American Economic Review* 90 (4): 1072–1092.

Landry, Craig E., Andreas Lange, John A. List, Michael K. Price, and Nicholas G. Rupp. 2006. "Toward an Understanding of the Economics of Charity: Evidence from a Field Experiment." *Quarterly Journal of Economics* 121 (2): 747–782.

Landry, Craig E., Andreas Lange, John A. List, Michael K. Price, and Nicholas G. Rupp. 2010. "Is a Donor in Hand Better Than Two in the Bush? Evidence from a Natural Field Experiment." *American Economic Review* 100 (3): 958–983.

Lange, Andreas, and Claudia Schwirplies. 2017. "A NIMBY Effect in the Private Provision of Public Goods: Using Donation Experiments to Inform Policy." Mimeo, University of Hamburg, Hamburg, Germany.

List, John A., and David Lucking-Reiley. 2002. "The Effects of Seed Money and Refunds on Charitable Giving: Experimental Evidence from a University Capital Campaign." *Journal of Political Economy* 110 (1): 215–233. http://www.jstor.org/stable/10.1086/324392.

Null, Clair. 2011. "Warm Glow, Information, and Inefficient Charitable Giving." *Journal of Public Economics* 95 (5–6): 455–465. http://www.sciencedirect.com/science/article/pii/S0047272710000836.

Rondeau, Daniel, and John A. List. 2008. "Matching and Challenge Gifts to Charity: Evidence from Laboratory and Natural Field Experiments." *Experimental Economics* 11 (3): 253–267.

Shang, Jen, and Rachel Croson. 2009. "A Field Experiment in Charitable Contribution: The Impact of Social Information on the Voluntary Provision of Public Goods." *Economic Journal* 119 (540): 1422–1439.

Soetevent, Adriaan R. 2005. "Anonymity in Giving in a Natural Context—A Field Experiment in 30 Churches." *Journal of Public Economics* 89 (11–12): 2301–2323. http://www.sciencedirect.com/science/article/pii/S0047272704001756.

Soetevent, Adriaan R. 2011. "Payment Choice, Image Motivation and Contributions to Charity: Evidence from a Field Experiment." *American Economic Journal: Economic Policy* 3 (1): 180–205. http://www.jstor.org/stable/41238089.

Vesterlund, Lise. 2003. "The Informational Value of Sequential Fundraising." *Journal of Public Economics* 87 (3–4): 627–657.

6 The Charitable Response to a Nondirected Matching Gift

Benjamin M. Marx

6.1 Introduction

A well-known fundraising technique involves charities obtaining a pledge from a major donor to match the gifts of other donors. These matching gifts have been shown to sometimes increase donations by other potential donors, often past givers, who are informed of the match by mail. This chapter examines a matching gift that was promoted online and covered all gifts to an anonymous organization by any donor, new or not. This matching gift was therefore nondirected in terms of which individuals could learn of and benefit from the match.

To what extent did the nondirected matching gift increase the amount of other donations to the recipient organization during the 2013–2014 holiday season? Answering this question is difficult, because the match took effect soon after a charity evaluator named the organization a top charity, an act that in itself most likely increased giving. Moreover, gifts may have grown from one year to the next with or without either of these occurrences. Fortunately, the organization provided the amounts and types of donations received around this time to enable estimation of the effect of the matching gift.

Estimates of the effect of the matching gift can be obtained from difference-in-difference strategies comparing giving to the charity by day in different months and years. The matching gift was available from late 2013 through January 31, 2014. A simple-difference estimate would compare gifts in January 2013 to gifts in January 2014. The simple-difference approach would attribute any increase in January gifts to the matching gift, but giving might have increased generally in 2014 for other reasons. To control for this general year-over-year difference, one can use the change in gifts received in February and March, since the match was not present in these months in either 2013 or 2014.

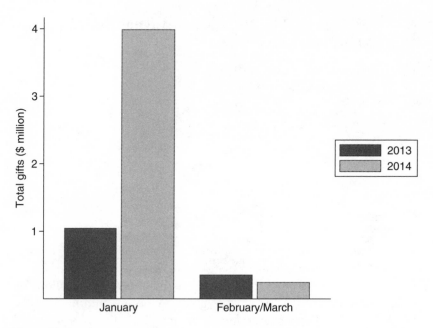

Figure 6.1
Total gifts, January and February 2014.

The intuition for the design is captured by figure 6.1. Between 2013 and 2014, gifts made in February and March declined by 31 percent, despite the announcement of the charity evaluator's recommendation. In contrast, January gifts grew by 282 percent year-over-year. Among these time periods, it was only in January 2014 that gifts were matched. Comparison of the growth in giving during January to that in later months should therefore capture the effect of the matching gift while controlling for the effects of the charity evaluator's recommendation and other changes from 2013 to 2014.

With regression analysis it is possible to improve on such comparisons and obtain estimates of the matching gift's effect that control for other potential confounding factors. More sophisticated sets of control variables can include calendar-day, day-of-week, and month-of-year effects. I also employ designs that allow changes in giving to vary over January to obtain a regression-discontinuity-inspired estimate of the effect right around the end date of the matching period on January 31, 2014.

The estimated effect of the matching gift is large. Across each regression specification, I find that the match more than doubled the amount of funds donated, a much larger effect than has been found for matching gifts promoted through mailings.

Several field experiments have identified the effect of mentioning a matching gift in a solicitation letter. Karlan and List (2007) find that a matching gift increases donations by about 20 percent whether the gift matches other donations dollar-for-dollar or more-than-dollar-for-dollar. Karlan et al. (2011) find smaller effects of smaller matches, with both increasing gifts by less than 5 percent. Eckel and Grossman (2003), Meier (2007), and Rondeau and List (2008) each examine a different setting, and none find an effect greater than 30 percent. Huck and Rasul (2011) and Huck et al. (2015) found larger effects of matching gifts, on the order of about 45 percent, in fundraisers for a German opera house. Karlan and List (2012) also obtained a roughly 50 percent increase in donations when approaching "cold list" individuals who were not recent donors to the fundraising organization. The largest of such estimates was found for a 3:1 match from the Bill & Melinda Gates Foundation, which roughly doubled gifts to a development organization from its recent donors (Karlan and List 2012). Still, none of these effects are as large as the smallest estimate presented in this chapter.

Several aspects of this matching gift may have contributed to its outsized success in attracting other donations. The caps on donations that could be matched, both per donor and in total, were relatively large. Large effects when caps are large would be consistent with some experimental evidence that match effects depend on the degree to which a subject believes her own donation will trigger matching (Gee and Schreck 2015). The grant also allowed the charity to respond by ramping up fundraising, much as Andreoni and Payne (2011) find that nonmatching grants to charities can induce crowd-out via charities' induced reductions to fundraising. The charity's response arises from the nondirectedness of the match, which may also increase its effectiveness by bringing in new donors. Nondirected matching gifts like the one studied here would be difficult to evaluate experimentally, because the nondirectedness by its very nature implies that there can be no control group for a single fundraising event. Nonetheless, future research may find ways to isolate and test these potential exlanations for the large effects.

Matching gifts are but one of a variety of techniques that have been found to increase donations. Laboratory experiments have documented increased generosity when an audience observes the decision (Andreoni and Bernheim 2009) or when the more-informed subject can overcome information asymmetry by donating first and announcing the donation (Potters et al. 2007). Morgan and Sefton (2000) found that well-designed lotteries could increase contributions several-fold. Field experiments indicate that social pressure can increase the number of small donations but can also trigger avoidance (DellaVigna et al. 2012, Andreoni et al. 2017). Landry et al. (2011) found larger effects when subjects received a book for giving over $25, a treatment that increased gifts by about 50 percent in the year of the intervention and roughly twice as much the following year. In some settings, simple information about others' donations has had a large effect. Huck and Rasul (2011) found that mentioning a lead donation as a seed gift had a larger effect than using it for matching. Shang and Croson (2009) found that announcing large gifts by a recent caller tripled expected revenues in a telethon, and List and Lucking-Reiley (2002) obtained similarly large effects by announcing seed money in a mail campaign. Thus the estimated effects of this nondirected matching gift are comparable in size to some of the most successful fundraising interventions in the literature.

The chapter proceeds as follows. Section 6.2 provides background on the matching gift and the recipient organization, including figures showing raw data. Section 6.3 describes the difference-in-difference empirical strategies. Section 6.4 presents the results, and section 6.5 concludes.

6.2   Background on the Organization and the Matching Gift

The organization studied (which preferred to remain anonymous in this study) is a public charity that promotes international development through unconditional cash transfers. Unconditional transfers of cash have recently gained attention from development economists as an aid strategy that may benefit recipients more directly than in-kind transfers or those that condition payment on some action of the recipient. Give-Directly uses data from a combination of public sources, door-to-door meetings, and independent sources (e.g., satellite imagery) to locate extremely poor households in Kenya and Uganda. It then connects them with electronic payment systems and transfers to them an amount equal to a one-year budget for a typical household. GiveDirectly thereby allows donors to make direct cash transfers to African households in verified poverty.

The charity studied here has regularly appeared on a list of about three top charities per year. This list is compiled by another organization called GiveWell, a nonprofit that helps donors decide where to give by identifying charities with strong evidence of impact and quantifiable cost effectiveness. GiveWell's endorsement of the charity helped attract the attention of a charitable foundation emphasizing global development and increasing the impact of philanthropy.

On December 3, 2013, the foundation announced a $5 million matching gift for donations made to the charity from December 3, 2013, through January 31, 2014. All donations of up to $100,000 per donor were eligible for matching. Gifts could be made through the the charity's website or through GiveWell or other intermediaries. The announcement stated that the funds were intended to help the charity attract new donors and encourage transfers to poor households in developing countries. The matching funds for the charity are part of a series of grants made by the foundation in recognition of GiveWell's charity recommendations for 2013, which were announced on December 1 of that year. The foundation also gave $2 million in unrestricted support to the charity in addition to the matching funds.

This study uses de-identified data provided by the charity. First, daily totals of traffic on the charity's website provide evidence of interest by potential donors. Second, transaction-level donation data enable estimation of the effect of the foundation's matching gift on donations to the charity. For each donation received, these data indicate the date, amount, and conduit (e.g., check, Google Checkout, or the GiveWell website). There is also an indicator variable for recurring donations, which distinguishes these from one-time gifts, but no donor information is included.

Figure 6.2 shows the charity's website traffic around the time of the matching gift period. In early December, around the time of announcements of both the repeated recommendation by GiveWell and the matching gift from the foundation, the daily number of visits to the organization's website tripled. It remained elevated into early January, suggesting that some combination of these announcements brought new attention to the charity's website.

Donations were also elevated during the period of the matching gift. Figure 6.3 shows the natural logarithm of the number of gifts from nonrecurring donors, by day. These gifts increased in 2013–2014 relative to their levels in the same months in earlier years. In particular, a visible increase took place around the December 3 announcement of the matching gift, and decrease occurred when it expired on January 31. No similar increase took place for recurring gifts, as can be seen in

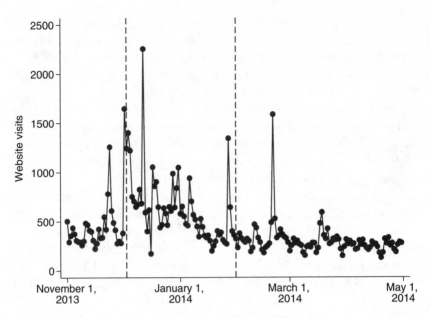

Figure 6.2
Website traffic, November 1, 2013–May 1, 2014. *Notes*: Dashed vertical lines mark the beginning of the matching gift period on December 3, 2013, and its end on January 31, 2014.

figure 6.4, indicating that the change occurred among new one-time gifts rather than increases among those already giving on a regular basis. A simple comparison of the size distribution of individual January gifts, depicted in figure 6.5, shows that gifts of all sizes increased in January 2014, at least for those above $20 ($\exp(3) \cong 20$).

Much of the effect of the matching gift may have occurred in December, between its announcement and the end of the tax year. However, the timing of the announcement shortly after the announcement that the charity was again a top GiveWell charity could conflate the effects of the two if one were to study the year-over-year increase in December giving. I instead focus on the end of the matching period on January 31, 2014. Figure 6.6 focuses on giving in the first quarter of 2014 and shows both raw daily totals and a smoothed averages using varying bandwidths. Regardless of the extent of smoothing, donations fall discretely from January 31 to February 1. These data are coarse for implementing a full regression discontinuity design, which requires a large number of observations for statistical power, and the opportunity for potential donors to retime their gifts around the end date would violate the assumptions of such a design. It is possible, however, to incorporate

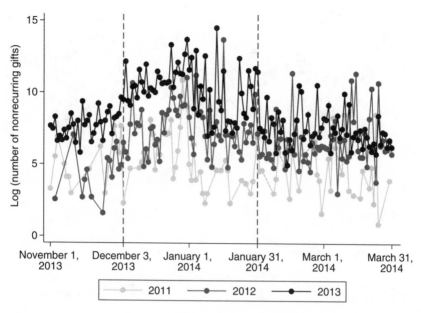

Figure 6.3
Number of nonrecurring gifts, by day, 2013 and 2014. *Notes:* Dashed vertical lines mark the beginning of the matching gift period on December 3, 2013, and its end on January 31, 2014. The natural logarithm of the number of nonrecurring gifts is plotted for a 5-month interval labeled by initial year (i.e., data for 2013 show log gifts from November 1, 2013 to March 31, 2014).

the regression-discontinuity concept of focusing on the threshold into a difference-in-difference design using year-over-year changes in giving at different times during the year.

6.3 Empirical Strategy

To estimate the effect of the matching gift on donations to the charity, I use generalized difference-in-difference estimation strategies. The basic strategy is to estimate the change in giving from January 2013 to January 2014 using the change from February–March 2013 to February–March 2014.

Let G_{yt} denote the natural log of total gifts received in year y on calendar day $t \in \{0,\dots,365\}$. The sample includes gifts received online during days from January 1 to March 31 in each of the years 2013 and 2014. The treatment dummy $T_{yt} = 1\{t \leq 31 \cap y = 2014\}$ identifies days in January 2014, the only days in the sample in which the matching gift

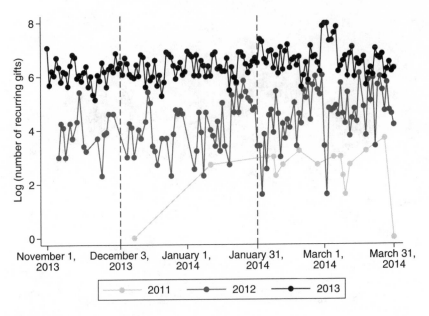

Figure 6.4
Number of recurring gifts, by day, 2013 and 2014. *Notes*: Dashed vertical lines mark the beginning of the matching gift period on December 3, 2013, and its end on January 31, 2014. The natural logarithm of the number of recurring gifts is plotted for a 5-month interval labeled by initial year (i.e., data for 2013 show log gifts from November 1, 2013 to March 31, 2014).

was available. The coefficient β on this treatment dummy describes the effect on log gifts, which can be exponentiated to give the percentage change in gifts. In the basic strategy, variation in the control variables gives different versions of the main comparison. Coefficients on the control variables are labeled α, and e_{yt} is the error term in each equation (i.e., the residual variation in G_{yt} that is not explained by any of the variables). All standard errors clustered by calendar day. I estimate four equations with different sets of control variables:

$$G_{yt} = \beta T_{yt} + \alpha_1 \cdot 1\{y = 2014\} + D_t \alpha_2 = e_{yt}. \tag{6.1}$$

Equation 6.1 includes a dummy variable for the year 2014 and a vector of dummies D_t for each calendar day t. This most basic equation is the most direct implementation of the general strategy. There are controls for day-to-day patterns, including the general decline in giving from January into February, and a control for year-over-year changes. Identification is obtained from the fact that T_{yt} allows the year-over-year change to be different in January than it is in February and March.

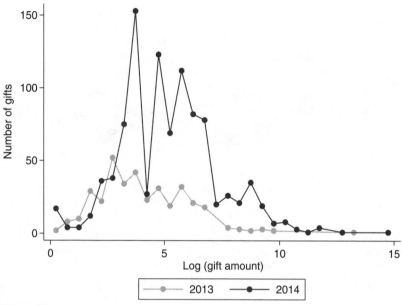

Figure 6.5
Number of gifts, by size of gift, January 2013 and January 2014. *Note*: The natural logarithm is used.

$$G_{yt} = \beta T_{yt} + \alpha_1 \cdot 1\{y = 2014\} + D_t \alpha_2 + \alpha_3 (31 - t) T_{yt} = e_{yt}. \tag{6.2}$$

Equation 6.2 includes the same controls found in equation 6.1. The additional control is a linear trend in calendar day during the treatment month (i.e., a continuous variable for the number of days before January 31). This control is inspired by the regression discontinuity design, and it focuses the estimation on changes occurring in the days just before the matching grant period expired. The linear control allows, for example, for lingering effects of late-2013 media exposure that die out over time. A sharp drop in the year-over-year increase in daily giving right after January 31 will be interpreted as the lapsing effect of the matching gift.

$$\begin{aligned} G_{yt} = \beta T_{yt} &+ \alpha_1 \cdot 1\{y = 2014\} + D_t \alpha_2 + \alpha_3 (31 - t) \\ &\cdot 1\{t \le 31 \cap y = 2014\} + D_w \alpha_4 = e_{yt} \end{aligned} \tag{6.3}$$

Equation 6.3 includes the days-before-January-31 term. The change relative to equation 6.2 is the use of day-of-the-week dummies D_d and week-of-the-year dummies D_w in place of the calendar-day dummies D_t. This specification is less demanding of the data, because while only

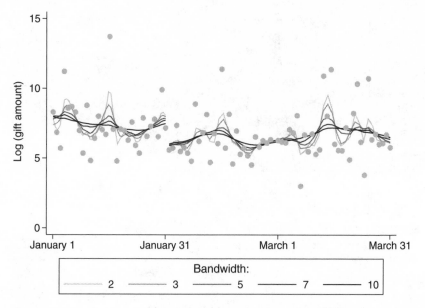

Figure 6.6
Number of gifts, by day, January 1–March 31, 2014. *Notes*: The natural logarithm of the total number of gifts is plotted. Shaded circles are data points. Curves represent local-linear smoothing, with varying bandwidths, using days before or after January 31.

two observations identify a calendar-day dummy (with two years of data in the sample), day-of-the-week dummies capture such factors as weekday versus weekend differences in giving with a larger number of observations. The comparisons also differ slightly because, for example, February 1, 2013, was a Friday, while February 1, 2014, was a Saturday.

$$G_{yt} = \beta T_{yt} + \alpha_1 \cdot 1\{y = 2014\} + D_d\alpha_2 + \alpha_3(31 - t) \cdot 1\{t \le 31 \cap y = 2014\} + P_t\alpha_4 = e_{yt}. \tag{6.4}$$

Equation 6.4 includes all variables from the third equation except the week-of-the-year dummies. Here seasonal changes are instead controlled for by using a polynomial in calendar day, P_t. With this approach one can control for seasonality with increasing flexibility (but increasing possibility of overfitting the model, given the data) by increasing the order of the polynomial P_t. The specification presented uses the order of the polynomial that minimizes the Aikake Information Criterion, which balances these concerns.

6.4 Results

The first row of table 6.1 shows the estimated effect of the match on log gifts, which translates to the percentage increases below. In all cases it is estimated that the match more than doubled the amount of other gifts.

While the estimated effect is always large, it varies quite a bit across different versions of the regression. Regression 6.1 most closely resembles the patterns shown in figure 6.1, as it gives the increase in daily gifts in January relative to the same increase for February and March. With this specification it is estimated that the match quadrupled the amount of other gifts (a 300 percent increase over the amount that would have been received without the match), and because the estimate is more than two standard deviations above zero, we can say with 95 percent confidence that the true effect was indeed positive. This would be an overestimate, however, if the GiveWell recommendation had a lasting effect that was greater in January 2014 than in the subsequent months. Regressions 6.2–6.4 control for this possibility by allowing the difference between 2014 and 2013 to be declining over time and focusing on the change in giving right around the January 31 end of the match. The three regressions control in different ways for the pattern of giving over time, providing estimates that differ in magnitude (but are not statistically distinguishable).

Overall, the estimates are imprecise but large. It appears very likely that the foundation's matching gift more than doubled other donors'

Table 6.1
Gifts.

	(1)	(2)	(3)	(4)
Effect on log gifts	1.39	1.05	1.49	1.65
	(0.67)**	(1.01)	(0.75)*	(0.74)**
Implied increase in gifts (%)	300	186	344	420
R^2	0.72	0.72	0.36	0.34
Number of observations	180	180	180	180

Notes: Sample includes days from January 1 to March 31 in 2013 and 2014. All standard errors clustered by calendar day. Controls: (1): year, day dummies; (2): year, day dummies, days before January 31, 2014; (3): year, day of the week dummies, week of the year dummies, days before January 31, 2014; (4): year, day of the week, days before January 31, 2014, 14th-order polynomial in day. The symbols ** and * indicate significance at the 5 percent and 10 percent levels, respectively.

gifts (a 64 percent likelihood based on the point estimate and standard error in the most conservative regression 6.2). The other estimates would indicate that the effect on January giving was much larger than this, and the excluded effects on December giving appear larger, if anything.

A few potential sources of bias in the matching-effect estimates should be mentioned. First, the GiveWell announcement may have had a positive effect that extended into January but not into February. The regression specifications controlling for day in January should control for this effect, but they may not adequately capture its pattern if it was nonlinear in day, which could bias results in either direction. Second is the possibility that quality-signaling effects of the matching gift may have had a lingering positive effect on gifts after January. This would cause the estimates to understate the true effect. Third, donors may have retimed gifts that would have been made after January so as to fall within the matching period. Following the logic in the "bunching" literature (e.g., Saez 2010), if retiming donations carries costs that are increasing in the number of days between the actual gift and the optimal timing, then we should see evidence of a dip in the first day(s) of February, followed by a rebound. Examination of the figures and regressions residuals shows little evidence of this retiming pattern.

6.5   Conclusion

In this chapter I estimate the effect of a nondirected (broadly announced and available) matching gift. Using 2013–2014 data on donations to the charity, I find that donations were 2–4 times greater during the a matching gift period than they would have been if the match had not been made available. While the estimates are imprecise, they are larger than the effect of matching gifts estimated in other papers. The results suggest that lead donors who want to use matching gifts to leverage the most contributions from others may want to broadcast announcements of the match and make it openly available to all possible contributors.

One reason nondirected matching gifts may have relatively large effects is that they may attract individuals who prefer to give to an organization they learn about from some source other than the organization itself. Another possibility is suggested by the fact that the charity had recently been named a top charity. A matching gift may be especially effective for an organization that is believed to be of high quality. Such complementarity could arise because potential donors who focus on benefits to organizations' clients should seek out high-quality charities and opportunities to contribute when the price of giving is lowered by a match. Other potential donors who are motivated more by warm glow may be less motivated by either matching gifts or quality ratings. Experiments with interacted treatments would provide evidence on these possibilities.

References

Andreoni, James, and B. Douglas Bernheim. 2009. "Social Image and the 50–50 Norm: A Theoretical and Experimental Analysis of Audience Effects." *Econometrica* 77 (5): 1607–1636.

Andreoni, James, and A. Abigail Payne. 2011. "Is Crowding Out Due Entirely to Fundraising? Evidence from a Panel of Charities." *Journal of Public Economics* 95 (5–6): 334–343.

Andreoni, James, Justin M. Rao, and Hannah Trachtman. 2017. "Avoiding the Ask: A Field Experiment on Altruism, Empathy, and Charitable Giving." *Journal of Political Economy* 125 (3): 625–653.

DellaVigna, Stefano, James A. List, and Ulrike Malmendier. 2012. "Testing for Altruism and Social Pressure in Charitable Giving." *Quarterly Journal of Economics* 127 (1): 1–56.

Eckel, Catherine C., and Philip J. Grossman. 2003. "Rebate Versus Matching: Does How We Subsidize Charitable Contributions Matter?" *Journal of Public Economics* 87(3–4): 681–701.

Gee, Laura K., and Michael J. Schreck. 2015. "Do Beliefs About Peers Matter for Donation Matching? Experiments in the Field and Laboratory." *Science of Philanthropy Initiative*, Working Paper Series No. 138, National Bureau of Economic Research, Cambridge, MA.

Huck, Steffen, and Imran Rasul. 2011. "Matched Fundraising: Evidence from a Natural Field Experiment." *Journal of Public Economics* 95: 351–362.

Huck, Steffen, Imran Rasul, and Andrew Shephard. 2015. "Comparing Charitable Fundraising Schemes: Evidence from a Field Experiment and a Structural Model." *American Economic Journal: Economic Policy* 7 (2): 326–369.

Karlan, Dean, and John A. List. 2007. "Does Price Matter in Charitable Giving? Evidence from a Large-Scale Natural Field Experiment." *American Economic Review* 97 (5): 1774–1793.

Karlan, Dean, and John A. List. 2012. "How Can Bill and Melinda Gates Increase Other People's Donations to Fund Public Goods?" NBER working paper No. 17954, National Bureau of Economic Research, Cambridge, MA.

Karlan, Dean, John A. List, and Eldar Shafir. 2011. "Small Matches and Charitable Giving: Evidence from a Natural Field Experiment." *Journal of Public Economics* 95: 344–350.

Landry, Craig E., Andreas Lange, John A. List, Michael K. Price, and Nicholas G. Rupp. 2011. "Is There a 'Hidden Cost of Control' in Naturally-Occurring Markets? Evidence from a Natural Field Experiment." NBER working paper No. 17472, National Bureau of Economic Research, Cambridge, MA.

List, John A., and David Lucking-Reiley. 2002. "The Effects of Seed Money and Refunds on Charitable Giving: Experimental Evidence from a University Capital Campaign." *Journal of Political Economy* 110 (1): 215–233.

Meier, Stephan. 2007. "Do Subsidies Increase Charitable Giving in the Long Run? Matching Donations in a Field Experiment." *Journal of the European Economic Association* 5 (6): 1203–1222.

Morgan, John and Martin Sefton. 2000. "Funding Public Goods with Lotteries: Experimental Evidence." *Review of Economic Studies* 67 (4): 785–810.

Potters, Jan, Martin Sefton, and Lise Vesterlund. 2007. "Leading-by-Example and Signaling in Voluntary Contribution Games: An Experimental Study." *Economic Theory* 33 (1): 169–182.

Rondeau, Daniel, and John A. List. 2008. "Matching and Challenge Gifts to Charity: Evidence from Laboratory and Natural Experiments." *Experimental Economics* 11: 253–267.

Saez, Emmanuel. 2010. "Do Taxpayers Bunch at Kink Points?" *American Economic Journal: Economic Policy* 2 (3): 180–212.

Shang, Jen, and Rachel Croson. 2009. "A Field Experiment in Charitable Contribution: The Impact of Social Information on the Voluntary Provision of Public Goods." *Economic Journal* 119: 1422–1439.

7 Intuitive Donating: Testing One-Line Solicitations for $1 Donations in a Large Online Experiment

Samantha Horn and Dean Karlan

7.1 Introduction

In recent years, many experimental studies have been conducted to study charitable giving decisions, including whether to give, how much to give, and where to give. Typically these studies are done either in a laboratory experiment in which individuals are given information about charities and asked to make a decision, or in a nonlaboratory setting, such as direct marketing mail, email, or door-to-door.

Naturally, the channel and decision-making environment may influence charitable giving decisions, not merely in the level of giving but in the rank order of effectiveness of different messages (this is a specific example of the general point made by Deaton 2009). For example, some donation decisions are undoubtedly intuitive, instantaneous, and impulsive (akin to System I decisions in Kahneman 2003), whereas others are deliberative, protracted, and thoughtful (akin to System II decisions in Kahneman 2003). A channel that likely leads to deliberation, such as a laboratory setting in which participants know they are being studied, may yield different sets of results than one that allows only for minimal and fleeting attention before making a decision.

We study one end of this spectrum by analyzing data from an eBay and MissionFish (a partner of eBay) randomized control trial testing nine scripts that solicited $1 donations at the point of checkout for individuals purchasing an item on the eBay auction shopping website. Individuals also had an option to increase the gift beyond $1. As this is a fleeting decision made at checkout for only $1, we argue this is likely best categorized as a "System I" decision. Naturally, this cannot be perfectly categorized as such. For example, if someone has already deliberated extensively on which charities to support, they may simply react by remembering decisions already made in the past and repeating the decision. We consider this a critical contextual factor when interpreting the results of our study, in that we are starting by assuming that we are operating in System I decision-making mode and testing individuals' "intuitive" reactions to different donor appeals. An interesting extension would be to test the same scripts but in a more deliberative decision-making environment.

Several of the scripts focus on charity quality and effectiveness. Recent literature shows that individuals respond negatively to what they perceive as high overhead and administrative costs (Gneezy, Keenan, and Gneezy 2014), and that individuals are willing to pay more for information about overhead ratios than for information on claims of impact (Metzger and Günther 2016). This is not to say that quality signals have no effect, and indeed, some argue that one reason matching or leadership gifts work is through a quality signal mechanism (see Vesterlund 2003 for a theoretical analysis, and Karlan and List 2012 for experimental evidence). Furthermore, in work more directly relevant for the tests here, Karlan and Wood (2016) find that adding information about scientific evidence of impact to a direct marketing letter via postal mail to prior donors of an international poverty charity has no impact, on average, on giving. However, important heterogeneity was observed, in that larger prior donors responded positively to the information, and smaller prior donors responded negatively. This effect persisted even after controlling for income and education (aggregated at the zip code level, hence a far from perfect control for income and education). With appropriate caveats for the challenges in interpreting why some donors previously gave more or less, we posit that small prior donors may be behaving more as System I "intuitive" donors (i.e., not deliberating much about the donation), whereas the large prior donors are deliberating. As such, we would expect our results in our online experiment reported here to be more similar to the small prior donors in Karlan and Wood (2016) and to potentially respond negatively, relative to other appeals.

7.2 Methods

7.2.1 Study Population

Our sample frame consists of eBay users who made a purchase on the American eBay site, www.ebay.com, in one of three weeks beginning January 9, 2011, January 23, 2011, or February 27, 2011. There were no restrictions as far as we know on being included in the study, and so all individuals who made a purchase on the site during the weeks the intervention was running participated in the study.

7.2.2 Study Design

A message appeared on the full sample frame at the confirmation step in the payment process. Figure 7.1 shows an example of the display individuals saw on the eBay website. Individuals were given the option to make a donation, defaulted to be $1, to their payment in support of the charity mentioned in the script. Participants in a given week were randomly assigned without any stratification to receive one of 22 messages (which consists of permutations of nine different content messages and three different charities). Each of the three weeks differed (non-randomly) in terms of the set of messages over which eBay randomized. Analysis will control for the week of the transaction. Table 7.1 provides summary statistics for each of the messages and charities. Aside from the differences in message provided, the display for each individual was identical. The donation was directly added to the bill presented by eBay and could be cleared with the rest of the amount due for the transaction.

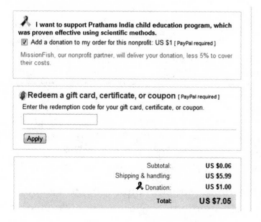

Figure 7.1
Screenshot for donation page on eBay website.

Table 7.1
Summary statistics.

Treatment	1000 × Likelihood of Donating $1 (average amount donated, $)			
	IPA	Pratham	UNICEF	All
Treatment 1: Fiscal efficiency	1.584 (1.295) $n = 1,444,940$	0.811 (1.285) $n = 3,028,671$	4.599 (1.274) $n = 1,913,616$	2.121 (1.284) $n = 6,387,227$
Treatment 2: Illustrating impact	3.586 (1.278) $n = 1,565,669$	1.499 (1.301) $n = 3,361,685$	1.953 (1.282) $n = 2,107,862$	2.099 (1.290) $n = 7,035,216$
Treatment 3: Proven impact: illustrating impact	2.660 (1.265) $n = 1,634,365$	1.017 (1.265) $n = 2,235,467$		1.711 (1.265) $n = 3,869,832$
Treatment 4: Expert signal		0.375 (1.335) $n = 596,859$	1.586 (1.317) $n = 2,881,419$	1.378 (1.320) $n = 3,478,278$
Treatment 5: Organizational focus on impact	1.551 (1.173) $n = 457,046$	1.254 (1.225) $n = 2,936,690$	–	1.294 (1.218) $n = 3,393,736$
Treatment 6: Popularity	0.959 (1.271) $n = 2,297,672$	0.593 (1.211) $n = 2,675,654$	1.471 (1.297) $n = 2,534,642$	1.002 (1.259) $n = 7,507,968$
Treatment 7: Matching grant		0.972 (1.307) $n = 1,650,515$	–	0.972 (1.307) $n = 1,650,515$
Treatment 8: Proven impact: specific program		0.810 (1.235) $n = 4,553,399$	–	0.810 (1.235) $n = 4,553,399$
Treatment 9: Quality signal		0.674 (1.274) $n = 1,050,902$	–	0.674 (1.274) $n = 1,050,902$
All	2.049 (1.270) $n = 7,399,692$	0.963 (1.261) $n = 22,089,842$	2.248 (1.295) $n = 9,437,539$	1.481 (1.271) $n = 38,927,073$

Notes: IPA, Innovations for Poverty Action. Each cell reports the proportion of views of each script for each charity that generated a donation (reported in tenths of basis points), the average amount donated of those that donated (in parentheses), and the sample size *n* per cell. The exact message scripts for each treatment are provided in table 7.2.

7.2.3   Study Intervention

Individuals were shown one of 22 one-line messages at the point of checkout on eBay. These scripts varied along two dimensions: nine different content messages (popularity, fiscal efficiency, impact per dollar donated, impact per dollar donated with reference to scientific evidence for the specific program, scientific evidence for the specific program, scientific approach used at the organization, scientific approach used at the organization and matching grant, expert signal by naming Hewlett Foundation as a supporter, and expert signal without naming any particular expert), and three different charities (Pratham, Innovations for Poverty Action, and UNICEF).

Table 7.2 presents the specifics of each of the scripts and also identifies how we categorized each into attribute qualities for the sake of carrying out a regression to examine how attributes influence likelihood and amount of donation.

We selected three different nonprofit organizations: two less well-known charities (Innovations for Poverty Action and Pratham), and one very well known multilateral fund (UNICEF). Pratham is based in India and focuses on childhood education, and Innovations for Poverty Action is a research and policy organization headquartered in the United States.[1] The specific Innovations of Poverty Action program mentioned in the messages related to child health in Kenya. UNICEF is a widely known multilateral organization targeting child well-being globally. Including multiple charities in the study allows us to ensure that sentiments toward particular organizations can be controlled for when detecting the impact of the different messages.

Certain limitations on the information available for UNICEF meant that the study was set up to run four of the treatments with all three organizations and the remainder with only Pratham and Innovations for Poverty Action. During the study, a technical error related to the display of messages in the eBay platform resulted in only four different messages being displayed for Innovation to Poverty Action: the scripts relating to expert signal, matching grant, scientific evidence for the specific program, and expert signal by naming Hewlett Foundation as a supporter were missed and thus data for donations related to this content for Innovations for Poverty Action cannot be included in the analysis. All other messages were deployed as expected.

7.2.4 Randomization

Individuals were randomized at point of payment through eBay's internal website programming, and the principal investigators were not privy to the specific algorithm used to randomize the messages. A calendar of messages by organization and by week was prepopulated and sent to the client before the start of the study.

7.2.5 Study Outcomes

The two outcomes in this study are whether the individual made any donation, and the average amount given for each treatment in each week (note that we do not have the individual-level data on the size of

Table 7.2
Treatment scripts and assigned attributes.

Treatment	Text of Script	Charity	Message Length (number of words)[a]	Depiction of Charitable Activity	Quantification of Impact	Matched Funds	Scientific Evidence	Expert Signal
Treatment 1: Fiscal efficiency	I want to support [organization's program], which has low overhead expenses.	All	14.7	X				
Treatment 2: Illustrating impact	I want to support [organization's program]. $1 provides [recipient] with one [program relevant outcome].[b]	All	19.0	X	X			
Treatment 3: Proven impact: illustrating impact	I want to support [organization's program], proven effective with scientific methods. $1 provides [recipient] with one [program relevant outcome].[b]	IPA, Pratham	19.0	X	X		X	
Treatment 4: Expert signal	I want to support [organization], whose methods have been approved by experts in international development.	Pratham, UNICEF	15.0					X
Treatment 5: Organizational focus on impact	I want to support [organization], which uses scientific methods to fight poverty.	IPA, Pratham	12.0				X	

Treatment 6: Popularity	I want to support [organization], one of the top nonprofits on eBay.	All	12.0		
Treatment 7: Matching grant	I want to support [organization], which uses scientific methods to fight poverty. My gift will be matched by a major foundation.	Pratham	21.0	X	X
Treatment 8: Proven impact: specific program	I want to support [organization's program], which was proven effective using scientific methods.	Pratham	16.0	X	X
Treatment 9: Quality signal	I want to support [organization], whose anti-poverty programs have been evaluated and supported by the Hewlett Foundation.	Pratham	17.0		X

Note: IPA, Innovations for Poverty Action.

a. Average across organizations. Actual length differs slightly by organization.

b. For program-relevant outcomes, the content was as follows. For Pratham, an Indian child education program, for which $1 provides a child with one semester of education; for IPA, a Kenya child deworming program, for which $1 provides a child with 2 years of medicine. For UNICEF, a safe drinking water for kids program, for which $1 provides a child with 40 days of clean water.

each donation, just the average for the treatment cell by week). No other data are available. Note that in the tables, the percentage of donations is given in tenths of basis points, so the value of the binary donated outcome is either 0 or 1000, not 0 or 1.

7.2.6 Sample Size and Statistical Analysis

We observed 38,927,073 eBay purchases. We do not know how many of those are multiple purchases by a single user. The randomization was done by transaction, and thus if a user bought more than one item, they were rerandomized for each transaction, independently of their last treatment assignment.

We conducted two sets of analyses. Both employ ordinary least squares (OLS) with one of two dependent variables (a binary for "donated anything," and the average amount donated).

The key independent variables in the first specification are indicator variables for eight of the nine content treatments. The specification also includes controls for the week of the experiment and the charity (because the randomization was conditional on week and charity). These results are presented graphically in figure 7.2 in section 7.3. Point estimates and standard errors for each treatment group are provided in the comments of the figure.

The key independent variables in the second specification are attributes of the content treatments. We assigned all treatments to a set of six attributes, since some of the messages overlap in the underlying theory they are intending to capture. The six attributes are as follows: message length, depiction of charitable activity, quantification of impact, matched funds, scientific evidence, and expert signal. Table 7.2 shows the mapping of the specific messages to these attributes. Table 7.3 in section 7.3 presents the OLS regression results, examining how each attribute predicts likelihood of donating and average donation size. These specifications, as with the first specification, include control for charity and week.

7.3 Results

Figure 7.2 presents the main results comparing the proportion of individuals who donate in response to each of the nine scripts (after controlling for charity and week). Given the sample size, the confidence intervals are small, and for almost all pairwise treatment comparisons, we can reject a null hypothesis of equality. Table 7.1 presents the means

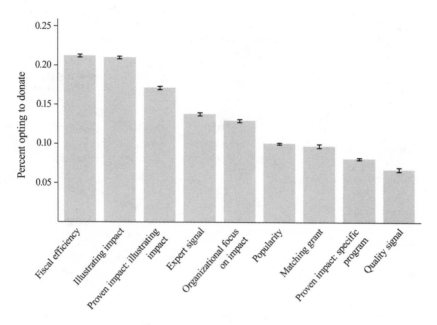

Figure 7.2
Donation rates by treatment. *Note*: Point estimates and standard errors (in parentheses) by treatment in terms of tenths of basis points are as follows: Fiscal Efficiency (Omitted Category): 2.872 (0.036), Illustrating impact: –0.079 (0.025), Proven impact: illustrating impact: –0.137 (0.027), Expert signal: –1.324 (0.032), Organizational focus on impact: –0.201 (0.027), Popularity: –1.277 (0.022), Matching grant: –0.240 (0.035), Proven impact: specific program: –0.544 (0.023), Quality signal: –0.539 (0.036).

for each treatment, broken down by charity, and reports the proportion who give (thus, it presents results that are similar to those shown in figure 7.2, except without controls for week) and the average amount donated.

Table 7.3 presents what we consider the main results, testing the impact of each attribute. The omitted category is the "popularity" treatment, which is coded as zero for all attributes. Thus all results in this table are the effect of a particular attribute compared to the popularity treatment. For the linear probability model (column 1 in the table) to predict likelihood of giving, we find, in order of magnitude, the following point estimates: matching (1.069, standard error [se] = 0.077), depiction of charitable activity (0.886, se = 0.030), quantification of impact (0.390, se = 0.039), scientific evidence (0.107, se = 0.016), and expert signal (0.027, se = 0.037). The coefficient on number of words in the message is –0.062 (se = 0.009), which means that the effect of going

Table 7.3
Effect of message attribute on likelihood of donating: OLS, probit.

Attribute	Donated (1000/0): OLS	Donated (1000/0): Probit	Average amount donated ($/1000): OLS
Message length (number of words)	−0.062 (0.009)***	−0.047 (0.002)***	−18.743 (0.006)***
Depiction of charitable activity	0.886 (0.030)***	0.300 (0.008)***	81.583 (0.019)***
Quantification of impact	0.39 (0.039)***	0.211 (0.009)***	91.21 (0.028)***
Matched funds	1.069 (0.077)***	0.545 (0.021)***	231.851 (0.039)***
Scientific evidence	0.107 (0.016)***	0.068 (0.004)***	−22.644 (0.012)***
Expert signal	0.027 (0.037)	0.094 (0.007)***	99.567 (0.019)***
Organization 1 (IPA)	−0.545 (0.025)***	−0.164 (0.005)***	−30.558 (0.015)***
Organization 2 (Pratham)	−1.604 (0.021)***	−0.381 (0.005)***	−34.075 (0.015)***
Week 1	−0.011 (0.022)	0.02 (0.005)***	−12.001 (0.022)***
Week 2	0.185 (0.020)***	0.058 (0.005)***	−40.197 (0.021)***
Constant	2.697 (0.121)***	−2.348 (0.029)***	1525.007 (0.092)***
Number of observations	38,927,073	38,927,073	38,927,073
Mean of dependent variable	1.481	1.481	1270.8

Notes: IPA, Innovations for Poverty Action; OLS, ordinary least squares. Estimates for columns 1 and 2 are in tenths of basis points (i.e., the dependent variable is either 1000 or 0, and the independent variables are indicator variables equal to 1 or 0). Depiction of charitable activity corresponds to treatments 1, 2, 3, and 8 in table 7.1; quantification of impact corresponds to treatments 2 and 3; matched funds corresponds to treatment 7; scientific evidence corresponds to treatments 3, 5, 7 and 8 expert signal corresponds to treatments 4 and 9. Probit results are marginal effects. Robust standard errors are shown in parentheses. The symbol *** indicates significance at the 1 percent level.

from the longest to the shortest message generates the same treatment effect as the quantification of impact treatment (relative to the popularity message, which is the omitted variable).

Column 3 reports the treatment effects on the average amount given. Matching funds generates the largest treatment effect. The main change in ordering, compared to column 1, is for scientific evidence, which lowers average amount given compared to the omitted category (popularity). In contrast, for likelihood of giving, the scientific evidence generated a small (relative to the other treatments) but positive treatment effect. Furthermore, the expert signal did not generate a statistically significant treatment effect on likelihood of giving, but it did lead to a statistically significant increase in average amount given.

7.4   Conclusion

To interpret our results, we start by assuming that the decision-making environment triggered System I "intuitive" thinking. We then use this experiment to learn which treatments work well in a no-deliberation, "intuitive" decision-making environment. The results are, ahem, fairly intuitive:

- shorter messages are good;
- matching grants (which is a common marketing tool and hence requires little thought) work well;
- depiction of charitable activities works well (it provides immediate and tangible understanding of what an organization does);
- quantification of impact does not work as well (this requires thinking: is $1 for 2 years of medicine a good deal? Is this a credible deal?);
- popularity does not work well; and
- scientific evidence has a weak result on the likelihood of giving and a negative result on average amount given.

On a practical level, there are many retail sites, both in person and online, which promote giving. These results are likely relevant for such efforts.

We stress obvious caveats: mapping these scripts to specific theories is difficult and tenuous. Furthermore, we lack any further data on the donors, which could be used to test richer theories. Further research examining heterogeneity across donors would be fruitful. In addition, we believe it would be fruitful to test the efficacy of these types of treatments in an environment that allowed researchers to randomize deliberation. To do so would allow us to make stronger statements than we can from our current data about what intuitive versus deliberative individuals respond most to for charitable giving. In addition, it would inform us about modeling of charitable giving more generally.

Notes

We thank MissionFish, eBay, and Clam Lorenz for collaboration and making the data available, and Matthew Grant and Nicole Mauriello at Innovations for Poverty Action for management and data analysis. All opinions and errors are our own.

1. Disclosure: Karlan is founder and chairman of Innovations for Poverty Action, and at the time of this experiment was the executive director.

References

Deaton, A. 2009. "Instruments of Development: Randomization in the Tropics, and the Search for the Elusive Keys to Economic Development." The Keynes Lecture, British Academy, London, January 2009.

Gneezy, U., E. A. Keenan, and A. Gneezy. 2014. "Avoiding Overhead Aversion in Charity." *Science* 346 (6209): 632–635. doi: 10.1126/science.1253932.

Kahneman, D. 2003. "Maps of Bounded Rationality: Psychology for Behavioral Economics." *American Economic Review* 93 (5): 1449–1475.

Karlan, Dean, and John List. 2012. "How Can Bill and Melinda Gates Increase Other People's Donations to Fund Public Goods?" Cambridge, MA: National Bureau of Economic Research. doi: 10.3386/w17954.

Karlan, Dean, and Daniel H. Wood. 2016. "The Effect of Effectiveness: Donor Response to Aid Effectiveness in a Direct Mail Fundraising Experiment." *Journal of Behavioral and Experimental Economics* 66: 1–8. doi: 10.1016/j.socec.2016.05.005.

Metzger, Laura, and Isabel Günther. 2016. "Making an Impact? The Relevance of Information on Aid Effectiveness for Charitable Giving. A Laboratory Experiment." Working paper, ETH Zurich, Zurich, Switzerland.

Vesterlund, Lise. 2003. "The Informational Value of Sequential Fundraising." *Journal of Public Economics* 87 (3): 627–657.

8 It's Not the Thought That Counts: A Field Experiment on Gift Exchange and Giving at a Public University

Catherine C. Eckel, David H. Herberich, and Jonathan Meer

8.1 Introduction

Donor premiums—gifts from a charity to a potential donor—are one of the most popular fundraising tools used to induce donors to give: Sixty percent of solicitations involve some form of donor premium (Koop 2005), with two general approaches. Front-end unconditional gifts, such as address labels, are included with the solicitation, irrespective of a donation. Back-end conditional gifts are sent only in response to a donation. For a premium to be effective, donors must respond positively. This response may be a result of the gift inducing a desire or obligation to reciprocate, or because the premium itself enhances the reputation of the donor by signaling that they are a supporter of the charity, thereby enhancing their social image (Benabou and Tirole 2006; Lacetera and Macis 2010b). Sending a gift may also serve as a signal of the quality of the organization, thereby increasing donations. But donor premiums can also backfire. Donors may react negatively if they disapprove of the premium as an unnecessary fundraising expense, or if the "incentive" inherent in the provision of premiums crowds out the inherent motive to donate (Lacetera and Macis 2010a; Newman and Shen 2012; Gneezy, Keenan, and Gneezy 2014).[1] Even among practitioners, there is disagreement. Some insist that "donors love premiums" (The NonProfit Times 2013), even as surveys show that nearly two-thirds of donors say "they do not want to receive token gifts of any kind so that as much of their gift as possible goes to the purpose to which they gave" (Cygnus Applied Research 2011).

We partner with the Association of Former Students (AFS) at Texas A&M University to conduct a natural field experiment during a regularly scheduled direct-mail fundraising campaign. The treatments are designed to elicit the mechanisms by which gift exchange might operate on potential donors. We vary whether the gift is unconditional (included with the solicitation, irrespective of a donation) or conditional (sent only in response to a donation). In the unconditional treatment, we provide a subset of potential donors with a higher quality version of the same gift (a leather vs. plastic luggage tag). We selected a donor premium that is branded with the university AFS logo and is therefore a signal of support for the organization (see appendix figure 8.A.1 for images of the tags). The treatment groups are designed to influence channels that impact both the extensive margin of whether or not to make a gift and the intensive margin of the size of the gift (conditional on giving).

If donors are motivated by a sense of reciprocity that increases with the value of the gift, then the higher-quality gift should yield more giving relative to the lower-quality gift, which in turn will be more effective than a baseline treatment with no gift. In contrast, if donors dislike overhead and fundraising expenditures, as they often claim they do, the relationship should go in the opposite direction.[2]

If the mere offer of a donor premium engenders feelings of reciprocity equal to those from having a gift actually in hand, then the conditional gift treatments should show the same patterns of donative behavior as the unconditional treatments. However, a conditional premium may not have the same motivational effect as the unconditional reward: its tit-for-tat character may instead crowd out intrinsic motivation to a greater extent than the unconditional premium. Thus donors may have a smaller response to conditional gifts.

To further investigate donor motives, we conduct two further treatments: giving donors the option to opt out from (or, symmetrically, opt in to) receiving the conditional gift. If donors are altruistically motivated to maximize the impact of their donations by avoiding fundraising costs, they should decline the gift to preserve the charity's resources. In addition, declining the gift can reduce social pressure to give a larger amount. However, the response to conditional premiums may be high and may produce a high rate of donations, along with a number of small, "token" donations, if donors want the item for its signaling or direct consumption value.

Prior research has investigated the effects of unconditional gifts in charitable giving. Falk (2007) mailed a solicitation including zero, one, or four postcards to previous donors of a children's aid charity, finding a slightly elevated giving rate for the small gift over the baseline and a much higher rate for the large gift. This intervention was highly profitable for the organization. Alpizar, Carlsson, and Johansson-Stenman (2008) offered a small gift during an in-person solicitation in a national park. They found a higher giving rate but a lower amount given. The result was driven by individuals in treatments without anonymity during the giving process, suggesting that social pressure may play a large role in gift exchange in this context; the treatment was not cost effective. These experiments do not, however, directly compare unconditional and conditional gifts, with their potentially differing mechanisms. In the experiment most similar to ours, Landry et al. (2011) conducted door-to-door solicitations with small and large gifts (a bookmark and a book) that were given unconditionally, conditionally for any gift, or conditional on a donation commensurate to the gift's value. They showed that while the unconditional treatments produce higher rates of giving, their proceeds did not cover their costs. Importantly, they found in follow-up solicitations that making the gift conditional "served as an effective screen of those who were truly interested in giving" (6).

Our approach differs in that we conduct a direct-mail experiment, in which social pressure to give in response to an unconditional gift is likely to be much lower relative to a door-to-door solicitation. We also enhance the comparability of the large and small gifts by varying the quality of an identical item. Most importantly, we offer donors the explicit option to decline (or, for completeness, require them to explicitly accept) the conditional gift. This innovation—which, to our knowledge, has not yet been examined in the literature—allows us to more thoroughly understand donors' motivations for responding to the charity's gift.

We find that the high-quality unconditional gift produces the highest giving rate, though this response is far from sufficient to cover the costs of the solicitation. There are no significant differences across the giving rates in the other treatments: All are indistinguishable from the baseline. Donors overwhelmingly preferred receiving the gift when offered the option—that is, they do not appear, for the most part, to be driven to maximize the charity's funds. There are no discernable effects on the size of the gift, conditional on giving, though this is unsurprising, given the structure of AFS's appeals.[3]

8.2 Experimental Design

We conducted a field experiment in partnership with the AFS at Texas A&M University in early 2014. We began in late January with 225,474 alumni who had not donated the prior year or were within the first few years after graduation. At AFS's request, we sequestered 84,832 members of the sample from the experiment in order to allow AFS's phone bank to continue to operate; these individuals were randomly chosen from the pool of alumni with a known phone number. The remaining 140,642 alumni were randomly assigned to seven treatment groups, balanced on year of graduation, gender, residence in Texas, and giving segment (nondonor; recently lapsed; and "distant lapsed," those whose last gift was more than 5 years prior). Table 8.1 shows the balance in observables across treatments: control (no gift); unconditional gift of a plastic AFS-branded luggage tag; unconditional gift of a leather AFS-branded luggage tag; conditional gift of a plastic luggage tag (the quality of the tag was not specified in the letter) with text on the envelope noting a "special offer"; conditional gift without the envelope text; conditional gift with an opt-out option; and conditional gift with an opt-in option. Each leather luggage tag cost $3.59, compared to $0.74 for the plastic luggage tag.

Letters were sent in early March, and those with known phone numbers were returned to the phone bank one month later. Other solicitations by mail began in early May; all follow-up solicitations were orthogonal to our treatments. We record gifts from March 10, 2014, to the end of our available data, November 10, 2014. We made one adjustment to our initial sample. There were 895 individuals who gave between the time of our randomization and the mailing of our solicitations. We removed them, leaving 139,747 in the sample that we use for the analysis.[4]

As shown in the appendix, the letters were identical across treatments with the exception of the text regarding the gift. The conditional treatments also included the text, "Look Inside for a Special Offer," on the envelope (except the "no text" treatment); removing the text made no appreciable difference to giving behavior.

Those in the control group received a standard solicitation letter, while the letter to those in the unconditional gift treatments (leather or plastic luggage tag) included the following paragraph:

As a token of appreciation for your Aggie pride, we are happy to enclose a former student luggage tag. To make your gift today, please mail in the attached gift form and mail it back in the included return envelope.

Those in the conditional gift treatments saw the following paragraph instead:

As a token of appreciation for your Aggie pride, we are happy to send you a former student luggage tag in response to your gift. To make your gift today, please mail in the attached gift form and mail it back in the included return envelope.

The opt-in and opt-out options were listed in a prominent position at the top of response form in those treatments.

Table 8.1
Balance table.

Subject Group	Treatment								
	Control	Unconditional Plastic	Unconditional Leather	Conditional	Conditional (No Text)	Conditional (Opt-Out)	Conditional (Opt-In)	Sequestered
Acquisition (%)	64.01	64.81	64.23	64.04	64.19	64.26	64.28	64.03
Distant Lapsed (%)	22.90	22.33	22.93	22.86	22.80	22.46	23.00	22.80
Recent Lapsed (%)	13.00	12.86	12.84	13.10	13.01	13.27	12.71	13.17
Texan (%)	75.93	75.49	74.91	76.22	75.54	75.36	75.80	78.41
Female[a] (%)	41.77	42.15	42.36	41.89	41.81	42.36	41.32	39.33
Phoneable[b] (%)	36.26	36.41	37.01	36.16	36.44	36.63	36.61	100.00
Years since graduation	22.77 (12.51)	20.78 (12.51)	20.90 (12.81)	22.64 (12.52)	22.70 (12.57)	22.66 (12.70)	22.73 (12.61)	22.78 (13.27)
Number of observations	22,418	20,282	7,436	22,488	22,343	22,459	22,321	84,832

a. The sequestered group is less likely to be female ($p = 0.000$).
b. The sequestered group is by definition phoneable.

8.3   Results

Table 8.2 summarizes the results for the giving rate and dollars given. The median gift is $100 in every treatment, and it is evident from the large standard deviations that there are a number of large gifts. To reduce their influence, we also show means winsorized at the 99th and 95th percentiles of the giving distribution. There are no significant differences in mean giving across treatments. Figure 8.1 shows that distributions of gift amounts for all treatments; there also are no significant differences in these distributions ($p = 0.139$).

The response rates are quite low in all treatments, though generally within the typical range of rates from direct-mail solicitations. However, the giving rate for the unconditional leather treatment stands out as twice as large as the control (0.97 percent vs. 0.47 percent); the difference is statistically significant at $p = 0.000$. The unconditional plastic treatment has a slightly higher giving rate than the control, though it is not significant at conventional levels ($p = 0.12$); it is significantly lower than giving in the higher-quality treatment ($p = 0.000$). These results suggest that a sense of reciprocity drives giving, and donors are therefore more responsive to higher-quality gifts. Further, despite claims to the contrary in other studies, donors are not averse to fundraising costs in this particular context.

Turning to the conditional treatments, there is no difference among the four ($p = 0.312$), nor between them and the control group ($p = 0.463$). However, the conditional donation rate is lower than the unconditional rate (conditional vs. unconditional plastic, $p = 0.08$; comparing the conditional donation rate across all treatments to the overall unconditional rate is significant at $p = 0.000$). It does seem that the offer of a conditional gift does not have quite the same gift exchange effect as an unconditional gift. It also appears that this offer does not reduce giving rates relative to the baseline through crowding out of intrinsic motivation or distaste for overhead costs. We also saw no indication of a greater prevalence of token donations in order to receive the gift for a minimal expenditure. However, we cannot say whether social norms preclude this behavior or that donors did not believe that the value of the gift would exceed the cost of even a small donation plus the effort to mail it in.

Offering prospective donors the option to opt out of (or into) receiving the gift did not have a significant impact on giving behavior. However, table 8.3 and figure 8.2a show that donors strongly preferred

Table 8.2
Giving rates and amounts by treatment.

Treatment	(1) Rate of Giving	(2) Average Giving Amount	(3) Winsorized 99%	(4) Winsorized 95%
Unconditional vs. Conditional				
Control	0.47%	157.42 (178.97)	157.42 (178.97)	142.14 (117.97)
Unconditional plastic	0.57%	136.02 (166.35)	131.74 (134.35)	123.56 (85.08)
Unconditional leather	0.97%	150.59 (194.59)	150.59 (194.59)	130.04 (111.63)
Conditional	0.45%	144.78 (147.85)	144.78 (147.85)	135.02 (98.83)
Conditional with no text	0.53%	121.32 (90.42)	121.36 (90.36)	120.69 (86.01)
Opt In vs. Opt Out				
Conditional opt-out	0.42%	199.21 (335.39)	172.89 (212.74)	151.26 (138.85)
Conditional opt-in	0.43%	138 (108.22)	138 (108.22)	136.96 (104.12)

Note: Mean and standard deviations (in parentheses) in columns 2–4.

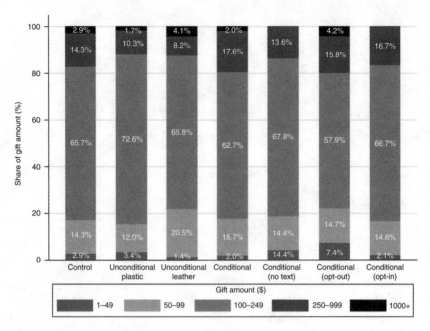

Figure 8.1
Distribution of giving amounts.

Table 8.3
Donation frequency and amounts in the opt-in and opt-out treatments.

Subject Group	Opt-In Treatment	Opt-Out Treatment
Chose Opt-In		
N	58	83
Percent taking the option	60.4%	88.3%
Mean amount given	$142.67 (122.39)	$210.90 (354.70)
Chose Opt-Out		
N	38	11
Percent taking the option	39.6%	11.7%
Mean amount given	$130.87 (83.12)	$120.00 (129.23)
Total	96	94

Note: Standard deviations in parentheses.

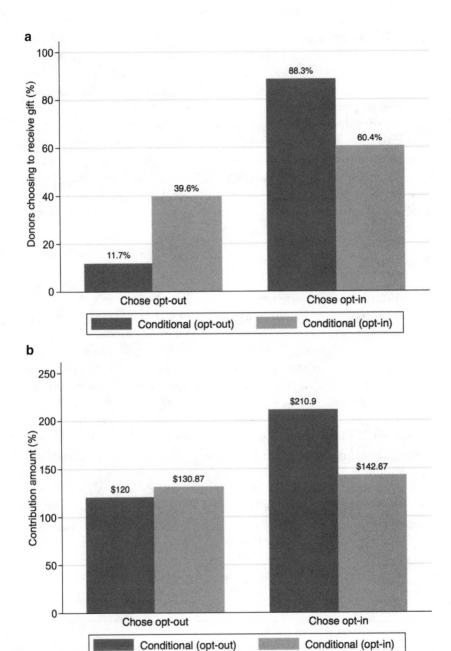

Figure 8.2
Conditional distributions.

to receive the gift in both treatments. When requiring an active decision to opt out, 88.3 percent chose to receive the gift, while 60.4 percent chose to do so when actively required to opt in; overall, three-quarters of donors making a gift in this treatment elected to receive the luggage tag. This provides evidence that donors are not motivated by the desire to maximize the impact of their donation, which could be thought of as a more altruistic motivation. Instead the motivation appears to be, at least in part, a desire for the item itself, whether for its direct value or the signaling value of an AFS-branded tag. Finally, Figure 8.2b shows that contributions were higher on average for those who chose to receive the tag in both treatments, but this difference is not statistically significant.

8.4 Conclusion

We conducted a field experiment at a large state university to investigate the mechanisms underlying gift exchange in philanthropy. We find that donors are responsive to unconditional gifts, particularly higher-quality ones. This suggests that reciprocity plays a role and that donors are not overly concerned with fundraising expenditures in this context. Despite the higher giving rate in the unconditional leather tag treatment, the expense of shipping the item to all prospective donors swamped the higher return, yielding a loss of nearly $3 per solicitation, compared to a net gain of $0.26 in the baseline treatment. The unconditional plastic tag treatment, with its lower-cost item, still lost $0.70 per solicitation.[5]

We further show that the promise of a gift through a conditional offer does not have the same impact as a gift in hand. Yet conditional offers do not appear to reduce donative behavior, either through distaste for fundraising costs or crowding out of intrinsic motivation. Donors overwhelmingly prefer to receive the gift when offered the option to decline it, providing evidence against purely altruistic motivations for giving.

8.A   Appendix

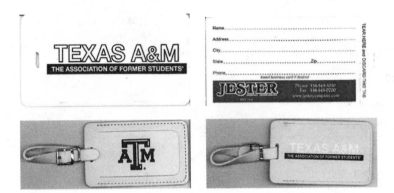

Figure 8.A.1
Tags offered as gifts.

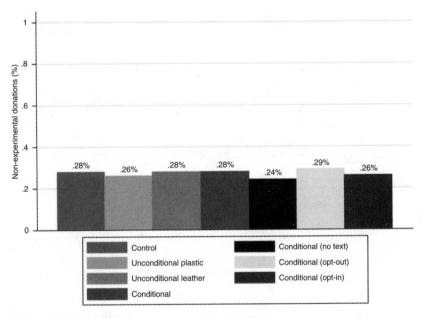

Figure 8.A.2
Nonexperimental donations: By mail (during and after).

Figure 8.A.3
Envelope without additional text.

The Association
OF FORMER STUDENTS®

TEXAS A&M UNIVERSITY®

**...and help our
students stay
a step ahead!**

John Doe
The Association
505 George Bush Dr.
College Station, TX 77840

Howdy, John Doe!

The Aggie experience is something that is truly special. In great measure because former students, like YOU, have stepped forward to ensure that each student has the opportunity to be a part of something bigger than themselves. Students who attend Texas A&M are already well on their way to being the leaders of tomorrow. Their lives will change significantly and for the better because they get the opportunity to attend this great university. Now, we are calling on YOU to help them stay a step ahead of the rest.

By making a gift to Texas A&M University through The Association of Former Students, you will be supporting organizations like Fish Camp, T-Camp, Big Event, and many more. You have the opportunity to help develop leaders through student organizations, enable students to attend college through scholarships, and develop respect through time-honored traditions. Without your gift, the Aggie experience would be just like any other but because of your loyalty and your support, these students can stand tall in knowing that they've made the best decision of their lives.

What an incredible opportunity to be a part of that magic. Don't miss another day—another opportunity to help Texas A&M students. "We are the Aggies, the Aggies are we. True to each other as Aggies can be." You can help shape student experiences at Texas A&M and help them stay a step ahead so that they'll be inspired to continue the legacy of giving back, because they benefited from your gift.

In the Aggie Spirit,

Marty '87

Marty Holmes '87
Vice President, Marketing and Programs

Figure 8.A.4
Standard solicitation letter.

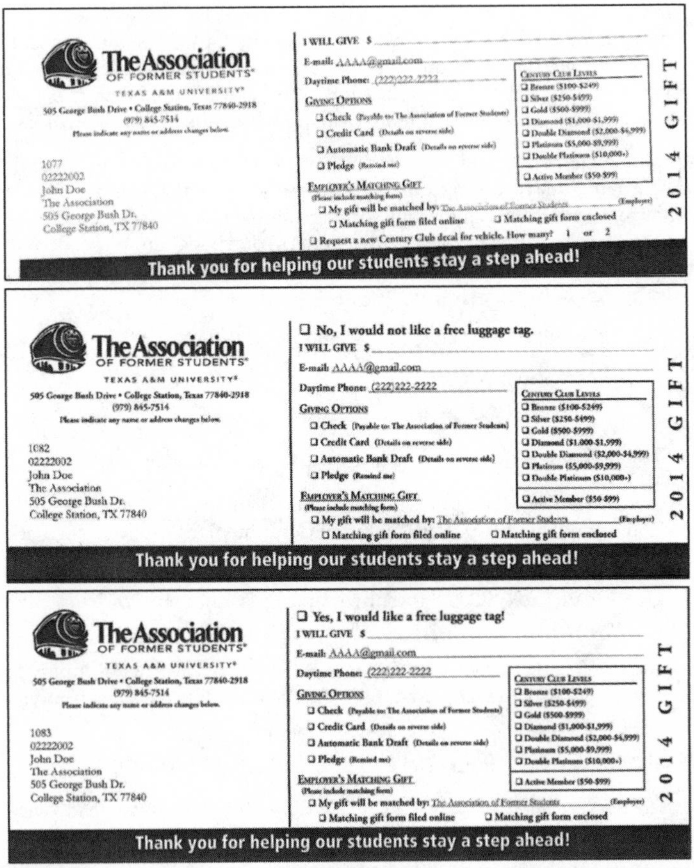

Figure 8.A.5
Donation reply cards.

Notes

We are grateful to the Association of Former Students at Texas A&M University for their cooperation, particularly to Chanee Carlson, Larry Cooper, and Marty Holmes. Wei Zhan provided excellent research assistance. We gratefully acknowledge financial support from the National Science Foundation through grant number SES-1338680.

1. Other possible mechanisms include that the gift serves as a proxy for the charity's quality, or that donors dislike spending on fundraising (Gneezy, Keenan, and Gneezy 2014; Meer 2014).

2. We can rule out that the gift serves as a signal of the charity's quality, since all recipients are alumni of Texas A&M University and are familiar with AFS, which serves both as the alumni organization and the fundraiser for the annual fund.

3. AFS's appeals revolve around membership in the "Century Club," which requires a $100 donation; more than half of the donations in our data are for this amount. As Harbaugh (1998) shows and we confirm in our data, donors tend to bunch at the bottom of giving levels, and the next suggested level is $250. It is perhaps overly optimistic to expect that our treatments would cause donors to more than double an already substantial gift.

4. In response to mailings other than our solicitations or through AFS's web page or phone bank, 5,432 donors gave during our data collection period. These donors are included in the experimental population, but we include them as not having donated during our experiment. There is no systematic pattern of giving for these donors ($p = 0.951$). Nonexperimental donations that occurred during and after the experimental period are shown in appendix figure 8.A.2.

5. These approaches may still be profitable in the long run if the act of giving creates a habit (Meer 2013).

References

Alpizar, Francisco, Fredrik Carlsson, and Olof Johansson-Stenman. 2008. "Anonymity, Reciprocity, and Conformity: Evidence from Voluntary Contribu- tions to a National Park in Costa Rica." *Journal of Public Economics* 92 (5/6): 1047–1060.

Benabou, Roland, and Jean Tirole. 2006. "Incentives and Prosocial Behavior." *American Economic Review* 96 (5): 1652–1678.

Cygnus Applied Research. 2011. "The Cygnus Donor Survey … Where Philan- thropy Is Headed in 2011." http://www.cygresearch.com/files/free/US-2011-Cygnus-Donor-Survey Report-Executive Summary.pdf.

Falk, Armin. 2007. "Gift Exchange in the Field," *Econometrica* 75 (5): 1501–1511.

Gneezy, Uri, Elizabeth A. Keenan, and Ayelet Gneezy. 2014. "Avoiding Overhead Aversion in Charity." *Science* 346 (6209): 632–635.

Harbaugh, William. 1998. "What Do Donations Buy? A Model of Philanthropy Based on Prestige and Warm Glow." *Journal of Public Economics* 67: 269–284.

Koop, Amy. 2005. "Focus On: Premiums: Here Donor, Donor." http://www.nonprofitpro .com/article/ premiums-vital-many-direct-mail-donor-acquisition-progams-but-address-labels- alone-might-not-do-job-33129/all/.

Lacetera, Nicola, and Mario Macis. 2010a. "Do All Material Incentives for Pro-social Activities Backfire? The Response to Cash and Non-cash Incentives for Blood Donations." *Journal of Economic Psychology* 31 (4): 738–748.

Lacetera, Nicola, and Mario Macis. 2010b. "Social Image Concerns and Prosocial Behavior: Field Evidence from a Nonlinear Incentive Scheme." *Journal of Economic Behavior & Organization* 76 (2): 225–237.

Landry, Craig, Andreas Lange, John List, Michael Price, and Nicholas Rupp. 2011. "Is There a 'Hidden Cost of Control' in Naturally-Occurring Markets? Evidence from a Natural Field Experiment." NBER working paper 17472, National Bureau of Economic Research, Cambridge, MA.

Meer, Jonathan. 2013. "The Habit of Giving." *Economic Inquiry* 51 (4): 2002—2017.

Meer, Jonathan. 2014. "Effects of the Price of Charitable Giving: Evidence from an Online Crowdfunding Platform." *Journal of Economic Behavior & Organization* 103: 113–124.

Newman, George E., and Y. Jeremy Shen. 2012. "The Counterintuitive Effects of Thank-You Gifts on Charitable Giving." *Journal of Economic Psychology* 33 (5): 973–983.

The NonProfit Times. 2013. "Direct Response … Tests Show Gifts Might Not Return Premium Donor." http://www.thenonprofittimes.com/, http://www.thenonprofittimes .com/newsletter.php?id=623#One.

9 Charitable Donations of Time and Money: Complements or Substitutes? Evidence from UK Data

Sarah Brown and Karl Taylor

9.1 Introduction and Background

In this chapter we explore the determinants of unpaid labor supply, specifically, how many hours of unpaid labor are volunteered by individuals. Recent figures for the United Kingdom from the Office for National Statistics (ONS 2013) indicate that in 2012 about 2.29 billion hours were volunteered, which equates to an average of 8 hours per individual, worth £25.6 billion to the economy.[1] Not surprisingly, given these figures, this topic has entered the political agenda. Prior to the 2015 UK general election, the then Prime Minister David Cameron pledged that such activity should be recognized and that the Working Time Regulations would be amended so that people are annually entitled to 28 days of paid vacation and 3 days of paid volunteering.[2] Clearly, understanding what influences volunteering behavior at the individual level is important, given the contribution of unpaid volunteering to the economy. An abundant literature has explored monetary donations to charity (for a detailed review, see Andreoni and Payne 2013); in contrast, the literature on volunteering (i.e., the supply of unpaid labor) is relatively sparse.

In this chapter we make a number of contributions to the existing literature. First, using the latest UK data from Understanding Society, the UK Household Longitudinal Study (UKHLS), we investigate donations of time, in particular, how many hours of unpaid labor are volunteered by individuals. To our knowledge, our study is the first in the economics literature to conduct such an analysis for the United Kingdom. Second, we also have information on whether individuals make monetary donations to charity and, if so, how much. This enables us to provide an insight into whether donations of time and money are complements or substitutes, which has not been investigated in the United Kingdom.

The existing literature for the United States and other developed countries, reviewed below, has typically found that the two activities are positively correlated. This is also confirmed by a report by the Charities Aid Foundation (2016). Ascertaining whether money and time donations are complements or substitutes is important for policy analysis. For example, if they are complements, then a tax deduction for cash gifts has the additional benefit of increasing the amount of time volunteered (Andreoni 2006).[3] What follows is a brief overview of the existing literature.

The paper by Menchik and Weisbrod (1987) was one of the first in the economics literature to explicitly investigate the supply of volunteer labor. These authors found that in the United States, price and income effects were important determinants of volunteering time, a finding similar to that of monetary donations (see, e.g., Andreoni and Payne 2013). In an influential paper, Freeman (1997) noted that volunteering is a substantial economic activity in the United States, yet it receives no monetary compensation. By adopting standard labor supply side analysis, he argued that volunteering is a "conscience good or activity" that individuals feel morally obligated to undertake because of, for example, peer or social pressure.[4] Moreover, contrary to the labor supply model, he finds little evidence that the amount of time volunteered is influenced by the opportunity cost of time (in a standard labor supply model, people should volunteer less when the wage offer is high).

Cognitive ability has been found to be associated with a number of social and economic outcomes (e.g., labor market outcomes, as in Heckman, Stixrud, and Urzua 2006) but has attracted limited attention in the economics literature on charitable behavior. In terms of volunteering, one particular cognitive skill—verbal proficiency—has been found in the wider social sciences literature to be positively associated with membership in voluntary organizations (see Hauser 2000 and Bekkers 2010). More generally, it has been argued that individuals with higher levels of cognitive ability may be better able to identify with the needs of distant others (see Wiepking and Maas 2009; James 2011).

The Brown and Lankford (1992) paper was one of the first in the economics literature to explicitly investigate whether monetary and time donations were complements or substitutes. They simultaneously estimated the determinants of both types of charitable behavior, allowing for censoring at zero (i.e., some individuals donate neither time nor money). Based on a unique US sample, they found evidence in favor of complementarity. More recently, the literature has continued to investigate donations of time and money in a bivariate framework (e.g., Apinunmahakul, Barham, and Devlin 2009; Cappellari, Ghinetti, and Turati 2011; and Bauer, Bredtmann, and Schmidt 2013), thereby allowing for potential simultaneous decision making.

Based on a large Canadian cross-sectional sample of individuals, Apinunmahakul, Barham, and Devlin (2009) examine the number of hours volunteered and the amount donated to charity in 1997. They find a positive correlation in the unobservables between time and money donations, suggesting complementarity between the two forms of charitable behavior. Using cross-sectional data for Italian individuals, Cappellari, Ghinetti, and Turati (2011) also find evidence in favor of complementarity. In addition, they report differences across gender, relating in particular to the responsiveness of males to changing opportunity costs. Using data from the European Social Survey for nineteen countries, Bauer, Bredtmann, and Schmidt (2013) focus on the role of income and opportunity costs in influencing time and money donations and the extent to which the different types of charitable behavior are interrelated. They report positive associations between monetary and time donations, although the extent of the correlation varies according to the type of charitable organization—being largest for religious organizations. In accordance with the existing literature, those with a lower opportunity cost of time, for example part-time workers or those without dependent children, are more likely to volunteer time.

9.2 Data and Methodology

We use data drawn from the UKHLS to investigate what factors influence donations of time (i.e., unpaid volunteering) and the relationship between volunteering and monetary donations. The UKHLS is designed to capture life in the United Kingdom and how it is changing over time. The survey builds on its predecessor, the British Household Panel Survey, which covered the period 1991 to 2008. Participants live in Scotland, Wales, Northern Ireland, and England. The survey contains information about people's social and economic circumstances, attitudes, behaviors, and health. In the first wave of the UKHLS, more than 50,000 individuals were interviewed between 2009 and 2011; correspondingly in the latest wave (wave 5), over 41,000 individuals were interviewed between 2013 and 2015. Questions regarding charitable donations of time and money are not asked in all five available waves of the UKHLS, being available only in waves 2 and 4.

Interviews for wave 4, which were conducted between 2012 and 2014, contain information on the number of hours of unpaid labor volunteered in the past 4 weeks and the monetary amount donated to charity over the past 12 months. As discussed in the previous section, when investigating whether donations of time and money are substitutes or complements, much of the literature has adopted a bivariate modeling framework. However, in the UKHLS the questions regarding donating behavior differ substantially in terms of the period covered (i.e., the past 4 weeks for volunteering and the past 12 months for monetary donations) and arguably render bivariate analysis inappropriate. We argue that, due to the timing difference between the questions of interest on time and money donations, it seems more appropriate to condition volunteering during the previous month on monetary donations over the past year rather than the other way around.

Table 9.1 shows that the average number of hours volunteered during the past 4 weeks is just over 2, and for nonzero values (i.e., those who volunteer, which accounts for about 15 percent of individuals), the average amount of time volunteered is 12 hours over the past 4 weeks.

Figure 9.1 shows a histogram of unpaid labor supply for volunteers, where it is apparent that the distribution is not normal. Consequently, we model hours volunteered as a count outcome.

Table 9.1
Summary statistics—dependent variable.

Variable	Mean	Standard Deviation	Minimum	Maximum
Number of hours volunteered in past 4 weeks	2.2265	9.5639	0	200
Number of observations	31,409			
If not equal to zero				
Number of hours volunteered in past 4 weeks	12.1995	18.6712	1	200
Number of observations (% nonzero)	4,601 (14.65%)			

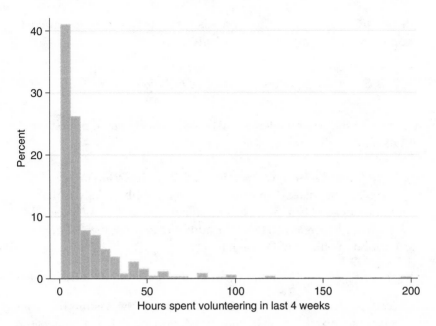

Figure 9.1
Number of hours volunteered in the past 4 weeks (volunteers only). *Source*: UKHLS.

9.2.1   Exogenous Monetary Donations

Volunteering during the past 4 weeks by individual i is denoted by vol_i ($i = 1, 2, 3 \ldots, 31{,}409$), which takes values $0, 1, 2, \ldots, 200$ and is determined by a set of exogenous covariates x_i and (in order to explore the relationship with monetary donations) the amount don_i that the individual donated to charity during the past 12 months. The expected value of volunteering conditional on the covariates is then

$$E\left\{vol_i \mid x_i, don_i\right\} = \exp(x_i' \, \boldsymbol{\beta} + \phi \, don_i). \tag{9.1}$$

The probability of a given outcome, for example whether individuals volunteer 1 hour, that is, $\mathrm{prob}\{vol_i = 1 \mid x_i,\, don_i\}$, can be determined by assuming that volunteering has a poisson distribution with expectation

$$\lambda_i = \exp\left(x_i' \, \boldsymbol{\beta} + \phi \, don_i\right) \tag{9.2}$$

and with the probability mass function of vol_i conditional on the covariates given by

$$\mathrm{prob}\left\{vol_i = v \mid x_i, don_i\right\} = \frac{\exp(-\lambda_i)\lambda_i^{v}}{v!}, \tag{9.3}$$

where $v = 0, 1, 2, \ldots, 200$. The model is estimated by maximum likelihood with the likelihood function L given by

$$\log L(\boldsymbol{\beta}, \phi) = \sum_{i=1}^{N} \left\{ [-\exp(x_i'\boldsymbol{\beta} + \phi \, don_i) + v_i(x_i'\boldsymbol{\beta} + \phi \, don_i) - \log v_i!] \right\} \qquad (9.4)$$

The sign of the ϕ parameter estimate will indicate whether donations of time and money are substitutes or complements.

9.2.2   Robustness—Overdispersion and Zero Inflation

A particular drawback of the aforementioned methodology is that the poisson model implies that the conditional variance of vol_i is equal to λ_i (i.e., equi-dispersion). Hence in addition to equation 9.1 and the assumption in equation 9.3, we have

$$V\{vol_i | x_i, don_i\} = \exp(x_i' \boldsymbol{\beta} + \phi \, don_i). \qquad (9.5)$$

We consider how robust the results are (under the assumption that monetary donations are exogenous) to allowing for overdispersion, whereby

$$V\{vol_i | x_i, don_i\} = E\{\epsilon_i^2 | x_i, don_i\} > \exp(x_i' \boldsymbol{\beta} + \phi \, don_i) \qquad (9.6)$$

by estimating a generalized negative binomial regression model, where

$$V\{vol_i | x_i, don_i\} = \{1 + \alpha^2 \exp(x_i' \boldsymbol{\beta} + \phi \, don_i)\} \exp(x_i' \boldsymbol{\beta} + \phi \, don_i) \qquad (9.7)$$

and the maximum likelihood estimator is consistent. Overdispersion is explicitly accounted for (relative to the poisson regression model), with the amount of overdispersion increasing in the conditional mean of volunteering, where a test of overdispersion is whether $\alpha^2 > 0$.

Given the preponderance of zeros (see table 9.1; 85 percent of respondents do not volunteer), we also estimate two-part count regression models, namely, the zero-inflated poisson and the zero-inflated negative binomial models (see Greene 2008). In such models, there is a participation equation or hurdle and then an equation for the event that is conditioned on actually participating (in our application, volunteering). The structure of the zero-inflated approach starts with the participation (or selection) equation based on a latent variable framework, which determines whether individuals volunteer, y_i^*, conditional on a set of covariates c_i:

$$y_i^* = c_i' \delta + \varepsilon_i,$$
$$y_i = \mathbf{1}(y_i^* > 0) \tag{9.8}$$

with the associated probability of volunteering being given by

$$\text{prob}\{y_i = 1 | c_i\} = 1 - \Pi(c_i' \delta). \tag{9.9}$$

The latent poisson (or negative binomial) model, where F denotes the functional form, determines the nonzero level of hours volunteered and is given by

$$vol_i^* | x_i, don_i \sim F(vol_i^* | x_i, don_i) \tag{9.10}$$

with conditional mean

$$E\left\{vol_i^* | x_i, don_i\right\} = \exp(x_i' \beta + \phi \, don_i) = \lambda_i. \tag{9.11}$$

The observational mechanism is

$$vol_i = y_i \times vol_i^*. \tag{9.12}$$

If individuals do not volunteer (so that $y_i = 0$), then the observed number of hours volunteered must also be zero (irrespective of the latent value of vol_i^*), that is, $vol_i = 0$. For those individuals who do volunteer, then $y_i = 1$ and the poisson or negative binomial variable (which could still be zero) is observed.

9.2.3   Robustness—Endogeneity of Monetary Donations

A potential problem with the above analysis is that monetary donations might be endogenous. Hence we also investigate this issue by employing an instrumental variable poisson regression model to allow for such endogeneity. Adopting a count poisson modeling approach, where monetary donations are allowed to be endogenous with unit mean errors ϵ_i, gives

$$vol_i = \exp(x_i' \beta + \phi \, don_i) \epsilon_i. \tag{9.13}$$

With multiplicative errors, this leads to the following error function:

$$u(vol_i, x_i, don_i, \beta, \phi) = vol_i / \exp(x_i' \beta + \phi \, don_i) - 1. \tag{9.14}$$

Given a set of instrumental variables z_i, the population conditions of the GMM estimator are:

$$E\{\tilde{z}_i u(vol_i, x_i, don_i, \beta, \phi)\} = 0,$$ (9.15)

where the vector $\tilde{z}_i$ is partitioned as (x'_i, z_i). The sample-moment conditions are formed by replacing the expectation with the corresponding sample mean. The generalized method of moments (GMM) estimator solves a minimization problem to make the sample-moment conditions as close to zero as possible. The GMM estimators of $\hat{\beta}$ and $\hat{\phi}$ are the values of β and ϕ that minimize the following function:

$$Q(\beta, \phi) = \left\{\frac{1}{N} \Sigma \tilde{z}_i u_i(vol_i, x_i, don_i, \beta, \phi)\right\}'$$

$$C_N \left\{\frac{1}{N} \Sigma \tilde{z}_i u_i(vol_i, x_i, don_i, \beta, \phi)\right\}$$ (9.16)

for a $q \times q$ weighting matrix C_N, where q is the dimension of $\tilde{z}_i$.

An alternative method to take account of endogeneity is to adopt a control function approach, where it is assumed that a certain structural relationship exists between the endogenous covariate (monetary donations) and the exogenous covariates. This approach uses functions of first-stage parameter estimates to control for the endogeneity in the second stage (see Wooldridge 2010). The structure of the model is

$$vol_i = \exp(x'_i \beta + \phi \, don_i + \omega'_i \rho + e_i)$$ (9.17)

$$don_i = \tilde{z}'_i \psi + \omega_i,$$ (9.18)

where e_i is independent of both ω_i and z_i. The inclusion of $\omega'_i \rho$ controls for the endogeneity of don_i. The parameter ρ measures the strength of endogeneity, and if $\rho = 0$ then monetary donations are exogenous.

Throughout we report incidence-rate ratios (IRRs) and heteroscedastic consistent standard errors. Omitting subscripts for brevity and defining $w = (x', don)'$, $\gamma = (\beta, \phi)$, then adding 1 to the kth independent variable in w (i.e., a unit change), the above functional form of the model implies the following:

$$\frac{E\{vol \mid w, (w_k + 1), \epsilon\}}{E\{vol \mid w, w_k, \epsilon\}} = \frac{E\{vol \mid w_1, w_2, ..., (w_k + 1), \epsilon\}}{E\{vol \mid w_1, w_2, ..., w_k, \epsilon\}} = \exp(\gamma_k)$$ (9.19)

where, given that the outcome of interest is a count variable, the normalized effect $\exp(\gamma_k)$ is the IRR for a one-unit change in w_k. A priori based on the evidence from other countries, we envisage complementarity between monetary donations and volunteering (i.e., hence in terms of the IRR $\phi > 1$).

Covariates in x_i include gender; age (specifically, aged 16–24, 25–34, 35–44, 45–54, 55–64, and 65–75; over 75 is the reference category); the number of children in the household aged 2 or under, between 3–4, between 5–11, and between 12–15; the number of adults in the household; married or cohabiting; highest educational qualification, that is, degree (undergraduate or postgraduate), Advanced (A) level, General Certificate of Secondary Education (GCSE), and all other qualifications (no education is the omitted category);[5] the natural logarithm of monthly labor income; the natural logarithm of monthly nonlabor income; the natural logarithm of monthly savings; labor force status, specifically, whether employed, self-employed, or unemployed (all other labor market states constitute the reference category);[6] housing tenure, whether the home is owned outright, owned via a mortgage, or privately rented (all other types of tenure make up the omitted category); religious denomination, whether Church of England, Roman Catholic, other Christian, Muslim, or other religion (no religion is the reference category); active membership of a church or religious group; to capture peer effects, the number of friends the individual has and whether the individual currently belongs to a social website; current health state, specifically, whether in excellent health, very good health, good health, or fair health (with poor and very poor health as the reference category); whether currently living in an urban area; measures of cognitive ability,[7] specifically, word recall (respondents were asked to remember a list of 10 words and repeat them back to the interviewer immediately), numeric ability (a series of short number puzzles to measure the use of numbers in everyday life),[8] verbal fluency (the number of animals that the respondent can correctly name in a minute); 11 region of residence controls (with London as the reference category); and 11 month of interview binary controls (with January as the reference category).

Following Freeman (1997) and Bauer, Bredtmann, and Schmidt (2013), to proxy the opportunity cost of time associated with providing unpaid labor, we include the total amount of time spent in paid employment,[9] doing housework and traveling to work. We also control for whether the individual is completely dissatisfied with the amount of leisure time and the number of hours spent caring per week, specifically whether up to 4 hours, 5–9 hours, 10–19 hours, 20–34 hours, 35–49 hours, 50–99 hours, and 100 hours or more (no time spent caring is the omitted category).

When allowing for the endogeneity of monetary donations, we employ two instruments. The first instrument we use is whether the individual has made a monetary donation to charity in previous years. Given that the UKHLS is longitudinal, we can track people over time. Although the data we use was collected in wave 4 (where interviews were conducted between 2012 and 2014), in wave 2 comparable information is also available on monetary donations; hence lagged donations are used as an instrument. The second instrument we employ is the proportion of individuals donating by local area district (LAD) for age-specific reference groups (the age categories are as defined above). The idea here is that individual monetary donations may be influenced by the monetary donations of those in the same social reference space (i.e., the LAD-age group; see Andreoni and Scholz 1998), but that there is no direct effect on volunteering. When estimating the zero-inflated models, the identifying variable used in equation 9.8 is the number of individuals in the respondent's household (excluding the respondent) who volunteered in wave 2. The motivation for this choice is that whether the individual decides to volunteer in the current period might be influenced by the past volunteering behavior of those close to the individual.

Summary statistics for the endogenous variables, the selection (i.e., hurdle equation) variable, and the instruments used are given in table 9.2. The corresponding information is provided in table 9.3 for all other covariates, where about 44 percent are male; 39 percent are aged between 35 and 54; 37 percent have a degree as the highest educational achievement; and approximately 28 hours per week are spent in paid employment, commuting, and doing housework. In the sample, 67 percent of individuals donated money to charity during the past year, and the natural logarithm of the monetary amount donated to charitable causes during the past year is 2.89, or approximately £142. Evaluated as a weekly amount (i.e., £2.73), this figure is comparable to that found by Smith (2012) using an alternative UK data source, the Living Costs and Food Survey (LCFS).[10]

Figure 9.2 is a scatter plot of the number of hours volunteered versus the amount donated to charity for those who volunteer, donate, or both (i.e., nonzero values). The raw data clearly show a positive correlation, as can be seen from the line of best fit. This trend implies that donations of time and money are complements. We now further investigate this finding and identify the factors associated with volunteering.

Table 9.2
Summary statistics—endogenous variables, selection, and instruments.

Variable	Mean	Standard Deviation	Minimum	Maximum
don_i—endogenous variables				
Whether donated to money to charity over past 12 months	0.6659	0.4717	0	1
Natural logarithm of charitable donations over past 12 months	2.8905	2.3418	0	9.2100
Charitable donations as a proportion of annual income	0.0067	0.0145	0	0.1259
c_i—inflation variable				
Number in household who volunteered in 2010–2012	0.5813	1.4119	0	8
z_i—instrumental variables				
Whether donated to charity in 2010–2012	0.6595	0.4747	0	1
Percent donating at local area district level, by age (16 and older)	73.0751	15.0885	35.7143	100
Number of observations	31,409			

9.3   Results

Table 9.4 presents the results of estimating the model, where monetary donations are initially assumed to be exogenous. There are three pairs of columns, in which IRR and t-statistics based on heteroscedastic consistent standard errors are reported. In the first column pair, we condition volunteering on whether the individual donated money to charity. In the second column pair, this control is replaced by the amount donated; in the final column pair, we use monetary donations as a proportion of total income.

The results show that the effects of age, where statistically significant, are positive: relative to those aged older than 75, individuals in the age groups from 45 to 74 volunteer more of their time. These findings are consistent with those of Menchik and Weisbrod (1987) and Freeman (1997) for the United States. Similarly, a statistically significant relationship is apparent between the composition of the family and volunteering. It should be noted that this effect exists after controlling for time commitments. For example, the number of children aged 2 or under is inversely associated with the number of hours volunteered, where, on average, individuals with children in this age category volunteer 50 percent less time than those without children in this age category.

Table 9.3
Summary statistics—explanatory variables.

x_i Explanatory variable	Mean	Standard Deviation	Minimum	Maximum
Aged 16–24	0.0763	0.2654	0	1
Aged 25–34	0.1385	0.3454	0	1
Aged 35–44	0.1942	0.3956	0	1
Aged 45–54	0.1952	0.3964	0	1
Aged 55–64	0.1645	0.3708	0	1
Aged 65–75	0.1461	0.3532	0	1
Male	0.4365	0.4960	0	1
Number of children aged 2 or under	0.0988	0.3298	0	3
Number of children aged 3–4	0.0741	0.2757	0	3
Number of children aged 5–11	0.2547	0.5928	0	5
Number of children aged 12–15	0.1534	0.4223	0	5
Number of adults in household	1.9915	0.9080	1	15
Married or cohabiting	0.5477	0.4977	0	1
GCSE	0.2017	0.4013	0	1
A level	0.1980	0.3985	0	1
Degree	0.3686	0.4824	0	1
Other qualification	0.0991	0.2988	0	1
Natural logarithm of monthly labor income	4.4467	3.5979	0	9.6158
Natural logarithm of monthly nonlabor income	4.4003	3.0683	0	11.9476
Natural logarithm of monthly savings	1.8073	2.2499	0	10.1266
Employed	0.5108	0.4999	0	1
Self-employed	0.0764	0.2657	0	1
Unemployed	0.0373	0.1895	0	1
Home owned outright	0.3370	0.4727	0	1
Home owned on a mortgage	0.3922	0.4883	0	1
Home privately rented	0.0997	0.2997	0	1
Church of England	0.2157	0.4113	0	1
Roman Catholic	0.0743	0.2622	0	1
Christian	0.0345	0.1825	0	1
Muslim	0.0355	0.1850	0	1
Other religion	0.1135	0.3172	0	1
Active member of religious group	0.1269	0.3329	0	1
Number of friends	4.1689	2.0866	0	7
Health excellent	0.1576	0.3643	0	1
Health very good	0.3417	0.4743	0	1

(continued)

Table 9.3 (continued)

x_i Explanatory variable	Mean	Standard Deviation	Minimum	Maximum
Health good	0.2957	0.4564	0	1
Health fair	0.1421	0.3492	0	1
Member of social website	0.4497	0.4975	0	1
Lives in an urban area	0.7366	0.4405	0	1
Opportunity cost of time[a]	27.7783	18.5194	0	168
Dissatisfied with leisure time	0.0458	0.2092	0	1
Cares up to 4 hours per week	0.0703	0.2557	0	1
Cares 5–9 hours per week	0.0365	0.1875	0	1
Cares 10–19 hours per week	0.0286	0.1667	0	1
Cares 20–34 hours per week	0.0232	0.1506	0	1
Cares 35–49 hours per week	0.0055	0.0742	0	1
Cares 50–99 hours per week	0.0045	0.0671	0	1
Cares 100+ hours per week	0.0158	0.1248	0	1
Word recall	0	1	–3.6716	2.1652
Numeric ability	0	1	–3.2449	1.2487
Verbal fluency	0	1	–3.1111	8.2773
Number of observations	31,409			

Note: GCSE, General Certificate of Secondary Education.
a. Opportunity cost of time is calculated as the sum of total hours spent per week in employment, doing housework, and commuting to work.

There is a positive association between savings and time volunteered, where a 1 percent increase in the amount of monthly savings is associated with about a 2 percent increase in the number of hours of unpaid labor volunteered. In terms of income effects, perhaps surprisingly, labor income is statistically insignificant in determining time volunteered. This may be because we explicitly control for the opportunity cost of time, which includes the number of hours in employment, although Bauer, Bredtmann, and Schmidt (2013), who follow a similar modeling approach, still found a role for income. However, their measure is based on household labor income rather than that of the individual.

Peer effects may influence volunteering, operating, for example, through the prestige motive whereby individuals seek social approval (Ellingsen and Johannesson 2009). Social connections appear to be important: The number of friends that the individual has and being an active member of a religious group are both positively related to time

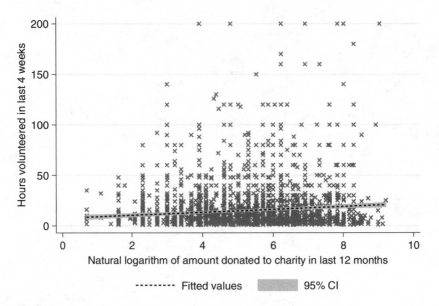

Figure 9.2
Hours volunteered and amounts donated. *Source*: UKHLS. *Note*: For volunteers and donators only.

spent volunteering. Those individuals who are members of a church or a religious organization volunteer twice as much time (i.e., about 140 percent) compared to those who are not members of a religious group. Having one more friend increases the amount of time volunteered by about 8 percent. Membership in social networks is also found to be important: Those individuals who are members of a social website are found to volunteer 29 percent more hours than corresponding individuals who are not members of such networks. These findings endorse the importance of social networks in influencing charitable behavior, as discussed by Andreoni and Payne (2013).

We define the opportunity cost of time as the sum of the number of hours per week spent in paid employment, doing housework, and commuting to work. As argued by Clotfelter (1985), if labor markets are imperfect, then focusing on hours in paid employment is relevant for determining volunteer labor supply rather than focusing on income from employment. In accordance with Bauer, Bredtmann, and Schmidt (2013), as expected a priori, we find a negative association between the proxy for the opportunity cost of time and hours volunteered. An extra hour spent per week in employment, housework, and commuting to

Table 9.4
Modeling hours volunteered—the role of monetary donations (exogenous).

| | Number of Hours Volunteered | | | | | | Donation as Proportion of Total Income | |
| | Whether Donated | | Amount Donated | | | | | |
Parameter	IRR	t-stat	IRR	t-stat	IRR	t-stat
Intercept	0.3173	-4.61	0.2890	-5.02	0.3283	-4.50
Aged 16–24	1.2163	1.07	1.4065	1.84	1.1868	0.94
Aged 25–34	1.1750	1.03	1.3007	1.68	1.1521	0.90
Aged 35–44	1.1271	0.84	1.2245	1.43	1.0881	0.60
Aged 45–54	1.3292	2.18	1.4082	2.64	1.2987	2.01
Aged 55–64	1.5377	3.85	1.6129	4.30	1.5002	3.62
Aged 65–75	1.5936	4.81	1.6293	5.07	1.5905	4.79
Male	1.0928	1.66	1.1006	1.81	1.1010	1.80
Number of children aged 2 or under	0.5096	-3.31	0.5172	-3.26	0.5071	-3.33
Number of children aged 3–4	0.8578	-1.53	0.8584	-1.53	0.8503	-1.61
Number of children aged 5–11	1.0425	0.93	1.0440	0.97	1.0343	0.74
Number of children aged 12–15	1.0584	0.93	1.0572	0.91	1.0571	0.91
Number of adults in household	0.9531	-1.28	0.9642	-0.97	0.9529	-1.28
Married or cohabiting	1.0922	1.51	1.0720	1.19	1.0791	1.31
GCSE	1.4364	3.52	1.4037	3.31	1.4533	3.63
A level	1.7018	4.87	1.6474	4.59	1.6926	4.82
Degree	2.1934	7.77	2.0556	7.12	2.2236	7.92
Other qualification	1.3857	2.61	1.3696	2.53	1.3862	2.61

(continued)

Table 9.4 (continued)

Parameter	Number of Hours Volunteered					
	Whether Donated		Amount Donated		Donation as Proportion of Total Income	
	IRR	t-stat	IRR	t-stat	IRR	t-stat
Natural logarithm of monthly labor income	0.9773	−1.28	0.9733	−1.51	0.9881	−0.66
Natural logarithm of monthly nonlabor income	1.0256	2.15	1.0221	1.89	1.0330	2.73
Natural logarithm of monthly savings	1.0287	2.81	1.0173	1.70	1.0283	2.75
Employee	0.7585	−2.03	0.7535	−2.08	0.7478	−2.14
Self employed	0.6489	−3.24	0.6589	−3.11	0.6554	−3.21
Unemployed	1.2674	1.69	1.3100	1.92	1.2596	1.64
Home owned outright	1.2072	2.06	1.1540	1.57	1.2041	2.04
Home owned on a mortgage	0.9707	−0.34	0.9358	−0.75	0.9711	−0.33
Home privately rented	0.9112	−0.81	0.9035	−0.88	0.9116	−0.80
Church of England	1.0788	1.17	1.0749	1.11	1.0870	1.29
Roman Catholic	0.9132	−0.92	0.9053	−1.00	0.9248	−0.79
Christian	1.3727	3.06	1.3259	2.73	1.2909	2.35
Muslim	0.9426	−0.36	−0.8666	−0.87	0.9486	−0.32
Other religion	1.4569	5.01	1.4086	4.57	1.4484	4.87
Active member of religious group	2.1469	14.07	1.9486	12.12	2.0827	13.34
Number of friends	1.0832	6.38	1.0757	5.82	1.0813	6.20
Health excellent	1.8505	4.46	1.7838	4.20	1.8004	4.22
Health very good	1.9656	5.17	1.9159	4.98	1.9799	5.21
Health good	1.9368	5.08	1.8978	4.92	1.9571	5.15
Health fair	1.5830	3.37	1.5646	3.28	1.5917	3.40
Member of social website	1.2975	4.76	1.2914	4.70	1.2844	4.53

	Model 1 IRR	z	Model 2 IRR	z	Model 3 IRR	z
Opportunity cost of time	0.9933	-2.59	0.9928	-2.78	0.9929	-2.74
Dissatisfied with leisure time	0.9884	-0.11	0.9952	-0.04	0.9948	-0.05
Cares up to 4 hours per week	1.2685	3.28	1.2451	3.03	1.2780	3.39
Cares 5–9 hours per week	1.3894	3.47	1.3558	3.24	1.3311	2.85
Cares 10–19 hours per week	1.3466	2.42	1.3328	2.36	1.3466	2.40
Cares 20–34 hours per week	0.9692	-0.19	0.9488	-0.32	0.9832	-0.10
Cares 35–49 hours per week	0.7476	-1.38	0.7782	-1.19	0.7558	-1.33
Cares 50–99 hours per week	0.7021	1.18	0.7068	-1.16	0.7076	-1.15
Cares 100+ hours per week	1.1059	0.49	1.0883	0.42	1.1236	0.57
Lives in an urban area	0.8782	-2.36	0.8765	-2.40	0.8774	-2.37
Word recall	1.0631	1.99	1.0560	1.78	1.0609	1.93
Numeric ability	1.1096	3.22	1.0871	2.59	1.1046	3.11
Verbal fluency	1.1279	4.32	1.1180	4.02	1.1298	4.35
Whether donated in past 12 months	1.1447	2.24	—		—	
Natural logarithm of amount donated	—		1.1078	7.24	—	
Amount donated as a proportion of income	—		—		1.0117	5.62
Pseudo R-squared	0.1531		0.1609		0.1566	
Number of observations	31,409					

Notes: Other controls include region dummies. GCSE, General Certificate of Secondary Education; IRR, incidence-rate ratio.

work is associated with a decrease in the number of hours volunteered by about 1 percent. However, whether the individual is dissatisfied with the amount of leisure time they have is, perhaps surprisingly, unrelated to hours volunteered. Interestingly, in terms of time spent caring for others per week compared to the omitted category of zero hours, spending up to 19 hours caring for others is associated with a higher number of hours volunteered.

Each measure of cognitive ability is found to be positively associated with volunteering, an effect over and above formal educational qualifications and income, which is consistent with James (2011). Verbal ability is the dominant cognitive skill, where a one standard deviation increase in verbal ability is associated with about a 12 percent increase in hours volunteered. The role found for verbal ability is consistent with the findings of Bekkers (2010) and Hauser (2000).

Turning to the role of monetary donations, from the first pair of data columns in table 9.4, it can be seen that those individuals who donated money to charity during the past year volunteered 14 percent more hours of unpaid labor (compared to those who do not donate money). Correspondingly, the second pair of data columns show that not only is the decision to donate money important but also the amount of money donated matters—a 1 percent increase in monetary donations is associated with 11 percent more hours volunteered. The proportion of the annual amount of money donated to charity relative to annual income is also positively associated with volunteering. These results are supportive of the underlying raw correlation in the data between money and time donations (see figure 9.2) and are consistent with the relationship between these different types of charitable behavior being complementary. This is in common with much of the existing literature, such as Apinunmahakul, Barham, and Devlin (2009), Hartmann and Werding (2012), and Bauer, Bredtmann, and Schmidt (2013).[11]

9.3.1   Robustness—Overdispersion and Zero Inflation

Next we explore how robust the results are under the assumption that monetary donations are exogenous by allowing for three models: (1) overdispersion, (2) zero inflation, and (3) zero inflation and overdispersion. We show the results of estimating models 1–3 in table 9.5 panels A–C, respectively. For the models incorporating overdispersion (models 1 and 3), we focus on the estimates of α. In addition, for the models incorporating zero inflation, we also report the parameter estimate from the inflation equation (i.e., δ) and the Vuong statistic, which tests zero inflation versus a count outcome (either poisson or negative binomial). Larger positive values of the Vuong statistic favor a zero-inflated approach (see Vuong 1989). Throughout each of alternative models, we are primarily concerned with the IRR on ϕ (i.e., whether monetary donations are still found to be complementary to volunteering time).

Focusing on panel A in table 9.5, the results of the negative binomial count model show that $\hat{\alpha} > 0$ and is statistically significant, implying overdispersion in the data. The IRR estimates of ϕ are consistent with those reported in table 9.4, which are based on the poisson regression model, in terms of magnitude and association. In particular, volunteering time and monetary donations are still found to be positively related, which is consistent with them being complementary. For example, a 1 percent increase in the amount of money donated to charity over the past 12 months is associated with 9 percent more hours volunteered. Both the zero-inflated poisson and the zero-inflated negative binomial models (see panels B and C, respectively) reveal that the number of people in the respondent's household in 2010–2012 who volunteered decreases the probability that the respondent does not volunteer in 2012–2014 (i.e., $\hat{\delta} < 0$). Furthermore, the Vuong statistics favor zero-inflated models over the standard poisson and negative binomial count estimators. However, the results are still consistent with complementarity between time and monetary donations, given that the IRR on ϕ is always above unity.

9.3.2   Robustness—Endogeneity of Monetary Donations

The above models are all based on the assumption that monetary donations are exogenous, but in table 9.6 we investigate whether the finding of complementarity remains once monetary donations are endogenized. An instrumental variable (IV) approach is adopted, in which the instrumental variables used are the past (i.e., lagged) monetary donating behavior of the respondent and the monetary donating behavior of those in the same social reference space (i.e., LAD-age group). The bottom part of table 9.6 shows Hansen's J statistic, which tests the overidentifying restrictions of the model where the null hypothesis that the excluded instruments are valid cannot be rejected.[12] Interestingly, the IRRs on the alternative controls for monetary donations to charity are consistent with complementarity. For example, considering the results of the second pair of columns , a 1 percent increase in monetary donations is associated with 7 percent more hours volunteered (compared

Table 9.5

Modeling hours volunteered—the role of monetary donations (exogenous) alternative specifications.

	Number of Hours Volunteered					
	Whether Donated		Amount Donated		Donation as Proportion of Total Income	
Parameter	IRR	t-stat	IRR	t-stat	IRR	t-stat
PANEL A: negative binomial						
Intercept	0.1992	−5.85	0.2014	−5.71	0.2859	−4.61
Whether donated in past 12 months	1.1698	2.21	—		—	
Natural logarithm of amount donated	—		1.0901	6.46	—	
Amount donated as a proportion of income	—		—		1.0601	6.85
$\hat{\alpha}$; p-value	21.4605; p = 0.000		21.3109; p = 0.000		21.1213; p = 0.000	
Wald statistic χ^2 (60); p-value	1163.73; p = 0.000		1165.45; p = 0.000		1283.29; p = 0.000	
Number of observations	31,409					
PANEL B: zero-inflated poisson						
Intercept	10.6033	6.36	10.0411	6.17	10.9599	6.68
Whether donated in past 12 months	1.1897	2.11	—		—	
Natural logarithm of amount donated	—		1.0136	7.68	—	
Amount donated as a proportion of income	—		—		1.0085	3.44
$\hat{\delta}$; p-value	−0.2747; p = 0.000		−0.2748; p = 0.000		−0.2748; p = 0.000	
Vuong statistic; p-value	41.47; p = 0.000		40.90; p = 0.000		41.62; p = 0.000	
Wald statistic χ^2 (60); p-value	5787.96; p = 0.000		5719.46; p = 0.000		6495.58.29; p = 0.000	
Number of observations	31,409					

PANEL C: zero-inflated negative binomial

Intercept	6.6760	10.49	6.4308	10.26	7.2237	10.87
Whether donated in past 12 months	1.1412	2.33	—		—	
Natural logarithm of amount donated	—		1.0243	3.08	1.0152	4.92
Amount donated as a proportion of income	—		—		—	
$\hat{\alpha}$; p-value	1.4104; $p=0.000$		1.4310; $p=0.000$		1.4075; $p=0.000$	
$\hat{\delta}$; p-value	−0.3112; $p=0.000$		−0.3126; $p=0.000$		−0.3114; $p=0.000$	
Vuong statistic; p-value	17.02; $p=0.000$		16.67; $p=0.000$		16.35; $p=0.000$	
LR statistic χ^2 (60); p-value	427.55; $p=0.000$		435.24; $p=0.000$		481.46; $p=0.000$	
Number of observations	31,409					

Notes: Other controls are as in table 9.4. The covariate used to inflate hours volunteered in panels B and C is the number of individuals in the household in wave 2 who volunteered (excluding the respondent).

Table 9.6

Modeling hours volunteered—the role of monetary donations (endogenous) generalized method of moments.

Parameter	Number of Hours Volunteered				Donation as Proportion of Total Income	
	Whether Donated		Amount Donated			
	IRR	t-stat	IRR	t-stat	IRR	t-stat
Intercept	0.3153	-4.09	0.2988	-4.24	0.3020	-4.31
Aged 16–24	0.9352	-0.30	1.0377	0.16	0.9296	-0.34
Aged 25–34	0.8269	-1.04	0.9111	-0.49	0.8725	-0.76
Aged 35–44	0.8997	-0.66	0.9558	-0.27	0.9304	-0.45
Aged 45–54	1.0346	0.23	1.0781	0.48	1.0712	0.46
Aged 55–64	1.4865	2.99	1.5282	3.08	1.4703	2.88
Aged 65–75	1.6965	4.39	1.6991	4.27	1.7689	4.71
Male	1.2357	3.41	1.2562	3.62	1.2758	3.91
Number of children aged 2 or under	0.5601	-3.30	0.5455	-3.52	0.5739	-3.24
Number of children aged 3–4	0.8493	-1.24	0.8503	-1.25	0.8140	-1.61
Number of children aged 5–11	1.0701	1.19	1.0783	1.29	1.0675	1.18
Number of children aged 12–15	1.2003	2.39	1.2008	2.40	1.1929	2.30
Number of adults in household	0.9146	-1.91	0.9177	-1.83	0.9146	-1.92
Married or cohabiting	0.9221	-1.11	0.9089	-1.30	0.8911	-1.59
GCSE	1.5354	3.44	1.4739	3.06	1.4797	3.12
A level	1.9763	5.00	1.9120	4.63	1.8673	4.58
Degree	2.5292	7.68	2.3892	6.91	2.4128	7.25
Other qualification	1.3820	2.34	1.3638	2.21	1.3898	2.37

Natural logarithm of monthly labor income	0.9472	-2.62	0.9413	-2.88	0.9695	-1.45
Natural logarithm of monthly nonlabor income	1.0191	1.37	1.0163	1.16	1.0297	2.11
Natural logarithm of monthly savings	1.0271	2.04	1.0201	1.47	1.0214	1.63
Employee	0.8383	-1.11	0.8565	-0.97	0.7860	-1.50
Self employed	0.6991	-2.47	0.7197	-2.26	0.6841	-2.62
Unemployed	1.6731	2.61	1.6935	2.69	1.7206	2.81
Home owned outright	1.1963	1.64	1.1377	1.14	1.1299	1.14
Home owned on a mortgage	1.1289	1.13	1.0960	0.83	1.1007	0.90
Home privately rented	0.9050	-0.79	0.8868	-0.95	0.8638	-1.21
Church of England	1.0358	0.47	1.0423	0.55	1.0564	0.75
Roman Catholic	0.8960	-1.04	0.8615	-1.35	0.8909	-1.09
Christian	1.5930	3.34	1.5236	3.03	1.4400	2.69
Muslim	1.1039	0.51	0.9512	-0.25	0.8980	-0.55
Other religion	1.5087	4.19	1.4533	3.70	1.4897	4.12
Active member of religious group	2.5045	13.37	2.3434	10.82	2.2138	10.39
Number of friends	1.0992	6.83	1.0971	6.56	1.0957	6.66
Health excellent	2.2230	4.47	2.1635	4.33	2.1812	4.60
Health very good	1.9928	4.26	1.9832	4.26	1.9419	4.23
Health good	1.9913	4.41	2.0084	4.40	2.0223	4.53
Health fair	1.9015	3.79	1.8883	3.74	1.8720	3.79
Member of social website	1.4897	5.71	1.4483	5.23	1.4781	5.82
Opportunity cost of time	0.9940	-2.24	0.9939	-2.30	0.9945	-2.09
Dissatisfied with leisure time	1.0549	0.40	1.0695	0.50	1.0791	0.56

(continued)

Table 9.6 (continued)

| | Number of Hours Volunteered | | | | | | Donation as Proportion of Total Income | |
| | Whether Donated | | Amount Donated | | | | | |
Parameter	IRR	t-stat	IRR	t-stat			IRR	t-stat
Cares up to 4 hours per week	1.3896	3.75	1.3755	3.56			1.3889	3.73
Cares 5–9 hours per week	1.6146	3.23	1.5739	3.07			1.6099	3.18
Cares 10–19 hours per week	1.6977	3.29	1.5828	2.88			1.5844	2.85
Cares 20–34 hours per week	1.4995	1.81	1.5532	1.94			1.5694	2.03
Cares 35–49 hours per week	0.5905	−2.05	0.6232	−1.82			0.6262	−1.82
Cares 50–99 hours per week	0.8181	−0.58	0.7768	−0.69			0.7550	−0.80
Cares 100+ hours per week	1.1193	0.46	1.0607	0.25			0.9531	−0.22
Lives in an urban area	0.8437	−2.62	0.8439	−2.58			0.8107	−3.25
Word recall	1.1329	3.41	1.1284	3.30			1.1337	3.50
Numeric ability	1.0872	2.29	1.0746	1.97			1.0698	1.86
Verbal fluency	1.1497	3.89	1.1318	3.25			1.1448	3.84
Whether donated in past 12 months	1.2531	1.60	—				—	
Natural logarithm of amount donated	—		1.0682	2.86			—	
Amount donated as a proportion of income	—		—				1.0231	2.53
Hansen J statistic χ^2 (1); p-value	1.3864; p = 0.2390		0.0262; p = 0.8715				0.0128; p = 0.9216	
Number of observations	31,409							

Notes: Other controls include region dummies. The instrumental variables used are whether the individual donated to charity during 2010–2012 and the percentage donating at the local area district level by age group (16 and older). GCSE, General Certificate of Secondary Education; IRR, incidence-rate ratio.

to 10 percent when monetary donations were treated as an exogenous variable; see table 9.4).

Table 9.7 presents results for when the endogeneity of monetary donations is modeled via a control function approach rather than by GMM. For each specification, the null hypothesis that $\rho = 0$ cannot be rejected.

Hence it would appear that monetary donations are exogenous, which might be attributed to the different period covered in the questionnaire for time and money donations. The two instruments employed—whether the individual has donated money in the past (i.e., 2010–2012) and the percentage donating money in the individual's LAD-age group—both increase the probability of donating money (see the first pair of columns in table 9.7) and the amount of money donated (see the second and third pairs of columns), which is consistent with a priori expectations. Again under this alternative approach for allowing for endogeneity, we find evidence that time and money donations are complements given that the IRR of $\phi > 1$.

9.4   Conclusion

In this chapter we have investigated the determinants of unpaid labor supply, namely, volunteering to charitable causes. The most recent large scale representative longitudinal data for the United Kingdom that contains detailed socioeconomic and demographic information is used to explore this facet of charitable behavior. This is the first contribution to the economics literature that sheds light on the factors that influence volunteering in the United Kingdom. Across a range of empirical techniques, we find that better educated individuals, those with higher savings, and those with higher cognitive ability are all associated with spending more time in voluntary activity. Conversely, more time spent in paid employment, commuting, and doing household chores is inversely related to time spent volunteering, which potentially reflects the opportunity cost of time. Similarly, having dependent children aged 2 years or under is also negatively associated with volunteering. Finally, the analysis also reveals that time spent volunteering and monetary donations made to charity are complements rather than substitutes. This finding is robust across alternative modeling approaches and prevails in an IV framework.

Clear policy implications arise from this finding: Tax breaks for monetary donations should not only increase the amount of money, on

Table 9.7
Modeling hours volunteered—the role of monetary donations (endogenous), control function.

| | Number of Hours Volunteered | | | | | |
| | Whether Donated | | Amount Donated | | Donation as Proportion of Total Income | |
Parameter	IRR	t-stat	IRR	t-stat	IRR	t-stat
Intercept	0.2609	-4.66	0.2764	-4.42	0.2668	-4.64
Whether donated in past 12 months	1.2525	2.39	—		—	
Natural logarithm of amount donated	—		1.0659	2.74	—	
Amount donated as a proportion of income	—		—		1.0156	2.83
Endogenous variable; $\hat{\psi}$						
Whether donated to charity in 2010–2012	0.2803	8.88	1.3975	5.73	0.4979	2.85
Percent donating at LAD level by age group (16 and older)	0.8042	6.32	0.3595	4.00	0.9442	10.29
ρ; p-value	-0.1481; $p=0.4031$		0.0143; $p=0.7228$		-0.0902; $p=0.1240$	
Number of observations	31,409					

Notes: Other controls are as in table 9.6 and region dummies. IRR, incidence-rate ratio.

average, that individuals donate to charity, but may also have spillover effects on volunteering. Specifically, due to the complementarity between the two types of charitable behavior, tax deductions should also increase the amount of time volunteered. Our most conservative estimates, based on IV analysis, suggest that a 1 percent increase in money donated to charity is associated with about 7 percent more time spent volunteering labor.

Notes

We are grateful to the Data Archive at the University of Essex for supplying Understanding Society (cited in the text as UKHLS), waves 1–4. We are very grateful to participants at the CESifo Venice Summer Institute Conference on "The Economics of Philanthropy," San Servolo, Venice, July 2016, and two anonymous referees for comments.

1. These figures are based on data on individuals who volunteer at least once per year.

2. The figure of 3 days comes from Community Life Survey (ONS 2013) estimates that a total of 15.2 million individuals are giving up their time freely, which is equivalent to 3 days of extra leave, where replacing such unpaid labor with paid staff would cost the UK economy £24 billion.

3. Although this conclusion holds if the complementarity is at the level of the individual, it is not clear that it would hold if the complementarity only captures a positive correlation between cash and time donations across individuals.

4. Prendergast and Stole (2001) show that volunteering time as opposed to more efficient monetary transfers may occur, because the latter can be considered too impersonal, which is consistent with Freeman's argument that volunteering is a "conscience good or activity."

5. GCSE level qualifications are taken after 11 years of formal compulsory schooling and approximate the US honors high school curriculum. The A level qualification is a public examination taken by 18-year-olds over a 2-year period studying between one and four subjects and is the main determinant of eligibility for entry to higher education in the United Kingdom.

6. This includes retirement, family care, full-time students, and the long-term sick or disabled.

7. For full details of the tests, see McFall (2013).

8. A similar test of cognitive ability has been used by Banks, O'Dea, and Oldfield (2010).

9. If labor markets are imperfect, then the individual's working hours become the theoretically relevant variable in determining voluntary labor supply rather than the market wage, since the latter is no longer measuring the opportunity cost of an additional hour of time (see Clotfelter 1985 and Brown and Lankford 1992).

10. The LCFS was formerly known as the Expenditure and Food Survey and the Family Expenditure Survey.

11. However, the finding of complementarity is at odds with Feldman (2010), who employs a full structural model of time and money donations to analyze the impact of a preferential tax on money donations.

12. We have experimented with using other instruments. First, we included the frequency of using the internet to account for the individual's social networks and frequency of access. In addition, monetary donations may be given online. Second, we also used indicators for how the individual receives news (i.e., via the radio, television, internet, or newspaper). Information sources, such as how news is acquired, may influence donating behavior. For example, media coverage of natural disasters, such as the 2004 Indian Ocean tsunami and Hurricane Katrina, may raise awareness of the need for donations (sometimes including specific appeals for donations in news bulletins), thereby increasing the amount given to charity. However, the inclusion of these instruments resulted in the model being overidentified.

References

Andreoni, J. 2006. "Philanthropy." In *The Handbook of the Economics of Giving, Altruism and Reciprocity*, edited by S. C. Kolm and J. M. Ythier, 1201–1269. Amsterdam: Elsevier North Holland.

Andreoni, J., and A. Payne. 2013. "Charitable Giving." In *Handbook of Public Economics*, vol. 5, edited by A. J. Auerbach, R. Chetty, M. Feldstein, and E. Saez, 1–50. Amsterdam: Elsevier North Holland.

Andreoni, J., and J. Scholz. 1998. "An Econometric Analysis of Charitable Giving with Interdependent Preferences." *Economic Inquiry* 36 (3): 410–428.

Apinunmahakul, A., V. Barham, and R. Devlin. 2009. "Charitable Giving, Volunteering and the Paid Labour Market." *Nonprofit and Voluntary Sector Quarterly* 38 (1): 77–94.

Banks, J., C. O'Dea, and Z. Oldfield. 2010. "Cognitive Function, Numeracy and Retirement Saving Trajectories." *Economic Journal* 120 (548): F381–F410.

Bauer, T. K., J. Bredtmann, and C. M. Schmidt. 2013. "Time vs. Money—The Supply of Voluntary Labor and Charitable Donations across Europe." *European Journal of Political Economy* 32 (Decemeber 2013): 80–94.

Bekkers, R. 2010. "Who Gives What and When? A Scenario Study of Intentions to Give Time and Money." *Social Science Research* 39 (3): 369–381.

Brown, V., and H. Lankford. 1992. "Gifts of Money and Gifts of Time: Estimating the Effects of Tax Prices and Available Time." *Journal of Public Economics* 47 (3): 321–341.

Cappellari, L., P. Ghinetti, and G. Turati. 2011. "On Time and Money Donations." *Journal of Socio-Economics* 40 (6): 853–867.

Charities Aid Foundation. 2016. "Gross Domestic Philanthropy: An International Analysis of GDP, Tax and Giving." https://www.cafonline.org/docs/default-source/about-us-publications/caf-gdp-report-v89c47ac334cae616587efff3200698116.pdf.

Clotfelter, C. T. 1985. *Federal Tax Policy and Charitable Giving*. Chicago: University of Chicago Press.

Ellingsen, T., and M. Johannesson. 2009. "Time Is Not Money." *Journal of Economic Behavior & Organization* 72 (1): 96–102.

Feldman, N. E. 2010. "Time Is Money: Choosing between Charitable Activities." *American Economic Journal: Economic Policy* 2 (1): 103–130.

Freeman, R. 1997. "Working for Nothing: The Supply of Volunteer Labor." *Journal of Labor Economics* 15 (1): S140–S166.

Greene, W. 2008. "Functional Form and Heterogeneity in Models for Count Data." *Foundations and Trends in Econometrics* 1 (2): 113–218.

Hartmann, B., and M. Werding. 2012. "Donating Time or Money: Are They Substitutes or Complements?" CESifo working paper 3835, Behavioural Economics, Center for Economic Studies, University of Munich.

Hauser, S. M. 2000. "Education, Ability, and Civic Engagement in the Contemporary United States." *Social Science Research* 29 (4): 556–582.

Heckman, J., J. Stixrud, and S. Urzua. 2006. "The Effects of Cognitive and Non-cognitive Abilities on Labor Market." *Journal of Labor Economics* 24 (3): 411–482.

Hill, M. 2012. "The Relationship between Volunteering and Charitable Giving: A Review of the Evidence." CGAP working paper, Consultative Group to Assist the Poor, Washington, DC.

James, R. 2011. "Charitable Giving and Cognitive Ability." *International Journal of Nonprofit and Voluntary Sector Marketing* 16 (1): 70–83.

McFall, S. 2013. "Understanding Society: UK Household Longitudinal Study: Cognitive Ability Measures." https://www.understandingsociety.ac.uk.

Menchik, P. L., and B. A. Weisbrod. 1987. "Volunteer Labor Supply." *Journal of Public Economics* 32 (2): 159–183.

ONS (Office for National Statistics). 2013. "Household Satellite Accounts: Valuing Voluntary Activity in the UK." http://www.ons.gov.uk/ons/rel/wellbeing/household -satellite-accounts/valuing-voluntary-activity-in-the-uk/art—valuing-voluntary -activity-in-the-uk.html.

Prendergast, C., and L. Stole. 2001. "The Non-monetary Nature of Gifts." *European Economic Review* 45 (10): 1793–1810.

Smith, S. 2012. "Increasing Charitable Giving: What Can We Learn from Economics?" *Fiscal Studies* 33 (4): 449–466.

Vuong, Q. H. 1989. "Likelihood Ratio Tests for Model Selection and Non-nested Hypotheses." *Econometrica* 57 (2): 307–333.

Wiepking, P., and I. Maas. 2009. "Resources That Make You Generous: Effects of Social and Human Resources on Charitable Giving." *Social Forces* 87 (4): 1973–1996.

Wooldridge, J. M. 2010. *Econometric Analysis of Cross Section and Panel Data.* 2nd ed. Cambridge, MA: MIT Press.

10 The Impact of Government Funded Initiatives on Charity Revenues

Bradley Minaker and A. Abigail Payne

10.1 Introduction

When a charity receives government funding, do total revenues increase? Does the charity undo the benefits of the funding by changing its behavior in seeking revenues from other sources (such as fundraising), or do donors change their behavior? Granting agencies may be concerned that the effect of their grant may be lessened if revenues from other sources decline and are displaced by funding provided by the grant (a phenomenon known as "crowd-out"). Recent research has suggested that much of the grant is crowded out, but that this crowd-out is not complete and that most of the crowd-out is due to reduced fundraising by the charity (see Andreoni and Payne 2003, 2011, 2013a, and Andreoni, Payne, and Smith 2014).[1] Can granting agencies change the structure of their granting program to ensure that their grants are not crowded out? It may be that certain types of grants, such as those that fund new initiatives (as opposed to those that fund existing programs), may lead to different levels of crowd-out.

This chapter studies the effects on total revenues of receiving a grant from a provincially funded foundation for the recipient charities operating in Ontario, Canada. We follow Andreoni, Payne, and Smith (2014), a study that examined the effects of a UK lottery grant program. Similar to the UK program, the funding from the Ontario foundation was to support community-based initiatives that were mostly new programs (Ontario Trillium Foundation 2016b). Initially, annual funding provided to the foundation was approximately $16 million per year,[2] and the grant recipients were human- and social service-based organizations. The funding program was restructured in 1999, and the provincial funds allocated to the foundation were substantially increased (~$100 million per year of funding). Although the focus of the programs operated by the foundation continues to be on the building and support of vibrant communities, the missions of the organizations eligible for funding were expanded to include community-oriented groups, such those in the arts and environmental conservation. We study the effects of the funding awards for the period 1999–2012. Our study covers those applications by single-applicant registered charities because of our ability to match their applications with annual data that captures revenues and expenses from their CRA information return. By matching information from these two data sources, we can explore the short term and persistent effects of the foundation grant on charity revenues.

The effects of the foundation grants on charity revenues are strikingly similar to those found for Andreoni, Payne, and Smith (2014). We find that the grants increase total revenues by 16 percent in the first year of funding and there continues to be growth in total revenues in subsequent years. This growth is observed for all sizes of charities except those with average revenues that are greater than $500,000.

How does this growth in revenues relate to the notion of crowd-out? If we explore the effect of the grant on 1 year of funding, then we would conclude that the grant crowds out other revenue. A $1 increase attributable to the foundation grant only increases total revenues by approximately 33 cents for small and medium-sized charities. Over a 3-year period, however, there is an increase in total revenues that remains less than $1 for small charities (~92 cents) but gets closer to $1 if we study the effect over a 5-year period (~$1.02), suggesting a neutral effect of the funding on small charity operations. For medium-sized charities, we do not observe any crowd-out over a 3-year period (a $1 increase in grants results in an $1.23 increase in total revenues), and some crowd-in is observed in the effect over a 5-year period (~$1.72 increase in total revenues). For larger charities, our estimates are small but imprecisely measured, suggesting that the foundation grant had relatively little impact on increasing revenues, which we attribute to the fact that the size of the grants to these charities represents a small proportion of these charities' total revenues.

The chapter proceeds as follows. Section 10.2 describes the funding program and discusses the importance of studying specific granting programs to understand better the issues surrounding crowd-out. Section 10.3 describes the data set and presents summary statistics. Section 10.4 presents the analysis for the overall effect of the grant and tests for crowd-in or crowd-out. Section 10.5 compares our results to those of Andreoni, Payne, and Smith (2014) and concludes.

10.2   Description of Program under Study

The granting foundation under study is one that was created by the provincial government as an arms-length organization in 1982 with the mission of distributing a portion of the proceeds collected from a provincially administered lottery to promote the development of vibrant communities (Ontario Trillium Foundation 2016b). The budget for the foundation in the early years was small, and the grants were distributed to organizations primarily focused on the delivery of human and social services. In 1999 the funding and the structure of organization of the foundation changed dramatically. The funding ceased to be tied to lottery proceeds and instead was allocated as part of the budget process, increasing to approximately $100 million per year. In addition, the types of organizations eligible to receive funding were expanded to include those providing services in the areas of arts and culture, the environment, and sports and recreation (Ontario Trillium Foundation 2016a).

Applications for funding to the foundation typically are considered under one of two main programs: community grants and province-wide grants. Across the province, there are 16 catchments that may receive funding. The province-wide program is for initiatives with a broad geographic focus, usually defined as covering three or more catchment areas. Our focus is on the distribution of funds under the community grants program. This program funds initiatives with an intent of having a clear and measurable impact on the local community and accounts for nearly 85 percent of all applications. The community grants program targets new initiatives by charities and nonprofit organizations engaged in community-oriented activities tied to services in arts and culture, social and human services, sports and recreation, and the environment.[3] The applications can be from a single organization or multiple organizations. This study focuses on single-charity applicants to the community program, given the ability to link information on applications to detailed financial information retrieved from the organization's information return filed with the CRA.

The community grant program is administered by local catchment grant review teams composed of approximately 18 to 25 volunteers who have applied for a position on the team.[4] Each member typically serves a renewable term that ranges from 1 to 3 years. The local review team is serviced by a foundation staff member who oversees the collection and evaluation of the applications. Once submitted, an application will be assigned to the relevant catchment area for evaluation. Until 2003, applications were accepted and evaluated on an ongoing basis. Between 2004 and 2005 the process switched to one in which an application deadline was imposed and the evaluations of the proposals were structured around these deadlines. By 2005 the foundation had converted to a process whereby applications are evaluated three times per year. The submission deadlines are March 1, July 1, and November 1.

Applications are first screened for basic eligibility criteria. This screening filters out applications that are either not eligible for funding or whose project does not fit the priorities of the grant program.[5] Projects with a request for greater than $100,000 are given a more thorough examination that may include on-site visits by foundation staff. The foundation staff compile the information from the applications and subsequent research and present a recommendation of either approval or rejection to the grant review team. The grant review team then meets to review the applications and to submit their recommendations. As the funding pot is fixed, the review team assists in deciding the ordering of applications, effectively influencing which applications are funded. These decisions are then finalized by the foundation's board of directors.

This granting program is interesting to study for a number of reasons. First, the granting program is very large. This provides a broad set of charities that are eligible to apply for a grant. Second, the granting foundation is well known and may result in a positive signal to donors about the quality of the charity, which may cause crowd-in of other sources of revenue (Payne 2001; Andreoni and Payne 2003; Vesterlund 2003; Andreoni 2006a). Third, and perhaps most important, we are able to observe information about all charities that apply for the grant, including those that do not receive a grant. Similar to Andreoni, Payne, and Smith (2014), we observe information about charities before and after they apply and so can compare charities that are successful with charities that are unsuccessful.

These grants are for specific programs and are typically programs that extend or expand an organization's operations. Thus, unlike a grant that supports the organization's general operations, we should query whether the organizations' and/or donors' reactions to learning about the receipt of a grant would be the same as it might be for grants that support the general operations of the organization. Similar to Andreoni, Payne, and Smith (2014), the foundation funding program under study allows us to study a relatively homogeneous set of organizations as well to utilize an identification strategy that focuses on studying organizations that apply for the funding versus just any organization.

During the period under study, the application process has changed a few times. The information collected through the process that is of interest to this study, however, has not changed. Common over the study period are requirements to describe a proposed project, to provide details on the level of funding requested and the time needed to complete the project, and to indicate whether the grant would support operating and/or capital expenditures. In addition to providing information and funding requests for the proposed project, organizations are expected to submit key information about finances, staff (e.g., number of volunteers and paid staff), and the types of services provided. We are able to utilize relatively consistently measured information from the application form and match this information to data points provided by the organization's information return filed with the CRA.

Our identification strategy is one that compares revenues within a charity before and after receiving the grant. After controlling for time-invariant characteristics of the charity we compare this difference to differences in revenues in the same catchment area and period of charities that applied but did not receive the grant. The strategy also controls for observable factors that might explain why some charities win grants and others are unsuccessful. In other words, we are employing a difference-in-differences strategy and will test for the sensitivity of this strategy.

Given the nature of the granting program, we might expect that a successful (funded) charity will expand and grow because it received funding to expand or add a new service. It could also use the resources to expand in one direction while contracting in another direction—a crowd-out scenario. In contrast, an unsuccessful charity can choose to continue to seek funding from other sources (including receiving funding from the same foundation in a future round) or choose to continue to operate without the proposed expansion or new service. If the unsuccessful charity acquires funding from another source in the same period as the funding is provided to the successful charity, then our identification strategy of comparing the growth in revenues for the two charities will be muted, or biased toward zero. Unfortunately, we cannot observe the actions of the charities in terms of their grant applications to other foundations and organizations.

In contrast, if there are stark differences between successful and unsuccessful applicants that would explain the differences in the success on the application and might also be correlated to the effectiveness of the charities, then our results could overstate the effectiveness of the granting program. Our identification strategy helps to mitigate this concern. Moreover, a good proportion of our charities eventually receive funding from the foundation, suggesting that the programs are fundable but are funded at different times. The differences in success rates could be attributable to budget constraints and/or preferences of the members adjudicating the proposals.[6]

10.3   Data and Summary Statistics

As explained previously, we are studying the effects of the grants for the period after the expansion of the funding program, post-1999 to 2012. During this period, applications were considered under two programs: a province-wide program that funded projects covering two or more catchment areas and a community program that funded projects covering one catchment area. Figure 10.1 depicts the total amount funded for these programs. The bulk of the funding is allocated to

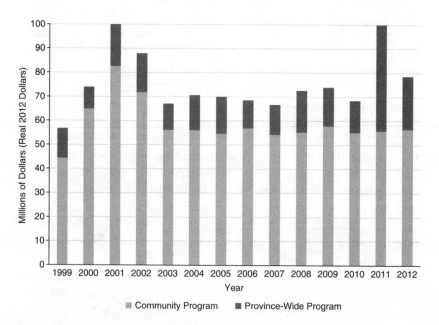

Figure 10.1
Total grants awarded, by program type and year.

projects under the community program. In most years, the level of funding awarded by the community programs is approximately four times the amount awarded for province-wide funding.

As our identification strategy relies on comparing charities operating in the same catchments, we focus our analysis on those grants awarded under the community program. This allows us to compare revenues of organizations located in similar areas while controlling for community characteristics that will help explain differences in programs offered across communities as well as within communities over time.

Applications to the community program can be organized into three groups: those submitted by registered charities, those submitted by nonprofits (but not registered charities), and those submitted by multiple organizations. The number of applications for each of these groups is depicted in figure 10.2. The dominant group of organizations are single applications for registered charities, representing 60 percent of the applications in most years. To be a registered charity, the organization must meet various regulatory requirements set forth by the CRA and submit an annual information return to CRA that reports the charity's

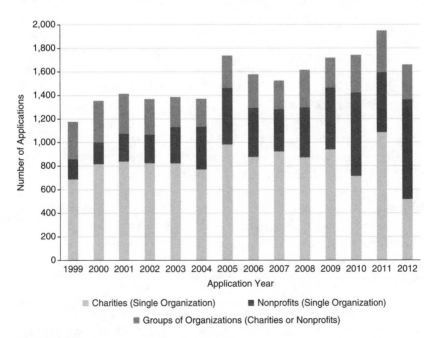

Figure 10.2
Number of applications, by type of organization.

activities, revenues, and expenditures. Organizations with registered charity status are permitted to issue tax receipts for donations.

The second group of applications are from nonprofits. While both nonprofits and registered charities are required to undertake activities that are for the public benefit, nonprofits have less onerous regulatory requirements in terms of compliance with CRA regulations and the submission of information. Nonprofits may receive donations, but they are not permitted to issue tax receipts to the donor. Over the sample period the number of applications by this group of organizations has increased. Our information on these organizations is limited to what is provided in the application to the funding agency. Thus we cannot observe revenues and expenditures for these organizations.

The third type of applications is from groups of organizations. Usually the lead organization is a registered charity or a nonprofit, but other types of organizations (e.g., local government groups) may also be participating in the application. The proportion of applications from this group has remained relatively constant over time. While we can observe the participating organizations on the group applications, we cannot observe how the funding is distributed across the organizations.

For the remainder of this chapter, our analysis will focus on the single applications by registered charities. In addition to matching information from the grant application to information from to the CRA data, we match in information on the characteristics of the neighborhood in which the charity operates based on sociodemographic measures from the 1996, 2001, 2006, and 2011 censuses. To properly reflect the neighborhood in which the charities operate, we use the forward sortation area (FSA), the first three characters of the postal code in which the charity operates, as our level of geography. The FSA represents approximately 8,000 households. The measures we use from the census include the average household income, total population, measures to capture the age distribution, and the percentage of the population who are immigrants. These measures help control for the environment in which the charity operates, both from the perspective of where potential funding sources may arise as well as with respect to the differential needs of the communities.[7]

Table 10.1 reports key information about the charities under study. We group the applications into 3-year intervals except for the last 2 years for ease of presentation. In the first two columns we report the number of applications and the success rate of these applications. Overall, the number of applications has not varied dramatically over

Table 10.1

Applications and funding for matched registered charities, by period.

Period of Funding	Total Number of Applications	Share of Applications That Are Funded (%)	Total Amount Requested ($ million)	Total Amount Awarded ($ million)	Median Amount Requested ($1,000)	Median Amount Awarded ($1,000)
	(1)	(2)	(3)	(4)	(5)	(6)
1999–2001	1,811	79.1	232.0	113.0	84.7	57.4
2002–2004	1,898	78.6	217.0	111.7	84.2	53.3
2005–2007	2,187	61.3	244.9	95.1	77.0	54.6
2008–2010	1,906	69.3	214.3	97.6	71.1	54.3
2011	671	53.9	89.3	29.7	78.3	62.8
2012	385	43.6	46.0	13.4	73.6	61.4
All years	8,858	69.0	1,043.5	460.5	77.3	55.3

Notes: These numbers reflect applications by single organization charities submitted to the community program funding grants in Ontario. All dollars are reported in real 2012 dollars the sample period. The success rate of the applicants, however, has varied. In the earlier periods nearly 80 percent of the applicants were successful. In the later periods the success rate has fallen substantially, to below 50 percent in the last year of our study. In columns 3 and 4 we report the total amount of funding requested and awarded for each period, respectively. There are far more projects pitched than can be funded by the foundation. Overall, the requests range from a few thousand dollars to well over $1 million. In columns 5 and 6, we report the statistics for the median amounts that were requested and awarded, respectively. The median requested amount is $77,000, and the median awarded amount is $55,000. In any given year, the maximum amount awarded under the community program is less than $500,000. Focusing on the successful applications, on average the amount awarded is 65 percent of the amount requested.

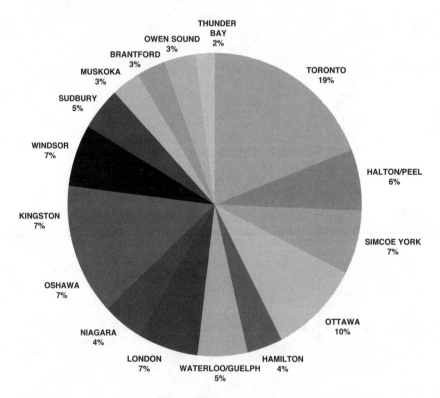

Figure 10.3a
Share of applications, by charities in region, 1999–2012.

Figure 10.3a depicts the distribution of applications by catchment area for the charities we study that applied to the community program. We have ordered the areas based on the total population for that area. The largest population is Toronto—and not too surprisingly, this is the area with the greatest share of applications. As we move across the catchment areas, however, population size and number of applications are not as strongly correlated as one might expect. Figure 10.3b depicts the share of awards granted in each region, which follows a similar pattern to the applications. For example, the populations of Hamilton, Waterloo/Guelph, and London range from 400,000 to 500,000. The share of the applications/awards from these cities range from 4 to 7 percent. In contrast, the populations of Windsor, Kingston, and Oshawa range from 100,000 to 200,000. Their shares of applications/awards also are similar to larger areas, ranging from 6 to 8 percent.

Thus far we have treated the applications as independent. It is not uncommon, however, for a charity to apply for funding more than once

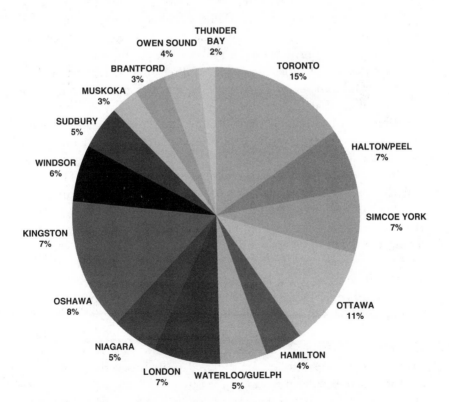

Figure 10.3b
Share of awards, by charities in region, 1999–2012.

Table 10.2
Number of applications.

Number of Applications Submitted by a Charity	Number of Charities	Share of Charities (%)	Share of Charities That Receive at Least One Award (%)	Share of Charities That Receive Two or More Awards (%)
	(1)	(2)	(3)	(4)
1	2,378	50.4	59.0	
2	1,285	27.2	84.4	53.0
3	669	14.2	93.6	80.3
4	279	5.9	97.8	92.5
5	78	1.7	98.7	89.7
6	28	0.6	100.0	100.0
7	3	0.1	100.0	100.0
Totals	4,720	100.0	74.2	33.7

and to observe more than one grant to a charity. Table 10.2 reports the distribution of applications based on the number of applications by a charity. Approximately 50 percent of the 4,720 charities in our sample apply for funding only once during the sample period. Approximately 94 percent of the charities apply for funding three or fewer times. In columns 4 and 5 we report the share of the charities grouped by number of applications that are observed being awarded once (column 3) or more than once (column 4). Although a few charities successfully obtain more than one award, nearly two-thirds of charities receive one or no awards. Table 10.3 reports the distribution of the awards based on the number of years of funding. Most of the awards are for 1 year of funding with the majority of awards covering 3 or fewer years of funding.

Table 10.4 further explores the number of awards per charity as well as the average number of months between the end of one award and the start of the next. Overall, approximately 26 percent of the charities never receive an award, and 41 percent of the charities receive only one award. While there are a few outliers, most charities receive three or fewer awards over the 13 years of study. The granting program places an emphasis on supporting new initiatives and discourages applications that simply support day-to-day operational expenditures. Thus, for the most part, we should assume that charities receiving multiple awards are seeking funding for different programs versus continued support of an existing program. Given that the average gap between the end of one award and the start of the next award is 31 months, the

Table 10.3
Length of awards.

Number of Years Covered by Grant	Number of Awards (1)	Share of Awards (%) (2)
1	3,456	57.8
2	1,227	20.5
3	1,123	18.8
4	84	1.4
5	86	1.4
Totals	5,976	99.9

Table 10.4
Grants awarded.

Number of Grants Awarded per Charity	Number of Charities (1)	Share of Charities in Sample (%) (2)
0	1,224	25.9
1	1,919	40.7
2	938	19.9
3	436	9.2
4	154	3.3
5	38	0.8
6	10	0.2
7	1	0.0

Notes: The number of months between the end of one award and start of another is calculated by the authors, using the decision dates for consecutive awards and the length of the grant. The number of grants per charity is conditional on the charity applying for a grant at least once.

data support this notion that charities receiving multiple awards are being funded for different programs.

Table 10.5 provides more detailed information from the applications and financial information. Panel A reports the mean and standard deviations of funding request, funding awarded, total revenue, private giving, and total government funding. Panel B reports the average and standard deviations of the numbers of paid employees and volunteers. In columns 1 and 2 we report the summary statistics for all applicant charities, regardless of size. In columns 3–8, we report the statistics based on the relative size of the charity. Size was determined by computing the mean total revenue excluding revenues from capital gains observed for the charity over the sample period. We define charity size

Table 10.5

Sources of funding for charities.

	All Charities		Small Charities (<$100,000 in Total Revenue)		Medium-Sized Charities (>$100,000 and <$500,000 in Total Revenue)		Large Charities (>$500,000 in Total Revenue)	
	Awarded Funding	Declined Funding	Awarded Funding	Declined Funding	Awarded Funding	Declined Funding	Awarded Funding	Declined Funding
	(1)	(2)	(3)	(4)	(5)	(6)	(7)	(8)
Number of charities	3,496	2,136	1,140	826	1,282	773	1,074	537
Number of applications	5,976	2,674	1,647	1,018	2,289	984	2,040	672
Panel A: Funding and Revenue								
Mean requested funding	115.8	121.6	64.9	83.3	113.1	130.7	160.1	166.2
(standard deviation)	(121.7)	(274.1)	(70.3)	(104.6)	(111.7)	(413.8)	(145.1)	(166.2)
Mean funding received if successful	75.2		41.1		73.0		105.1	
(standard deviation)	(67.9)		(36.0)		(62.0)		(79.5)	
Mean total revenues	821.8	680.2	62.0	45.2	264.1	252.0	2,052.3	2,262.9
(standard deviation)	(1,610.3)	(1,677.3)	(46.6)	(42.5)	(156.9)	(176.0)	(2,282.8)	(2,783.6)
Mean private giving	161.6	124.6	18.5	18.8	78.9	98.2	368.4	322.5
(standard deviation)	(465.8)	(334.8)	(26.7)	(28.9)	(104.4)	(127.3)	(743.9)	(602.8)
Mean government funding	448.3	359.9	20.2	6.3	92.6	58.5	1,193.1	1,336.8
(standard deviation)	(1,190.7)	(1,239.0)	(29.5)	(16.8)	(108.8)	(101.0)	(1,815.4)	(2,195.7)
Panel B: Characteristics								
Number of full-time employees	6.5	4.7	0.6	0.6	1.8	1.9	16.7	15.2
(standard deviation)	(17.4)	(14.2)	(3.1)	(2.9)	(3.7)	(9.4)	(26.5)	(22.6)
Number of part-time employees	6.2	4.8	1.3	1.2	3.0	3.0	13.6	12.8
(standard deviation)	(15.8)	(15.2)	(3.0)	(2.9)	(6.4)	(6.8)	(24.4)	(27.4)
Number of volunteers	118.2	83.4	45.5	38.8	89.4	73.2	209.1	166.0
(standard deviation)	(742.7)	(396.0)	(96.7)	(80.0)	(188.6)	(169.0)	(1,247.1)	(749.5)

Notes: All values in real 2012 dollars. Total revenues captures all revenues except capital gains/losses. Private giving captures all forms of private donations.

based on reported total revenues as follows: A small charity reports $100,000 or less; a medium charity reports between $100,000 and $500,000; and a large charity reports greater than $500,000.

Looking across all charities, the mean amount requested by successful applicants is similar ($115,800) to those that are rejected ($121,600). There is greater variance, however, for the rejected applicants. It also appears that successful applicants typically are larger, by almost 20 percent. Across the three groups of charities, the patterns are similar: The funding requested is uniformly lower for successful than for unsuccessful applicants, and the successful applicants are slightly bigger than the unsuccessful applicants.

Panel B of table 10.5 reports information from the applications from the charities about the number of volunteers and employees. Small charities have on average less than 1 full-time employee and about 1 part-time employee. Medium charities have closer to 2 full-time and 3 part-time employees, while large charities have around 17 full-time employees and 13 part-time employees. There are also differences in the number of volunteers, with charities that receive the funding having about 20 percent more volunteers than those charities that do not receive funding.

10.4   Effects of Successful Grants

10.4.1   Effect of Success on Total Revenue
Akin to the approach taken by Andreoni, Payne, and Smith (2014), we analyze the effect of the grant along two dimensions. First, we examine whether we observe differences in overall charity revenues when a charity is funded. This is the basic difference-in-differences specification that allows us to observe whether the total revenues increase as a result of receiving an award. We study these differences for a period (3 or 5 years) as well as allowing for separate effects for each year. Second, we study the effect of the dollar value of the grant on total revenue.

Figure 10.4a–d illustrates the basic effects of receiving a grant from the funding agency. The year of the application and/or the award would be observed on the information return and is identified as year t. Year $t+1$ represents the year after the decision and year $t-1$ represents the year prior to the decision. For all applications we use year $t-2$ as the base year and then compute the year over year percentage change in revenues reported on the CRA information return. For each box shown in the figure, the horizontal line in each box represents the

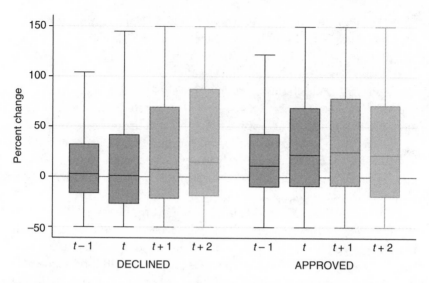

Figure 10.4a
Total revenue changes—all charities. *Note*: Changes capped at –50% and 150%.

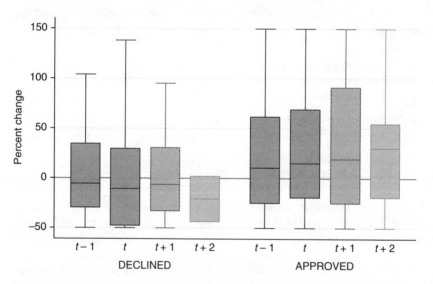

Figure 10.4b
Total revenue changes—small charities. *Note*: Changes capped at –50% and 150%.

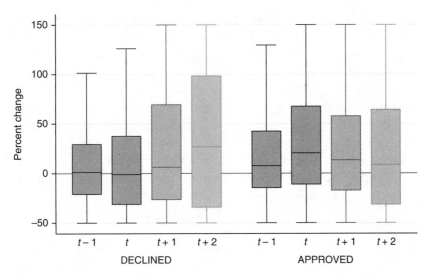

Figure 10.4c
Total revenue changes—medium charities. *Note*: Changes capped at –50% and 150%.

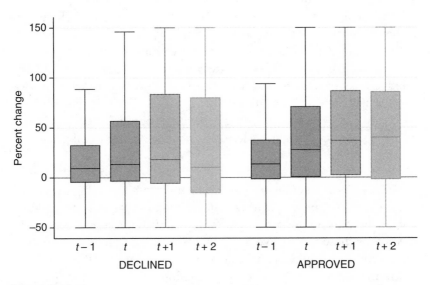

Figure 10.4d
Total revenue changes—large charities. *Note*: Changes capped at –50% and 150%.

median; the top and bottom edges of the box represent the 25th and 75th percentiles, respectively; and the outer horizontal lines represent the minimums and maximums, respectively. For ease of display, however, we capped the minimum at –50 percent and the maximum at 150 percent.

Focusing first on the applications that were declined, extending 2 years beyond the decision, the median change in revenue remains at zero. Near $t+2$, however, the distribution of the changes in revenue widens substantially, suggesting that some of the charities have done well despite having their applications declined. For the applications that were successful, we observe growth in revenues in years t and $t+1$, overall and at the median. The growth, however, starts to dissipate by year $t+2$. This is not too surprising, however, given we are measuring the year over year growth versus the growth since year $t-2$. Thus by year $t+2$, while the revenue growth has dissipated, the charities have continued to experience higher annual revenues compared to the period before receiving the grant.

Figure 10.4b–d depicts the differences based on charity size. There are striking differences for the small charities (figure 10.4b). Total revenues for unsuccessful charities are more likely to decline year over year, whereas the successful charities are more likely to experience growth over time. Unsuccessful medium charities (figure 10.4c) have relatively flat growth around the time of decision, whereas the successful charities have revenue growth that gradually declines. Finally, both successful and unsuccessful large charities (figure 10.4d) experience revenue growth, with the successful charities experiencing slightly greater growth.

Overall, figure 10.4 suggests that charities with successful applications experience revenue growth for several years following the award of the grant. Relying on these raw statistics, however, may be misleading, as there likely are other factors that contribute to this growth. To control for these factors, we move to a regression framework. We first focus on the overall effect of receiving an award on total revenue and follow the empirical framework by estimating a difference-in-differences model:

$$y_{itc} = \alpha_i + \lambda_t + \gamma_{cj} + \beta\, Post_{itc} + \delta\, Award_{itc} + \theta\, Controls_{itc} + \epsilon_{itc}, \qquad (10.1)$$

where y_{itc} is log total revenue for charity i, in year t and catchment c; α_i and λ_t are charity fixed effects and year dummy variables, respectively;

γ_{cj} is a dummy variable for the period of application j in catchment area c; *Post* is an indicator variable for the period after application for all charities that apply (with the period measured as either 3 or 5 years post application), *Award* is an indicator variable equal to 1 for the period following the award of a grant (again either a 3- or 5-year period). The vector of *Controls* includes neighborhood characteristics (average household income, total population, the share of the population aged 0–19, 55–64, and over 65, and the share of the population who are immigrants). The charity fixed effect controls for time-invariant characteristics of the charity (e.g., location, mission, operational structure), which helps control the differences across the charities applying for funding. The year dummy variables control for macro level changes that would affect all charities similarly (e.g., economic growth or downturn). Because our revenue information on the charities is provided on an annual basis, we effectively are comparing all applications by charities located in the same catchment area in the same year. The estimation clusters the standard errors at the FSA level, using cluster-robust Huber-White standard errors.

The coefficient β measures the effect on total revenues of the outcome for all charities that applied for funding and are located in the same catchment area and period after the application.[8] This coefficient helps control for factors that may affect all charities in that area (e.g., an economic, demographic, or weather event). Our main parameter of interest is δ, which captures the effect of receiving an award on total revenues for the period post award (3 or 5 years). As the value of the award is a dummy variable (0 if no award or 1 if awarded funding), then $\delta = 0$ suggests that there is complete crowd-out of the grant. If, however, $\delta > 0$, then there could be a partial crowd-out or a crowd-in effect of the grant.

In addition to equation 10.1, we estimate separate effects of receiving an award by year using equation 10.2:

$$y_{it} = \alpha_i + \lambda_t + \beta_s \sum_{s=0}^{2 \, or \, 4} Post_{i(t+s)} + \delta_s \sum_{s=0}^{2 \, or \, 4} Award_{i(t+s)} + \theta Controls_{it} + \epsilon_{it}. \qquad (10.2)$$

Table 10.6 presents the results for equations 10.1 and 10.2. Columns 1–4 reports the results when we run the analysis on all charities, regardless of size. The first two columns report the results when we allow the effect to extend 3 years and the latter two columns report the results when we allow the effect to extend 5 years. Overall, the results are very

Table 10.6
Results for effect of being awarded funding.

Dependent Variable: Log Total Revenue	Three Years — All Charities		Five Years — All Charities		Small Charities		Medium-Sized Charities		Large Charities	
	(1)	(2)	(3)	(4)	(5)	(6)	(7)	(8)	(9)	(10)
Awarded funding	0.157*** (0.015)		0.141*** (0.015)		0.225*** (0.028)		0.133*** (0.023)		0.043* (0.024)	
Awarded funding $t=0$		0.171*** (0.016)		0.187*** (0.017)		0.434*** (0.034)		0.153*** (0.025)		0.017 (0.025)
Awarded funding $t=1$		0.158*** (0.017)		0.176*** (0.017)		0.326*** (0.034)		0.180*** (0.026)		0.027 (0.026)
Awarded funding $t=2$		0.073*** (0.016)		0.100*** (0.017)		0.132*** (0.034)		0.123*** (0.026)		0.032 (0.027)
Awarded funding $t=3$				0.063*** (0.017)		0.034 (0.033)		0.102*** (0.026)		0.021 (0.029)
Awarded funding $t=4$				0.033* (0.017)		-0.008 (0.035)		0.080*** (0.027)		0.004 (0.028)
Controls	Charity, neighborhood, year, meeting date	Charity, neighborhood, year, meeting date	Charity, neighborhood, year, meeting date	Charity, neighborhood, year, meeting date	Charity, neighborhood, year, meeting date	Charity, neighborhood, year, meeting date	Charity, neighborhood, year, meeting date	Charity, neighborhood, year, meeting date	Charity, neighborhood, year, meeting date	Charity, neighborhood, year, meeting date
Number of observations	61,843	61,843	61,843	61,843	20,727	20,727	22,490	22,490	18,626	18,626

Notes: The measure awarded funding is a dummy variable that is equal to 1 for the first 3 years (column 1) or first 5 years (columns 3, 5, 7, and 9) of being awarded a grant from the foundation. The measure "Awarded funding; $t = X$" is a dummy variable equal to 1 for that particular year. The year $t = 0$ represents the year the grant is awarded and is first observed in the charity's information return. Coefficients represent the percentage increase in revenue from being awarded a grant. Small charities defined as having less than $100,000 in average total revenue, medium charities between $100,000 and $500,000, and large charities over $500,000. Charity and year fixed effects are included. Neighborhood controls are household income, percent immigrants, and the percentages of population aged between 0–19, 55–64, and 65+ years, respectively. Meeting date dummies are constructed for the largest meeting dates, where dates between large meeting dates are assigned to the closest large meeting date. The symbols ***, **, and * indicate significance at the 1 percent, 5 percent, and 10 percent levels, respectively.

similar to those reported in table 10.5. Receiving an award increases total revenues, on average, between 14 percent and 16 percent.

In table 10.5 we observed large differences in the size of the grant relative to total revenues for charities of different sizes, so we might expect the grant to affect charities differently depending on their size. Columns 5, 7, and 9 of table 10.6 report the overall effect of the grant for small, medium, and large charities, respectively, for the estimation of equation 10.1. Columns 6, 8, and 10 report the results for equation 10.2. We find that the effect is strongest for small charities, with the grant raising total revenues by 22.5 percent over a 5-year period. When we allow for separate effects by year, however, there are very strong effects in the first two years that quickly dissipate by years 4 and 5. For medium-sized charities we observe a positive effect of the grant, with the total revenues rising 13.3 percent over the 5-year period. This effect is smoothly distributed across the 5 years with a slower dissipation. The effect for large charities is essentially zero. These findings are consistent when what we observed in the raw summary statistics of table 10.5.

10.4.2   Crowd-In or Partial Crowd-Out?

The previous section presented evidence that the grant had a positive effect on total revenue for small and medium-sized charities and was completely crowded out for large charities. What the evidence presented failed to capture, however, was whether the grant increases total revenue dollar-for-dollar or by some other amount. If the grant increases the charities revenues by less than dollar-for-dollar, then the granting foundation may be concerned that the full impact of their grant is not being realized by the charities. If the grant causes total revenues to increase by more than the amount of the grant, then the granting foundation needs to take this into account when it makes funding decisions. To test for the level of crowd-out or crowd-in, we use the actual dollar value of the grant. Our analysis follows Andreoni, Payne, and Smith (2014), using the following specification:

$$O_{it} = \alpha_i + \lambda_t + \beta_s \sum_{s=0}^{4} Post_{i(t+s)} + \delta_s \sum_{s=0}^{4} Award_{i(t+s)} x \ Amount_{it}$$

$$+ \theta Controls_{it} + \epsilon_{it},$$

(10.3)

where everything is the same as in equation 10.2 except that *Amount* represents the total amount of the grant that the charity receives. The other exception is that the dependent variable is now measured in levels instead of logs. This allows us to test the level of crowd-out observed over a 5-year period. $\delta_0 + \delta_1 + \delta_2 + \delta_3 + \delta_4 = 0$ suggests that the award has been completely crowded out, $0 < \delta_0 + \delta_1 + \delta_2 + \delta_3 + \delta_4 < 1$ suggests partial crowd-out, $\delta_0 + \delta_1 + \delta_2 + \delta_3 + \delta_4 = 1$ suggests the grant has a neutral effect (raises total revenue dollar for dollar), and $\delta_0 + \delta_1 + \delta_2 + \delta_3 + \delta_4 > 1$ suggests crowd-in.

Table 10.7 presents the results for the effect of the grant over a 5-year period, with the coefficients representing the effect of each dollar of the grant on total revenue. First focusing on all charities (column 1), in the first year of funding, $1 of grant money raises total revenue by 39 cents. The coefficient is not statistically different from 0. For years 2 through 5, however, $1 of grant increases total revenue. Over a 3-year period, the sum of the effect of each dollar of the grant is $2.86, supporting the argument that the grant has a crowd-in effect. Over 5 years, each dollar from the grant raises total revenue by nearly $6.

In columns 2–4, we report the results from estimations that provide separate estimates based on charity size (small, medium, or large). The results for small charities are reported in column 2. Similar to what we observed in table 10.6 the strongest and biggest effects are observed in the first 3 years of funding. Aggregated over 3 years, the overall effect is just less than $1, at $0.92 and this coefficient is not statistically different from 1, suggesting the effect of the grant on total revenues is revenue neutral—the funding increased revenues by the amount of the award but did not result in an increase in revenue growth for the firm. Aggregated over 5 years, the overall effect equals $1, again suggesting a neutral effect.

Moving next to the results for medium-sized charities (column 3), we again observe a long-term effect of the grant on total revenues. Over a 3-year period we can reject a neutral effect at the 10 percent level. Over a 5-year period, the effect is close to $1.72 and is statistically different from $1, suggesting a crowd-in effect of the grant. Finally, we report the results for large charities in column 4. Interestingly, the effect in the first year of funding ($t = 0$) is imprecisely measured, and the effect in the second year of funding is only significant at a 10 percent level. We do not begin to observe significant effects until the third ($t = 2$) and later years. Given that the size of the awards are relatively small for large charities and the effects are lagged, we are not sure what to make

Table 10.7
Effect of grant amount on total revenue.

Dependent Variable: Total Revenue	All Charities (1)	Small Charities (2)	Medium-Sized Charities (3)	Large Charities (4)
Awarded funding $t=0 \times$ Amount of award	0.394 (0.340)	0.356*** (0.028)	0.319*** (0.048)	0.486 (0.590)
Awarded funding $t=1 \times$ Amount of award	1.392** (0.584)	0.357*** (0.029)	0.513*** (0.052)	1.916* (1.061)
Awarded funding $t=2 \times$ Amount of award	1.077*** (0.289)	0.206*** (0.027)	0.402*** (0.048)	1.316** (0.537)
Awarded funding $t=3 \times$ Amount of award	1.362*** (0.303)	0.075*** (0.024)	0.288*** (0.046)	1.657*** (0.541)
Awarded funding $t=4 \times$ Amount of award	1.512*** (0.362)	0.023 (0.025)	0.199*** (0.040)	1.959*** (0.637)
Sum of coefficients over 3 years	2.863	0.919	1.234	3.718
p-value, test $=1$	(0.061)	(0.249)	(0.090)	(0.141)
Sum of coefficients over 5 years	5.737	1.017	1.721	7.334
p-value, test $=1$	(0.001)	(0.875)	(0.000)	(0.021)
Controls	Charity, neighborhood, year, meeting date	Charity, neighborhood, year, meeting date	Charity, neighborhood, year, meeting date	Charity, neighborhood, year, meeting date
Number of observations	61,843	20,727	22,490	18,626

Notes: Coefficients represent the increase in total revenue for each dollar of grant awarded. Small charities are defined as having less than $100,000 in average total revenue, medium-sized charities between $100,000 and $500,000, and large charities over $500,000. Charity and year fixed effects are included. Neighborhood controls are household income; percent immigrants; and a percent of population aged between 0–19, 55–64, and 65+ years, respectively. Meeting date dummies are constructed for the largest meeting dates, where dates between large meeting dates are assigned to the closest large meeting date. The symbols ***, **, and * indicate significance at the 1 percent, 5 percent, and 10 percent levels, respectively.

of these estimates. We suspect there is more going on for the large chari-ties than we can explain by our analysis.

These results demonstrate a variation of effects based on size of charity, and likely reflect the importance of the grant to the charity as well as the ability of the charity to continue to provide additional ser-vices beyond the end of the grant. There is some evidence of limited crowd-out for grants to small charities over a 3-year period, but the grant appears to be revenue neutral over a 5-year period. For medium-sized and large charities, we see evidence of crowd-in from other sources. The patterns for charity sizes coincide with the results reported in tables and figures earlier in this chapter.

10.5 Conclusion

Our study closely follows that of Andreoni, Payne, and Smith (2014). In this section we compare our results to their findings. Panel A of table 10.8 presents the estimates of the overall effect of the grant from both studies (table 10.6 of this chapter and table 6 of Andreoni, Payne, and Smith 2014). The 2014 paper finds that grants increase total revenue by 22.2 percent. Our results suggest an increase of 14.1 percent. The pattern is similar in both studies, with the effect largest for small charities (Andreoni, Payne, and Smith, 40.4 percent; our study, 22.5 percent), slightly smaller for medium charities (Andreoni, Payne, and Smith, 18.4 percent; our study, 13.3 percent) and even smaller and insignifi-cant for large charities (Andreoni, Payne, and Smith, 4.3 percent; our study, 4.3 percent).

Panel B of table 10.8 shows similar patterns when accounting for the size of the grant (table 10.7 of our chapter; table 7 of Andreoni, Payne, and Smith 2014). The effect of each dollar (or pound) of the grant is largest for small charities, and is also largest in the first 3 years after the grant, with smaller (and sometimes insignificant) values for the fourth and fifth years after the grant is awarded. Testing for crowd-out or crowd-in reveals very similar patterns in both studies. The 5-year sum of the effect of the grant for small charities reveals nearly a dollar-for-dollar (or pound-for-pound) increase in total revenue for small charities, while medium charities show about a $1.54 (£1.64 for Andre-oni, Payne, and Smith 2014) increase in total revenue for each dollar (pound) of grant over a 5-year period.

Our study focuses on a provincially run grant program in a single province in Canada, while Andreoni, Payne, and Smith (2014) use a

Table 10.8
Comparing results with past research.

Panel A: Overall Effect of Grant

	This Study (Table 10.6)	APS
	(1)	(2)
All charities	0.141***	0.222***
Small charities	0.225***	0.404***
Medium-sized charities	0.133***	0.184***
Large charities	0.043*	0.043

Panel B: Effect of dollar value of grant

	Small Charities		Medium Charities	
	This Study (Table 10.7)	APS	This Study (Table 10.7)	APS
	(1)	(2)	(3)	(4)
Awarded funding $t = 0$	0.356***	0.223***	0.319***	0.242***
Awarded funding $t = 1$	0.357***	0.254***	0.513***	0.338***
Awarded funding $t = 2$	0.206***	0.302***	0.402***	0.347***
Awarded funding $t = 3$	0.075***	0.075	0.288***	0.198
Awarded funding $t = 4$	0.023	0.050	0.199***	0.518***
Sum of 3 years	0.919	0.879	1.234	0.927
p-value, test = 1	(0.249)	(0.165)	(0.090)	(0.692)
Sum of 5 years	1.017	1.005	1.721	1.643
p-value, test = 1	(0.875)	(0.973)	(0.000)	(0.079)

Notes: APS refers to Andreoni, Payne and Smith (2014). Coefficients in Panel A represent the percent increase in revenue from being awarded a grant. This chapter's definition of small charities is less than $100,000 in average total revenue; medium charities, between $100,000 and $500,000; and large charities, over $500,000. The APS definition of small charities is between £10,000 and £100,000 in revenue; medium charities, between £100,000 and £1 million; and large charities, between £1 million and £5 million. Panel A dependant variable is log total revenue. Panel B dependant variable is total revenue in dollars (this study) and in pounds (APS). The symbols *** and * indicate significance at the 1 percent and 10 percent levels, respectively.

national grant program in the United Kingdom. Despite the differences in both the scope of the grant program and the country in which the grant program takes place, we find remarkably similar results. Both studies show that the grant increases total revenue for charities, with the grant being revenue neutral for small charities, and the grant crowding-in revenue from other sources for medium-sized charities. In both countries the funding program was from a quasi-governmental source (lottery proceeds) and is perceived to be a highly respected source of funding. Both sources also promoted applications for new programs versus continuation or the coverage of day-to-day operational expenses. Separately, but further strengthened in combination, the results from both studies suggest that the structure of the granting program can affect the impact on overall revenue sources for charities.

Notes

We thank the Ontario Trillium Foundation for access to their data, and the PEDAL lab and staff for assistance in transforming and linking the data sets. We also thank participants of the CESifo Summer Institute Workshop on the Economics of Philanthropy for their comments as well as those of participants at presentations held at Canadian Institute for Advanced Research: Social Interactions, Identity, and Well-Being Study Group (Vancouver, Canada), Monash University (Melbourne, Australia), National Tax Association (Baltimore, Maryland), and the International Institute for Public Finance (Tokyo, Japan). Support for this research has been funded through Social Science and Humanities Research Council (Canada) insight and partnership development research grants.

1. For a review of past studies of crowd-out, see Andreoni (2006b) and Andreoni and Payne (2013b).

2. All dollar values reported are in Canadian dollars.

3. This can include such community groups as library boards and small municipal governments. The key difference between nonprofits and charities is that charities must use their resources for charitable activities—this constraint does not exist for nonprofits.

4. Volunteers wishing to apply to their local grant review team submit an application through the Public Appointment Secretariat. The secretariat maintains a list of candidates for each catchment area, and as vacancies arise, qualified candidates are considered for appointment to the grant review team (Ontario Trillium Foundation 2011).

5. It is unusual for an application to be screened out for not meeting the criteria of the grant program, because the types of programs funded is very broad.

6. If we limit our control sample to those charities that are both denied and awarded funded, our results are slightly bigger in magnitude than those reported in this chapter.

7. A detailed memorandum explaining the linking process is available from the authors.

8. There are 661 cases in which a charity applies more than once for a grant with the foundation during a single year. Some charities (115) receive more than one grant. For

the purpose of the analysis, we identify success based on there being at least one successful application during the year. For charities with more than one grant award in a given year, we sum the amounts of the award.

References

Andreoni, James, 2006a. "Leadership Giving in Charitable Fund-Raising." *Journal of Public Economic Theory* 8 (1): 1–22.

Andreoni, James, 2006b. "Philanthropy." In *Handbook of the Economics of Giving, Altruism and Reciprocity.* edited by S. C. Kolm and J. M. Ythier, 1201–1269. Amsterdam: Elsevier North Holland.

Andreoni, James, and A. Abigail Payne. 2003. "Do Government Grants to Private Charities Crowd Out Giving or Fund-Raising?" *American Economic Review* 93 (3): 792–812.

Andreoni, James, and A. Abigail Payne. 2011. "Is Crowding Out Due Entirely to Fundraising? Evidence from a Panel of Charities." *Journal of Public Economics* 95 (5–6) 334–343.

Andreoni, James, and A. Abigail Payne. 2013a. "Crowding Out: The Effect of Government Grants on Donors, Fundraisers, and Foundations in Canada." Working paper 2013-10, Department of Economics, McMaster University, Hamilton, Ontario.

Andreoni, James, and A. Abigail Payne. 2013b. "Charitable Giving." In *Handbook of Public Economics,* edited by Alan J. Auerbach, Raj Chetty, Martin Feldstein, and Emmanuel Saez, 1–50. Amsterdam: Elsevier.

Andreoni, James, A. Abigail Payne, and Sarah Smith. 2014. "Do Grants to Charities Crowd Out Other Income? Evidence from the UK." *Journal of Public Economics* 114 (C): 75–86.

Ontario Trillium Foundation. 2011. "How to Apply as a Volunteer." http://www.otf.ca /en/aboutUs/volunteer_apply.asp.

Ontario Trillium Foundation. 2016a. "FAQS." http://www.otf.ca/who-we-are/faqs.

Ontario Trillium Foundation. 2016b. "History." http://www.otf.ca/who-we-are/history.

Payne, A. Abigail. 2001. "Measuring the Effect of Federal Research Funding on Private Donations at Research Universities: Is Federal Research Funding More Than a Substitute for Private Donations?" *International Tax and Public Finance* 8 (5/6): 731–751.

Vesterlund, Lise. 2003. "The Informational Value of Sequential Fundraising." *Journal of Public Economics* 87 (3): 627–657.

11 Forgetful or Reluctant? Evidence on Reminder Response and Donor Behavior from Panel Data

Mette Trier Damgaard, Christina Gravert, and Laura Villalobos

11.1 Introduction

Many charities rely on continuous fundraising as their main source of income to support their cause. In the United States over 1 million charities compete for the attention of the roughly 200 million potential donors by sending out millions of letters, emails, and text messages to ask people for a donation or to join a membership program (National Center for Charitable Statistics 2017). The charities are right to assume that without these continuous asks, donations are unlikely. Previous research has shown that individuals are most likely to donate immediately when asked and seldom decide to donate without an external trigger (Damgaard and Gravert 2017). This lack of attention can be explained partly by forgetfulness. Donors might intend to give, but if they are asked at an inconvenient time when the transaction costs of reacting to the reminders are high, then they might delay giving and forget about it until the next reminder comes along (Taubinsky 2013; Karlan et al. 2016). If the next reminder reaches them at a more convenient time when their transaction costs are lower, they might give then instead (Huck and Rasul 2010).

However, as shown by Damgaard and Gravert (2018), reminders may also have adverse effects. Reminders impose annoyance costs on the receivers, as evidenced by the unsubscriptions that follow every reminder. In the long run, this might counteract the positive effect of reminders on giving.

This chapter provides further evidence on the potential two-sided effects of reminders and explores whether reminders impact generosity and hence the intent to give. We use panel data from a large US charitable institution and observe roughly 444,800 yearly membership and gift transactions made by the full sample of 113,652 membership program members over the 4 years from 2011 to 2014. The charity sends multiple reminders to members around the time that their annual memberships expire, and members may receive up to eight rounds of reminders to renew their membership.

We analyze reminder response behavior in each round and benchmark behavior patterns against a simple transaction cost argument (i.e., whether the reminder reaches them at a convenient time). The transaction cost hypothesis provides a natural starting point for measuring response rates, as it abstracts from any behavioral mechanisms (e.g., altruism and warm glow) and from heterogenous donor characteristics. Transaction cost theory predicts that low response rates to membership or donation reminders are due to time costs of making a decision or opportunity costs of other, more pressing activities at the time of solicitation. In section 11.3 we develop a basic theoretical framework for the transaction cost argument, showing the rate of decline in response rates over the reminder rounds. In sections 11.4.1–11.4.4 we then propose and provide empirical evidence for additional explanations for why we see a more rapid decline in response rates over the reminder rounds than predicted by transaction cost theory.

Part of the deviation from our theoretical predictions can be explained by the heterogeneity of donors, in particular, their commitment to the charity as measured by their tenure as a member and the willingness to pay higher membership fees. We find evidence that more committed donors respond earlier, and more marginal donors respond later. The results in section 11.4.2 suggest that more generous members and long-term members are more likely to renew in early rounds but less likely to respond in later rounds. In line with this hypothesis, we find that members with a $100 higher membership fee the previous year were 3.5 percent more likely to renew in the first reminder round than in the second reminder round. If we assume that transaction costs are randomly distributed among receivers, then committed and generous members receive a higher utility from donating, helping them overcome the transaction costs. This would suggest that those who renew in response to the later reminders are the more marginal and less committed members, for whom transaction costs need to be lower to generate positive utility from the renewal. We cannot rule out that multiple reminders might additionally have an annoyance effect on the receivers, which could lead to an adverse reaction to later reminder rounds, as shown by Damgaard and Gravert (2018), who use exogenous variation in reminder frequency to test this hypothesis.

Our dataset includes voluntary donations on top of the yearly membership fee. These donations are responses to spontaneous requests and are not tied to any membership benefits. In section 11.4.3 we use this additional measurement of generosity to show that individuals who gave an additional gift the previous year are more likely to renew within the first three reminder rounds than those who did not give an additional gift. While this result could be explained by these more generous individuals receiving a higher utility from giving, it could also be explained by wealth.

To circumvent controlling for wealth, in section 11.4.4 we show that renewing later (and thus receiving more reminders) in the previous year is negatively associated with the willingness to give additional gifts to the charity on top of the membership fee in the current year. We show this result by using fixed-effects regressions, exploiting variation in response time for each individual over time and thus controlling for time-invariant unobservables. The result is stable to including past donation amounts. If reminders were a neutral tool to curb forgetfulness, then they should have no or even a positive effect on additional giving. The negative effect hints at a more complicated relationship between reminders and giving.

While the results in this chapter do not allow for a causal interpretation of the relationship between reminders and giving, our findings point to several behavioral aspects that are relevant for responding to reminders in addition to the basic transaction cost model. This chapter thus extends the arguments made in Damgaard and Gravert (2018) that the response to reminders is complex and that senders should make an effort to understand their target group in order to maximize responses and avoid negative effects of reminders.

The remainder of the chapter is organized as follows: section 11.2 describes the institutional setting and our data, section 11.3 lays out the theoretical framework, and section 11.4 describes the results of our study. Section 11.5 concludes.

11.2   Institutional Setting and Data

Our donation data come from the Friends of the Smithsonian, the membership program of the Smithsonian Institution. Founded in 1846, the Smithsonian in Washington, DC, is the world's largest museum, education, and research complex, consisting of 19 museums and galleries, the National Zoological Park, and nine research facilities. For this study, we use the full sample of donors over a period of 4 years, from 2011 to 2014. Many donors had a membership for several decades; however, due to data availability on our main variable of interest, response to reminders, we restrict our analysis to data starting in 2011. There are several membership levels available with different membership rates and benefits. We restrict our data to the lowest four membership levels, as these levels are the most common membership levels and these members are mostly contacted through letters and campaigns. Members at levels higher than level four are called on the phone and contacted at events to ensure renewal of their memberships. The lowest membership level is achieved by a donation of $75–149, the second level by $150–249, the third by $250–499, and the highest by $500. However, occasionally campaigns give a discount for a yearly membership, so we do observe membership amounts below the $75 minimum. We have 113,652 individuals in our sample. For each individual, we observe whether they paid a membership fee in each of the 4 years. We have annual information for additional gifts made by each member on top of their membership fee. This gives us 444,818 monetary transactions. Actual transactions made by each member can be higher, as gifts are aggregated on the yearly level.

The reminder data are generated continuously throughout the year, because memberships can start at any point during a year. Memberships last for 12 months. See figure 11.1 for an illustration of the reminder process. Existing members receive the first request to renew their membership 3 months before the membership expires (i.e., 9 months after

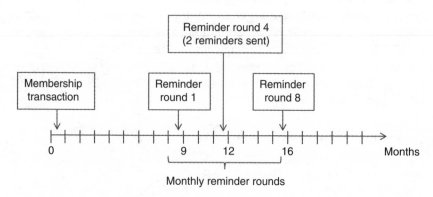

Figure 11.1
Timing of reminders.

their last membership transaction). We refer to this as the first *reminder round*. There is a total of eight reminder rounds—one every month from 3 months before the membership expires to 4 months after. Each reminder round consists of one reminder, except reminder round 4, which coincides with the month the membership expires (i.e., 12 months after the membership transaction). Reminder round 4 involves two separate reminders. As soon as members renew their membership, the reminders stop. If the member has not renewed after the eighth reminder, the reminders stop, and the former member is added to the reactivation pool, meaning that he or she will receive requests to start a new membership at other times throughout the year.

11.3 Theoretical Framework

The transaction cost model formalized by Huck and Rasul (2010) provides a useful benchmark for analyzing reminder response behavior. Let s denote the share of members who wish to renew if there were no transaction costs, no forgetting, and renewal was purely based on the expected utility from donating and becoming a member, as in the standard models of pure and impure altruism (Andreoni 1989, 1990). In the absence of transaction costs and liquidity constraints, the response rate to the first reminder round would be s, and no additional reminders would be necessary. The response rate in later reminder rounds would be zero. However, fundraising experiments have consistently found positive response rates for an additional reminder (Huck and Rasul 2010, Sonntag and Zizzo 2015, and Damgaard and Gravert 2018).[1]

The transaction cost model provides one possible explanation for why reminders are associated with positive response rates. Let transaction costs in period t be denoted by c_t, and suppose that a member only wishes to renew in period t if $c_t \le \tau$, with τ being the threshold for transaction costs below which renewing is optimal. Assume that transaction costs are identically and independently distributed across time and individuals. In addition, assume that every reminder triggers a new draw of transaction costs, and let $Pr(c_t \le \tau) = p$ denote the probability that transaction costs in period t are sufficiently low for a renewal to be made in period t. Then the response rate (i.e., the share of period t recipients who renew their membership in reminder round t) is given by

$$
r_t = \begin{cases}
ps & \text{if } t = 1 \\[2ex]
\dfrac{ps(1-p)^{t-1}}{1-s+s(1-p)^{t-1}} & \text{if } t \in \{2,3\} \\[3ex]
\dfrac{ps(1-p)^{t-1}+ps(1-p)^{t}}{1-s+s(1-p)^{t-1}} & \text{if } t = 4 \\[3ex]
\dfrac{ps(1-p)^{t}}{1-s+s(1-p)^{t}} & \text{if } t > 4.
\end{cases}
\tag{11.1}
$$

Note that members only get the reminders in reminder rounds 2–8 if they have not renewed in one of the previous reminder rounds. In addition, note that reminder round 4 consists of two reminders, and the expression above for $t = 4$ gives the combined response rate for both of the round 4 reminders together, because this is what is observable in the data. To get some intuition for the results, consider the special case where *all* members would renew in the absence of transaction costs (i.e., $s = 1$). Then expression 11.1 reduces to

$$
r_t = \begin{cases}
\dfrac{p}{1-p}+p & \text{if } t = 4 \\[3ex]
p & \text{otherwise.}
\end{cases}
$$

Hence, with identically and independently distributed transaction costs across time and individuals, the model predicts a uniform distribution of renewal over the eight reminder rounds except in reminder round 4, which consists of two reminders and therefore two independent draws from the transaction cost function for every recipient. So in this special case a pure transaction cost argument predicts that every additional reminder is as effective as the previous one.

However, the assumption that $s = 1$ is quite strong, even for our sample of dedicated, long-term members. Altruism and warm-glow from giving to this particular charity might vary from one year to the next as individuals gain new information about the charity or about competing charities. Changes in the donors' budgets might also have an effect on generosity. We therefore relax the assumption to $s < 1$, which implies lower response rates in all periods and the possibility that the response rate declines across reminder rounds. In the next section, we compare the response rate predicted by expression 11.1 for each reminder round with the corresponding proportion observed in

Table 11.1
Summary statistics.

Variable	Mean
Age (in 2015)	73.14
	(12.69)
Share female	0.46
	(0.50)
Share living in DC area	0.20
	(0.40)
Average years since first membership record	11.03
	(8.68)
Share of repeat members	0.85
	(0.36)
Average annual membership fee for members	$70.14
	(80.50)
Average annual gift conditional on giving	$63.87
	(121.73)
Number of observations	113,652

Notes: The table reports means and standard deviations (in parentheses) for the variables over the years 2011–2014. The sample consists of individuals who received a reminder from the Smithsonian at least once during 2011–2014.

the data. In this benchmarking exercise, we assume that the proportion of members who have renewed their memberships at least once during our observational period is a good approximation of s. This approach takes into consideration that some members will cease to remain members regardless of the actions of the charity.

11.4 Results

Table 11.1 shows descriptive statistics of our sample during the period of interest (2011–2014). The sample consists of individuals who received a reminder from the Smithsonian at least once in 2011–2014. Our unit of observation is the member-year. For the aggregate statistics of the time-variant variables, we take the averages over the 4 years. The average age of our donors is relatively high—73 years in 2015. The sample consists of slightly more males than females (46 percent). Although the Smithsonian is a local institution, only about 20 percent of the members live in Washington, DC, and the surrounding area. On average they first signed up as members 11–12 years ago. However, this does not mean that they have been members in all consecutive years since. By construction, all members in the sample got at least one reminder during the 4 years. On average 85 percent of our sample renewed their membership at least once. Conditional on being a member, individuals on average pay $70 in membership fees per year in the period of interest, and conditional on giving a gift to the Smithsonian, donors on average give $64.

11.4.1 Reminder Response Behavior

Figure 11.2 shows the observed and predicted response rates for each reminder round. The observed response rate is given by the share of recipients in each reminder round who renewed their membership in response to that reminder round (light gray bars). The observed response rate in round 1 is highest at 23.2 percent, and the response rate then gradually declines to about 3 percent in reminder rounds

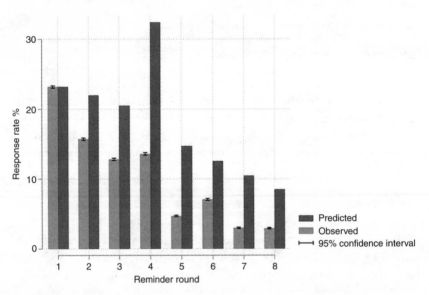

Figure 11.2
Observed and predicted response rate, by reminder round. *Notes:* Data pooled for 2011–2014. The observed series depicts the percentage of people who renewed their membership conditional on receiving that reminder and all previous reminder rounds. The predicted series is calculated using equation 11.1 with $s = 0.8518$ calibrated to the share of repeat members and $p = r_1/s = 0.2724$ calibrated to match the response rate in reminder round 1, r_1 given $s = 0.8518$.

7 and 8. As expected, we see an increase in the response rate in reminder round 4, which consists of two reminders. There is also an increase in round 6, which cannot be explained by the theory.

Equation 11.1 is used to predict response behavior that would be consistent with the transaction cost model. We calibrate the share of recipients who wish to renew if there were no transaction costs by the share of repeat members, that is, $s = 0.8518$. We use the share of repeat members as a proxy for s, because repeat members have shown an interest in renewing, although they may not necessarily have renewed 2 years in a row (e.g., due to high transaction costs). By not calibrating s to unity, we assume that not every member would renew if there were no transaction costs. Instead we allow for the possibility of some learning about the value of the membership that would reduce the willingness to renew. Given the calibration of s, we calibrate p to match r_1, the response rate in the first reminder round: $p = r_1/s = 0.2320/0.8518 = 0.2724$.

The transaction cost model with our calibration of the parameters leads to the predicted series shown in figure 11.2 (dark gray bars). Note that the calibration is such that the actual and predicted response rate for reminder round 1 coincide by construction. However, it is obvious that the actual response rates in all subsequent reminder rounds are smaller than predicted by the transaction cost model. Hence, sending out additional reminders is much less effective in terms of securing renewals than expected based on a transaction cost argument. We continue the analysis by exploring the gap between the transaction cost benchmark and the observed renewals.

11.4.2 What Drives Renewals?

These findings naturally raise two questions: What drives renewal in general, and what drives early renewal? In other words, what factors, apart from transaction costs, might explain the fact that we observe lower response rates than predicted by the model?

As a first step toward answering these questions, we run a simple probit model to determine which of the observables can explain whether or not recipients renew at all. Column 1 in table 11.2 shows the estimation results. Older individuals, women, and members living in the DC area are less likely to renew their memberships. The time since they first appeared in the member database and a higher membership fee paid in the previous year (conditional on being a member the previous

Table 11.2
What explains renewals?

Dependent Variable	Renewed at All (1)	Renewed in Rounds 1–3 (2)
Age (in 2015)	−0.003259*** (0.000)	−0.001328*** (0.000)
Female	−0.013943*** (0.002)	−0.018270*** (0.002)
Living in DC	−0.014380*** (0.002)	−0.018782*** (0.003)
Last year's membership fee	0.000385*** (0.000)	0.000423*** (0.000)
Last year's gift	−0.000279*** (0.000)	0.000028* (0.000)
Years since first membership	0.006436*** (0.000)	0.005520*** (0.000)
Number of observations	301,656	122,584

Notes: "Renewed at all" is a dummy equal to 1 if the member was registered as a member the following year. "Renewed in Rounds 1–3" is a dummy equal to 1 if the member received a reminder and renewed in rounds 1–3, conditional on renewing at all. The table reports marginal effects and standard errors (in brackets) from a probit model. All standard errors are robust. The symbols *** and * indicate significance at the 1 percent and 10 percent levels, respectively.

year) are positively associated with renewals. A higher additional gift the previous year is negatively associated with renewals in general.

In column 2 we regress the same variables on the probability of renewing early (i.e., in reminder rounds 1–3), conditional on receiving a reminder and renewing at all. Conditional on renewing, older people, women, and people living in the DC area are less likely to renew early. Higher membership dues,[2] larger previous gifts, and a longer time since first appearing in the membership database (which we take as proxies for commitment to the charity) are all positively associated with renewing earlier. The estimates suggest a small, positive association between responsiveness to reminders and commitment to the charity. We find the largest marginal effect for members living in the DC area. Since Smithsonian museums charge no entrance fees, museum visitors will often be asked to become a member when visiting a museum. It is thus likely that these visitors feel less attached to the membership, as they see it as a hidden entrance fee. They might be more likely to

Table 11.3
Conditional on renewing: What explains renewals in each round?

Renewal in reminder round	1	2	3	4	5	6	7	8
Age (in 2015)	-0.001473***	-0.000001	0.000248***	0.000432***	0.000175***	0.000308***	0.000146***	0.000164***
	(0.000)	(0.000)	(0.000)	(0.000)	(0.000)	(0.000)	(0.000)	(0.000)
Female	-0.025764***	-0.000066	0.004314***	0.007557***	0.003070***	0.005418***	0.002573***	0.002898***
	(0.002)	(0.000)	(0.000)	(0.001)	(0.000)	(0.001)	(0.000)	(0.000)
Living in DC	-0.024941***	-0.000271***	0.004078***	0.007318***	0.003005***	0.005342***	0.002258***	0.002912***
	(0.003)	(0.000)	(0.000)	(0.001)	(0.000)	(0.001)	(0.000)	(0.000)
Last year's membership fee	0.000358***	0.000000	-0.000060***	-0.000105***	-0.000043***	-0.000075***	-0.000036***	-0.000040***
	(0.000)	(0.000)	(0.000)	(0.000)	(0.000)	(0.000)	(0.000)	(0.000)
Last year's gift	0.000001	0.000000	-0.000000	-0.000000	-0.000000	-0.000000	-0.000000	-0.000000
	(0.000)	(0.000)	(0.000)	(0.000)	(0.000)	(0.000)	(0.000)	(0.000)
Years since first membership	0.006107***	0.000003	-0.001029***	-0.001792***	-0.000726***	-0.001278***	-0.000606***	-0.000680***
	(0.000)	(0.000)	(0.000)	(0.000)	(0.000)	(0.000)	(0.000)	(0.000)
Number of observations	122,584	122,584	122,584	122,584	122,584	122,584	122,584	122,584

Notes: The table reports coefficients and standard errors (in brackets) from an ordered probit model. The symbol *** indicates significance at the 1 percent level. Estimated coefficients and cutoffs are provided in table 11.A.1 in the appendix.

renew the membership once they again visit a museum and directly take advantage of the benefits, rather than through a mail reminder.

Now consider the probability of renewing for each reminder round. To determine what explains renewals at which stage of the reminder process, we run an ordered probit model. Table 11.3 shows the marginal effects for each of the eight possible reminder rounds, conditional on responding. Although the magnitude of the effects is modest, we confirm the findings from column 2 in table 11.2. Older recipients are less likely to respond in the first reminder round and more likely in all reminder rounds from round 3 on. People living in the DC area are less likely to respond in the two earliest rounds. Women are less likely than men to respond in early reminder rounds but more likely to respond in later rounds. A possible explanation could be that women, older donors, and people living in the DC area need to be more strongly persuaded to renew their membership and are more marginal donors. An alternative explanation could be that they delay more, which might be rational. Without an exogenous variation in the type of ask, we are not able to distinguish between the two possible explanations.

The results further suggest that, conditional on renewing, people who paid a larger membership fee last year and people who first appeared in the membership database a long time ago are more likely to renew in earlier rather than later reminder rounds. This is consistent with the hypothesis that more committed members renew earlier but might also suggest that loyal members react adversely to multiple reminders, for example, because they are annoyed by repeated reminders or because they are angered by them. For the individual reminders the marginally significant effect of last year's gift disappears.

11.4.3   Are Late Donors More Marginal?

These estimation results thus suggest that response behavior is explained partly by personal characteristics and partly by differences in the commitment to the charity. One explanation for why the reminder response behavior cannot be explained by the transaction cost model (as discussed in section 11.4.1) could be that the utility from donating differs by individual (DellaVigna, List, and Malmendier 2012, DellaVigna et al. 2013). In other words, it could be that the members with the highest utility from donating renew early, whereas people who renew later on are more marginal donors. Under this hypothesis, by the eighth reminder round the pool of the receivers consists mainly of marginal donors, who are difficult to convince. Donors may be marginal if they have a low income (and thus are truly budget constrained) or if they choose to allocate less of their income to the charity. As we do not have any income data in our sample, we cannot disentangle these two reasons. Instead we provide more evidence consistent with the idea that the donors who renew later are more marginal.

To explore whether the utility from donating differs depending on when donors renew, we use the total amount of money donated to the Smithsonian on top of the membership fee as an indication of the (altruistic and warm-glow) utility from donating to the charity in a given year. Being a member brings a number of member benefits, such as a monthly magazine, savings in the museum shop, and invitations to special events. Further, being a member has some social image value as well, which can be demonstrated by wearing membership pins or going to member-only events. In contrast, additional gifts given do not create any further benefits and are thus more likely to reflect fluctuations in the altruism and warm-glow toward the Smithsonian.

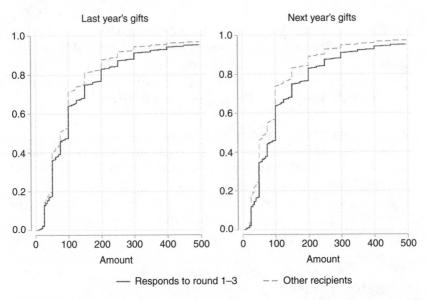

Figure 11.3
Cumulative distribution function for gifts given last year and next year conditional on giving. *Notes:* Gifts in the range (0, $500) are included. Data are pooled for 2011–2014. The differences in the distribution are statistically different using a two-sample Kolmogorov–Smirnov test. For last year giving, the Kolmogorov–Smirnov statistic is $D = 0.0722$ (p-value < 0.000) and for next year giving, $D = 0.1180$ (p-value < 0.000).

In line with the hypothesis that people who renew early also have a higher utility from donating, we find that 11.6 percent of the people who renewed in rounds 1–3 gave a gift to the Smithsonian the previous year, while the corresponding number is 9.3 percent for all others (Pearson $\chi^2(1)$ p-value < 0.000). Figure 11.3 plots the cumulative distribution function (CDF) of last year's gifts conditional on giving. The CDF for individuals who renew in rounds 1–3 is consistently below the CDF for other recipients. This is also consistent with the hypothesis that people who respond late or never are more marginal donors. The difference becomes even stronger when we only consider members paying a fee of \$75 a year or less (Pearson $\chi^2(1)$ p-value < 0.000). For higher levels, this effect decreases (Pearson $\chi^2(1)$ p-value < 0.063). Thus the difference in response rates is not driven by differences in membership levels but instead comes from the different commitment of lower level donors. Furthermore, similar patterns exist between response behavior and gift giving next year. Among the people who renew in rounds 1–3, 12.3 percent give a gift next year. Among other recipients the corresponding figure is 10.0 percent (Pearson $\chi^2(1)$ p-value < 0.000). Again we see an even larger difference when we only consider the low value donors (Pearson $\chi^2(1)$ p-value < 0.000), and the difference disappears for high level donors (Pearson $\chi^2(1)$ p-value < 0.389). This suggests that people who consistently respond early are more committed to giving money to the charity than people who respond late.

11.4.4   Unobserved Drivers of Our Results

So far we have shown that (1) both the length of time since registering as a member for the first time and higher past membership fees increase the probability of renewing in general; (2) higher membership dues, larger previous gifts, and a longer time since first appearing in the membership database increase the probability of responding to early reminders; and (3) early renewers are more likely to donate more in the following year.

However, in our previous regressions there might be an omitted variable bias from unobserved characteristics, such as general altruism, warm-glow, wealth, or interest in the mission of the charity. In this section, we add additional evidence on the effects of the reminders on the probability of additional gifts in the following year by controlling for time-invariant differences across individuals. As there is variation both in the number of reminders that each member received and in the renewal response for different years, we can estimate an individual

Table 11.4
Effect of reminders on additional gifts, in dollars.

Dependent Variable	Amount Given in Addition to Membership Fees in Year t		
	(1)	(2)	(3)
Reminder round in period $t-1$	−0.705132***	−0.361633	−0.685356***
	(0.204)	(0.280)	(0.201)
Reminder round in period t		−0.362123	
		(0.332)	
Gift in period $t-1$			−0.163636***
			(0.056)
2013	0.690901	1.088464*	−0.027131
	(0.526)	(0.581)	(0.510)
2014	1.613200***	3.834358***	1.174485*
	(0.584)	(0.660)	(0.611)
Number of observations	116,297	72,682	116,297
R^2	0.00	0.00	0.06

Notes: Fixed-effects regression of gift given in addition to the membership fee. The table reports coefficients, and standard errors are given in parentheses. The reference year is 2012. The symbols *** and * indicate significance at the 1 percent and 10 percent levels, respectively.

fixed-effects model. Table 11.4 shows the output of the fixed-effects regressions with different specifications. In column 1 we explore the effect of the lagged reminder round (a variable between 1 and 8 that indicates in which round the individual responded in the previous year) on the amount given in gifts in addition to the membership fee this year. We control for time trends by adding year dummies to the regression. If reminders are purely a tool to remember to renew the membership and if individual level altruism or warm-glow is time invariant, then we should find a zero effect of when people respond to reminders on additional gifts given. However, we find a significant effect of lagged reminder round on additional gifts. Each round that the member responds later is associated with a $0.71 decrease in giving the following year. This is about the same effect as the change caused by between-year variation from 2012 to 2013. In column 2 we add the current year reminder round as an additional control. While the current reminder round variable is not significant, it does appear to be correlated with last year's response time, as the estimate for the lagged reminder round decreases to −$0.36 and is no longer significant. Last, we add a lagged version of the total amount given as additional gifts in column 3. The coefficient of the lagged reminder round stays stable, indicating that last year's gift and last year's response time is largely uncorrelated. We find a small but precisely estimated negative effect of last year's gift on this year's gift, which is about a quarter of the effect of an additional reminder round in the previous year.

The evidence presented shows that there is a significant negative relationship between when members respond to reminders and how much they give the following year in addition to the membership fee. Reminders therefore do not appear to be a neutral tool to target the effects of forgetting. Instead there is indication of interactions between response behavior and donation behavior: Relatively more marginal donors (who give less) renew later in subsequent years, and in addition late renewers give less the following year. As we have no exogenous variation in the number of reminders, we cannot disentangle whether responding late is an indication of being reluctant or whether receiving more reminders creates annoyance costs that are later deducted from total giving.

11.5   Conclusion

Using panel data from a large charity's membership program, we analyzed member reactions to renewal reminders. We used the traditional transaction cost model, with a random variation in transaction costs across time and individuals, as a benchmark to understand responses to reminders. Responses decline more rapidly than predicted by the model. In several steps we explore additional explanations for the decline. We show what donor characteristics are useful in predicting renewal behavior and whether they lead to heterogeneous patterns in renewal times. Responsiveness to reminders may be correlated with generosity or commitment to the charity such that more committed members (as measured by their membership tenure and donor level) respond earlier, and more marginal donors respond later. Late renewers are the more marginal members, who are usually on the lowest membership level. An additional reminder is therefore less effective than the previous one, because the sample receiving the reminder changes with an increasing fraction of more marginal individuals. We use data on additional, membership-independent, donations to estimate the relationship between response time and generosity. If reminders were a neutral tool to curb forgetting, we should not see any significant relationship between response time and additional giving. However, in a fixed-effects regression controlling for time-invariant unobservables, we find significant evidence that later responses are related to lower voluntary donations the following year. This is evidence in line with an adverse reaction to multiple reminders. As shown in Damgaard and Gravert (2018), annoyance costs and feeling pushed can decrease the willingness to donate. Exogenous variation in the number of reminders would be optimal to determine the causal effect of multiple reminders on response rates and subsequent additional donations during the following year. Charities should be aware that reminders can have heterogenous effects on donors and should aim to uncover ideal reminder frequencies through data analysis and rigorous testing.

11.A Appendix

Table 11.A.1
Ordered probit estimates of response behavior.

Dependent Variable	Reminder Round
Age (in 2015)	0.0038***
	(0.0003)
Female	0.0669***
	(0.0062)
Living in DC	0.0651***
	(0.0077)
Last year's membership fee	−0.0009***
	(<0.0001)
Last year's gift	<0.0001
	(<0.0001)
Years since first membership	−0.0158***
	(0.0004)
Cut 1	−0.2730
	(0.0204)
Cut 2	0.2518
	(0.0204)
Cut 3	0.6514
	(0.0205)
Cut 4	1.1333
	(0.0207)
Cut 5	1.3338
	(0.0207)

(continued)

Table 11.A.1 (continued)

Dependent Variable	Reminder Round
Cut 6	1.7751
	(0.0213)
Cut 7	2.1021
	(0.0219)
Number of observations	122,584
R^2	0.01

Note: The table reports coefficients and standard errors (in parentheses). The symbol *** indicates significance at the 1 percent level. Reminder round is a discrete variable indicating the reminder round that donors renewed in, conditional on renewing.

Notes

1. Positive effects of reminders on behavior have also been found in several other contexts (Vervloet et al. 2012; Allcott and Rogers 2014; Altmann and Traxler 2014; Calzolari and Nardotto 2017; Gilbert and Zivin 2014; Bhargava and Manoli 2015; Karlan et al. 2016).

2. One could argue that the level of last year's membership fee is endogenous. We therefore estimate both regressions without this variable and find that the model is robust to excluding it.

References

Allcott, H., and T. Rogers. 2014. "The Short-Run and Long-Run Effects of Behavioral Interventions: Experimental Evidence from Energy Conservation." *American Economic Review* 104 (10): 3003–3037.

Altmann, S., and C. Traxler. 2014. "Nudges at the Dentist." *European Economic Review* 72: 19–38.

Andreoni, J. 1989. "Giving with Impure Altruism: Applications to Charity and Ricardian Equivalence." *Journal of Political Economy* 97 (6): 1447–1458.

Andreoni, J. 1990. "Impure Altruism and Donations to Public Goods: A Theory of Warm-Glow Giving." *Economic Journal* 199 (401): 464–477.

Bhargava, S., and D. Manoli. 2015. "Psychological Frictions and the Incomplete Take-Up of Social Benefits: Evidence from an IRS Field Experiment." *American Economic Review* 105 (11): 3489–3529.

Calzolari, G., and M. Nardotto. 2017. "Effective Reminders."*Management Science* 66 (9): 2915–2932.

Damgaard, M. T. and C. Gravert. 2017. "Now or Never! The Effect of Deadlines on Charitable Giving: Evidence from Two Natural Field Experiments." *Journal of Behavioral and Experimental Economics* 66: 78–87.

Damgaard, M. T., and C. Gravert. 2018. "The Hidden Costs of Nudging: Experimental Evidence from Reminders in Fundraising." *Journal of Public Economics* 157: 15–26.

DellaVigna, S., J. A. List, and U. Malmendier. 2012. "Testing for Altruism and Social Pressure in Charitable Giving." *Quarterly Journal of Economics* 127 (1): 1–56.

DellaVigna, S., J. A. List, U. Malmendier, and G. Rao. 2013. "The Importance of Being Marginal: Gender Differences in Generosity." *American Economic Review: Papers and Proceedings* 103 (3): 586–590.

Gilbert, B., and J. G. Zivin. 2014. "Dynamic Salience with Intermittent Billing: Evidence from Smart Electricity Meters." *Journal of Economic Behavior & Organization* 107, Part A: 176–190.

Huck, S., and I. Rasul. 2010. "Transaction Costs in Charitable Giving." *B.E. Journal of Economic Analysis & Policy* 10 (1): article 31.

Karlan, D., M. McConnell, S. Mullainathan, and J. Zinman. 2016. "Getting to the Top of Mind: How Reminders Increase Saving." *Management Science* 62 (12): 3393–3411.

National Center for Charitable Statistics. 2017. "Quick Facts about Nonprofits." http://nccs .urban.org/data-statistics/quick-facts-about-nonprofits.

Sonntag, A., and D. J. Zizzo. 2015. "On Reminder Effects, Drop-Outs and Dominance: Evidence from an Online Experiment on Charitable Giving." *PLoS One* 10 (8): e0134705.

Taubinsky, D. 2013. "From Intentions to Actions: A Model and Experimental Evidence of Inattentive Choice." Working paper, Harvard University, Cambridge, MA.

Vervloet, M., A. J. Linn, J. C. M. van Weert, D. H. de Bakker, M. L. Bouvy, and L. van Dijk. 2012. "The Effectiveness of Interventions Using Electronic Reminders to Improve Adherence to Chronic Medication: A Systematic Review of the Literature." *Journal of the American Medical Informatics Association* 19 (5): 696–704.

12 The Donation Response to Natural Disasters

Sarah Smith, Mark Ottoni-Wilhelm,
and Kimberley Scharf

12.1 Introduction

On December 26, 2004, a massive earthquake occurred in the Indian
Ocean near the west coast of Sumatra. It sent killer waves radiating
from its epicenter, causing an estimated 250,000 deaths and affecting
an estimated 5 million people across 14 countries. There was an unpre-
cedented public response in the aftermath of the tsunami, not only in
the amount of money raised (£10 billion globally) but also in the speed
with which money was pledged or donated. In the United Kingdom,
an emergency appeal was launched on December 29, 2004, and set a
new world record for the amount donated online in a 24-hour period:
£392 million was donated to the official disaster appeal in the United
Kingdom—nearly three times the amount raised by any other emergency appeal in the same period of time, before or after. In this chapter
we study donor responses to this type of emergency situation caused
by natural disasters. We shed light on what determines the magnitude
of responses to disaster appeals—focusing on the scale of the disaster
and the role of disaster appeals.

Previous literature has used two measures for the scale of a disaster—
the number of people reported killed and the number of people reported
affected. The latter includes the number with physical needs, such
as accommodations, as well as the number injured (Eisensee and
Stromberg 2007, Stromberg 2007, Evangelidis and Van den Bergh 2013).
Looking to the findings from previous studies, there are seemingly
inconsistent results on the relative importance of these two dimensions
in driving aid responses to disasters. Stromberg (2007) found that both
measures—the number of people killed and the number of people
affected—were correlated with whether governmental aid was given in
response to a disaster. In contrast, Evangelidis and Van den Bergh (2013)

found that only the number killed mattered, not the number affected, for private voluntary (nongovernmental) aid, both for whether aid was given and for the amount of aid. Evangelidis and Van den Bergh (2013) argued that the number affected better captures the extent of need that donors should be responding to.

In this chapter we investigate further the relationship between the scale of the disaster—measured by the two indicators—and the aid response. We show that the results are sensitive to the functional form specification, and we argue in favor of including the number killed and the number affected in logs rather than levels. One reason the regression results are sensitive to specification is because some very large-scale disasters, including the East Asia tsunami, that are associated with a high level of impact in terms of the number of people killed and/or the number of people affected and also associated with a big donor response. We show that it is important that estimation take proper account of such "big disasters." With a specification that includes donations and disaster scale in logs, we are able to reconcile the findings from the earlier studies, both with each other—and also with results from a new source of data on the responses to emergency appeals launched by the UK Disasters Emergency Committee (DEC).[1] The consistent findings are that both the number killed and the number affected matter equally for whether aid is given. The number killed has a stronger effect than the number affected on the amount given—and a few of the deadliest disasters have a particularly powerful effect.

We then discuss one factor that may explain the people affected–donation association being smaller relative to the people killed–donation association: error in measuring the number of people killed. It may be that the number of people killed gives donors a clearer sense of the devastating impact of the disaster that is more directly comparable across disasters.

A second factor is media coverage. Media coverage played an important part in the big response to the East Asia tsunami. Dramatic pictures of devastation were broadcast around the world at Christmas, a time when people typically watch a lot of television and also when there may be few competing news stories.[2] Of course, large disasters are more likely to be covered in the media, so to pin down the effect of media coverage, Eisensee and Stromberg (2007) used an instrumental variable approach, exploiting competing news events to instrument coverage of disasters, to show that television coverage has a causal effect on whether aid is provided in the case of natural disasters. Brown and Minty (2008) found a similar effect. The exact mechanism is not clear, but media coverage is likely to provide information on the scale of the need, make the need salient, create identifiable victims by showing images of real people who are suffering (Loewenstein and Small 2007), and reduce the social distance between donor and potential recipients (Fong and Luttmer 2007). Focusing on the DEC appeals, we present new evidence on the importance of public appeals in driving donations. We present stylized facts on donor responses to disaster appeals, exploiting a uniquely detailed dataset that allows us to track donations day by day around the time that the appeal is launched. We present striking evidence that appeals have an immediate and powerful effect on donations to DEC and its member charities. Moreover, we pin down the timing of the response to show that it is linked to the date of the appeal rather than to the date of the disaster itself.

The plan of the chapter is as follows. In section 12.2 we discuss data sources that have been used in this literature to estimate the relationship between scale and donation response. In section 12.3 we revisit existing studies and look at whether we are able to reconcile findings, paying close attention to functional form specifications. Section 12.4 presents new evidence on the dynamics of donor responses to disaster appeals. Section 12.5 concludes.

12.2 Data and Estimation Issues

A key source of data in this literature is the Centre for Research on the Epidemiology of Disasters (CRED), which provides comprehensive coverage of disasters via their Emergency Disaster Database (EM-DAT). This dataset records a "disaster" if 10 or more people are reported killed, 100 or more people are reported affected, or if a disaster is declared.

CRED reports the number of deaths following each disaster, defined as both the number reported dead and the number reported missing and presumed dead. These numbers are based on official measures where available. CRED also reports the number of people who are affected by each disaster, defined as the number of people requiring immediate assistance during a period of emergency (i.e., requiring such basic survival needs as food, water, shelter, sanitation, and immediate medical assistance). For many disasters both the number of people killed and number of people affected are estimated—in the immediate

Sarah Smith, Mark Ottoni-Wilhelm, and Kimberley Scharf

aftermath of major disasters, it may not be possible to collect precise information on the number killed/affected.

Table 12.1 presents summary information from CRED on the number reported killed and the number reported affected for all natural disasters during 1968–2015. As might be expected, the number of people reported killed is typically smaller than the number of people reported affected—only in 3 percent of disasters is the relationship the other way around. Perhaps surprisingly, the number killed and the number affected are not strongly correlated (the p-value is equal to 0.037). Thus it should be possible to identify the separate effects of the two measures of scale on the donation response. The strength of the relationship between the two measures of scale does vary considerably across types of disasters, however. The correlation is stronger for landslides, earthquakes, and floods and weaker for extreme temperature and wildfire. This makes it important to control for disaster type when looking at the relationship between different measures of disaster scale and the aid response.

Table 12.1 draws attention to another feature of the scale of disasters: Some disasters stand apart from the others in terms of the numbers of people killed and affected. The mean number killed across all reported

Table 12.1
Number reported killed and number reported affected, natural disasters, 1968–2015.

	Number of People Killed	Number of People Affected	Correlation
Mean (standard deviation)	477	927,508	0.037
	(7,528)	(8,897,949)	
Minimum	0	0	
Maximum	300,317	300,000,000	
By type (mean)			
Drought	1,156	3,560,346	0.012
Earthquake	2,005	280,759	0.275
Epidemic	253	27,392	0.102
Extreme temperature	412	233,247	−0.006
Flood	123	1,499,187	0.241
Landslide	85	22,086	0.379
Storm	494	591,101	0.076
Volcano	160	38,364	0.002
Wildfire	7	22,526	−0.003
Number of observations	12,470	12,470	12,740

Source: Data on natural disasters from the Emergency Disaster Database, provided by the Centre for Research on the Epidemiology of Disasters.

natural disasters is around 500, but the worst disasters are associated with the deaths of hundreds of thousands of people. Similarly, the mean number affected is just under 1 million, but the worst disasters affect more than 300 times that number. The presence of such outliers is likely to make estimation of the effect of scale of the disasters sensitive to the functional form specification. Table 12.A.1 in appendix 12.A lists the 20 worst disasters over this period, defined by the number of people killed and, separately, by the number of people affected. The profiles of the type and location of the very worst disasters differ, depending on the measure used. Strikingly, there is no overlap in the two lists of the 20 worst disasters.

There are also outliers when looking at the amounts of aid given—some disasters attract many times more aid than others (e.g., see the set of DEC disaster appeals summarized in table 12.B.1 in appendix 12.B). This is a potential issue when analyzing the magnitude of the aid response. Stromberg (2007) and Eisensee and Stromberg (2007) look only at whether aid is provided in response to a disaster, focusing on aid provided by the US Office of Foreign Disaster Assistance during 1968–2002. In contrast, Evangelidis and Van den Bergh (2013) look both at whether aid is given and also at the amount of aid. They exploit information on private donor responses from the Financial Tracking System of the UN Office for the Co-ordination of Humanitarian Aid. They study a much smaller sample than do Stromberg (2007) and Eisensee and Stromberg (2007), focusing on 381 disasters during 2000–2011 for which aid was given in 124 cases. In this chapter we present new analysis of the amount of aid given, focusing on the appeals launched in the United Kingdom by DEC. During 1968–2015, DEC launched 65 appeals—appendix B gives full details. All DEC appeals result in some aid being given, and our analysis therefore focuses on what determines the amount that is raised by each appeal. Although a relatively small sample, it allows for comparison with the Evangelidis–Van den Bergh data.

Several implications follow for any empirical analysis that attempts to relate the scale of disasters to aid given. First, estimating the effect of the number killed and of the number affected is going to be affected by a few very big disasters (and these very big disasters will differ according to the two measures of scale). Second, the disasters associated with the most aid will influence estimates regardless of specification. In the next section we show that, indeed, regression results are sensitive to functional form specification and, in the case of amount of aid, to specific high-aid disaster appeals.

12.3   Reconciling Estimates on Aid Responses

12.3.1   Whether Aid Is Given

The studies by Stromberg (2007) and Evangelidis and Van den Bergh (2013) examine the relationship between the scale of the disaster and whether or not aid is given. The main regression results from Stromberg (2007) are repeated in table 12.2; they show that that whether or not aid is given is correlated with both the number killed and the number affected. These numbers are expressed on a base 10 log scale. In the ordinary least squares (OLS) specification in column 1, a change in the number killed has a stronger effect on aid than a change in the number affected. This specification includes a control for news coverage. In the Instrumental Variables specification, where news coverage is instrumented with the presence of competing news, the relationship is reversed, and the effect of the number killed becomes insignificant. The results indicate that part of the observed effect of the number killed is likely because deaths drive news coverage.

Table 12.2
Stromberg's (2007) results.

Dependent Variable	Ordinary Least Squares Regression	Instrumental Variable Regression
Number killed (log 10)	0.10***	0.02
	(0.01)	(0.04)
Number affected (log 10)	0.06***	0.04***
	(0.01)	(0.01)
Real GDP per capita (log10)	−0.08***	−0.23***
	(0.03)	(0.07)
Disaster in the news (0/1)	0.09***	0.76**
	(0.02)	(0.32)
Number of observations	4,755	4,755

Source: These results are taken from Stromberg (2007).
Notes: The dependent variable is a binary variable: Whether aid is provided in response to a natural disaster. Regressions additionally control for year, continent, disaster type, month, and for (log) population. Disaster in the news is instrumented with presence of competing news stories (e.g., the Olympics). Robust standard errors, clustered by recipient country, are in parentheses. The symbols *** and ** indicate significance at the 1 percent and 5 percent levels, respectively.

Evangelidis and Van den Bergh (2013) include the number killed and the number affected *in levels* in their regression specification. Column 1 in table 12.3 replicates their approach:[3] Whether or not aid is given is regressed on the number killed, the number affected (in units of 100,000s), and an indicator for whether an appeal was launched. The regression also controls for location and type of disaster. In this level specification, the number of people killed is associated with the probability that there are private voluntary donations in response to the disaster, but the number of people affected is not. On the face of it, these results appear at odds with Stromberg's findings. However, when the same relationship is estimated using a log specification (column 2), both the numbers of people killed and affected are associated with the probability of donations, a qualitatively similar set of findings to those of Stromberg (2007).

Table 12.3
Replication of Evangelidis and Van den Bergh's (2013) level-specification, and new results in logs.

	OLS Levels	OLS Logs
Number of people killed (β_1)	.118[a,b]	.041***
	(.075)	(.012)
Number of people affected (β_2)	.0001[a]	.030***
	(.0002)	(.010)
Appeal	.544***	.408***
	(.067)	(.068)
p-value: ($\beta_1 = \beta_2$)	.115	.546
R^2	.206	.275
J–test evidence against the model *t*-statistic	6.392	−1.879
p-value	$.0004 \times 10^{-6}$	.061
Number of observations	381	381

Source: Data are from Evangelidis and Van den Bergh (2013).
Notes: The dependent variable is a binary variable: Whether aid is provided in response to a natural disaster. Estimates are from linear probability models. In column 1 the numbers of people killed and affected are in levels; in column 2 the numbers are in logarithms. Both specifications include controls for continent, disaster type, and year trend. Standard errors are in parentheses. OLS, ordinary least squares. The symbol *** indicates significance at the 1 percent level.
a. Numbers in units of 100,000. For example, and additional 100,000 people killed is associated with a .118 point increase in the probability of donations.
b. $p = .114$.

There are some reasons for preferring a log specification. Theoretically, the difference in aid in response to 1,000 additional people killed between one disaster and another, both of whose scale of people killed is in the hundreds, would be expected to be larger a priori than would be the difference in aid in response to 1,000 additional people killed between one disaster and another, both of whose scale of people killed is in the hundreds of thousands. Empirically, formal tests indicate that including measures of the scale of disaster in logs provides a better description of the data. The R^2 in the log specification is much higher (.275 compared to .206), indicating that the log specification is a much better description of the whether-aid-is-given–scale relationship. This is confirmed by the J test: although the level model does provide some evidence against the log model ($p = .061$), the log model provides much stronger evidence against the level model ($p = .0004 \times 10^{-6}$).

12.3.2   How Much Aid Is Given

Next we focus on the relationship between the scale of the disaster and how much aid is given. As previously discussed, there are outlying observations both in the distribution of the amount of aid and in the numbers killed/affected; ideally the regression specification will be robust to these outliers. Table 12.4 uses the Evangelidis–Van den Bergh data to explore the effects of different specifications: The top and bottom panels contain level and log specifications, respectively. Across the columns we drop potentially influential observations to investigate how this affects both the estimated coefficients and the specification tests. The estimation is OLS on the subsample of 124 disasters for which aid was given. The specification tests are comparisons of the values of R^2. For the log model, the R^2 is the squared-correlation coefficient between the predicted amount donated in levels and the actual amount donated.

The first column drops no observations. The level specification in the top panel produces estimates similar to those presented by Evangelidis and Van den Bergh (2013). For every person killed, donations are \$9,254 higher; for every person affected donations are 4 dollars lower (not significant.). The R^2 is .635. In the log specification in the bottom panel, aid is also more responsive to the number killed than to the number affected, but the association with the number of people affected is in the expected positive direction and the gap is smaller: A 10 percent increase in the number of people killed is associated with a 4.71 percent increase in donations; a 10 percent increase in the number

Table 12.4
Level and log specifications, with specification tests.

Parameter	(1) None dropped	(2) Drop 2004 tsunami — East Asia	(3) Drop 2010 earthquake — Haiti	(4) Drop 2011 tsunami — Japan	(5) Drop 2010 floods — Pakistan
Level specification					
Number killed (β_1)	9,254.**	3,864.***	1,109.[c]	714.*	886.**
	(3,922.)	(1,376.)	(669.)	(404.)	(403.)
Number affected (β_2)	-4.	-1.	0.	1.	0.
	(5.)	(2.)	(1.)	(1.)	(0.)
Appeal	7,074,574.	-7,970,189.	1,362,605.	13,518,647.	3,584,683.
	(33,294,007.)	(17,887,581.)	(15,946,616.)	(10,451,346.)	(3,106,515.)
p-value: ($\beta_1 = \beta_2$)	.020	.006	.101	.081	.030
R^2	.635	.637	.183	.274	.595
Log specification					
Number killed (β_1)	.471***	.427***	.401***	.351***	.338***
	(.093)	(.090)	(.093)	(.086)	(.088)
Number affected (β_2)	.123	.135[b]	.129	.139[d]	.112
	(.084)	(.084)	(.084)	(.085)	(.083)
Appeal	1.626***	1.514***	1.518***	1.667***	1.598***
	(.401)	(.387)	(.394)	(.383)	(.379)
p-value: ($\beta_1 = \beta_2$)	.012	.023	.042	.085	.071
R^2 [a]	.220	.817	.234	.317	.607
Number of observations	124	123	122	121	120

Notes: The dependent variable is how much aid is provided (>0). Ordinary least squares estimates use the sample of disasters in which donations were received. All regressions control for continent, disaster type, and a year trend. Standard errors are in parentheses. The symbols ***, **, and *indicate significance at the 1 percent, 5 percent, and 10 percent levels, respectively.
a. For the log specification, the R^2 is calculated by first predicting the amount donated in levels (using the estimates from the log specification), and then calculating the squared-correlation coefficient with the actual amount donated in levels.
b. $p = .109$.
c. $p = .101$.
d. $p = .105$. Data source: Evangelidis and Van den Bergh (2013).

of people affected is associated with a smaller (1.23 percent) increase in donations ($p = .148$).

Comparing the R^2 values would at first suggest that the level specification is preferred. However, the estimates from the level specification change considerably on dropping the 2004 East Asia tsunami (the biggest disaster in terms of amount of aid). The people killed–donation association drops by more than half, and the appeal–donation association becomes counterintuitively negative. The people affected–donation association remains essentially zero. Also note the large decrease in the standard errors. The estimates from the log specification also change but by much less. And the standard errors are stable. The R^2 log value is now larger than the R^2 level value (.817 compared to .637).

The level results continue to change (both the estimated coefficients and the R^2) on dropping other high-aid disasters, including the 2010 Haitian earthquake in column 3. Changes in the log specification are much more modest. Overall, the greater insensitivity of the log specification to the influential observations, its sensible positive (borderline significant) estimate for the people affected–donation association, its sensible positive significant appeal–donation association, and its larger R^2 suggest that it is the better of the two specifications. To be sure, in the log specification the people killed–donation association remains larger than the people affected–donation association, and the difference is significant (see the penultimate row in the table 12.4). That said, the people affected–donation association is not irrelevant.

These results highlight the result that high-aid disasters are influential in the estimation. Even in the log specification, the estimate falls by about one-third (.471 to .338) on dropping four influential observations. This motivates re-estimation of the log specification, using a spline for both the number of people killed and the number of people affected. For the spline in the number of people killed, the knot is placed at the point of separation between the 8 standout disasters in the Evangelidis–Van den Bergh sample and the remaining 116 disasters. The knot for the spline in the number of people affected is placed to separate out the 9 standout disasters; it turns out that only 5 of these received donations to help the victims.[4]

Table 12.5 presents the estimates for the spline specification. Column 1 reproduces table 12.4 (column 1, panel b) to facilitate comparison. The spline in the log specification indicates that donated amounts increase by 15.05 percent in response to a 10 percent increase in the number of people killed among the most deadly disasters, a much larger response

Table 12.5
Spline specification in logs.

	Linear in logs[c]	Spline in logs
	(1)	(2)
Number of people killed	.471*** (.093)	
Number of people killed less than 5,778[a]		.257** (.102)
Number of people killed more than 5,778		1.505*** (.264)
Number of people affected	.123[d] (.084)	
Number of people affected less than 14 million[b]		.097[e] (.098)
Number of people affected more than 14 million		.726[e] (.657)
Appeal	1.626*** (.401)	1.505*** (.389)
Number of observations	124	124
R^2	.593	.645
Adjusted—R^2	.545	.596

Notes: The dependent variable is how much aid is provided (>0). Ordinary least squares estimates use the sample of disasters in which donations were received ($N = 124$). Both regressions control for continent, disaster type, and a year trend. The R^2 values are based on the sum of squares of the log amount donated. The symbols ***, **, and * indicate significance at the 1 percent, 5 percent, and 10 percent levels, respectively.
a. The number of people killed in the 2006 earthquake in Indonesia.
b. The number of people affected in the 2007 flood in Bangladesh was 13,771,380.
c. Estimates repeated from table 12.4.
d. $p = .148$.
e. Test of the hypothesis that both coefficients are 0 has $p = .116$.

than the 2.57 percent increase in response among the less deadly disasters. The difference in response is significant ($p = .0001$). The same pattern occurs in the response to the number of people affected: larger percentage donation responses are associated with percentage increases in the number of people affected among disasters that affect larger numbers of people. The adjusted R^2 values indicate that the spline improves the model fit: .596 compared to .545.

For further evidence on the donation response to disasters, we look to confirm the main patterns from the Evangelidis-Van den Bergh data using a dataset on responses to the DEC appeals. This is narrower in scope than the Evangelidis–Van den Bergh data, because the DEC data only record disasters for which there was an appeal. There were 33 DEC appeals for natural disasters in 1968–2015 for which we also have data on the numbers of people killed and affected. Results for this subsample of the DEC sample are reported in table 12.6.

For comparison, we repeat the results from table 12.4 (column 1, panel b) for the Evangelidis–Van den Bergh data. In column 2 we also report results for a subgroup of 37 disasters in the Evangelidis–Van den Bergh for which an appeal was launched—this is more directly comparable with the DEC appeal data (although these disasters occurred in 2003–2011). Note that the magnitude of the coefficients increases in the subsample compared to the full sample, consistent with a stronger response to larger disasters/appeals. Column 3 reports results for the DEC data that confirm previous findings that the number killed has a stronger effect on the amount of aid than the number affected. The magnitude of the coefficients is smaller than the Evangelidis–Van den Bergh data. Columns 4 and 5 drop the two largest disasters from the analysis. The effect of the number of killed is reduced, confirming that deadly disasters have a particularly powerful effect on donations. The gap in the estimated coefficients on the number killed and the number affected is also reduced, although the significance of the individual coefficients does not change.

Summing up our analysis of the response to disasters, several key insights emerge. First, the presence of outliers makes estimation of the effect of disaster scale on aid sensitive to regression specification. Second, log specifications are more stable than level specifications and are generally preferred on the basis of theoretical considerations and formal specification tests.[5] Third, whether any aid is given depends both on the number of people killed and on the number of people affected— and both measures of the scale of a disaster have a similar relationship. Finally, how much aid is given is more strongly affected by the number killed than by the number affected. The number of deaths has a particularly strong effect among a small number of very deadly disasters.

Evangelidis and Van den Bergh (2013) argue that the stronger effect of the number killed (compared to the number affected) is an indication that aid is misdirected, since, in their view, the number affected provides a stronger indication of the level of need following a disaster than the number killed. A plausible alternative explanation for the smaller association with the number affected may be that this number is harder

Table 12.6
Analysis of DEC appeals.

	(1)	(2)	(3)	(4)	(5)
	Evangelidis All (>0)	Evangelidis Appeals	DEC Appeals	DEC (drop Tsunami)	DEC (drop Haiti)
Number killed (β_1)	0.471*** (0.093)	0.779** (0.171)	0.304** (0.105)	0.238** (0.087)	0.225** (0.086)
Number affected (β_2)	0.123 (0.084)	0.300 (0.203)	0.031 (0.220)	0.095 (0.175)	0.099 (0.171)
Appeal launched (0/1)	1.626*** (0.401)	—	—	—	—
p-value: ($\beta_1 = \beta_2$)	[.012]	[.144]	[.323]	[.490]	[0.530]
Number of observations	124	37	33	32	31

Notes: The dependent variable is how much aid is provided (in logs). Regressions estimated using ordinary least squares on data from Evangelidis et al. (2013) and on data from DEC appeals compiled by the authors. All regressions control additionally for year, continent, and disaster type. Robust standard errors are in parentheses. DEC, UK Disasters Emergency Committee. The symbol ** indicates significance at the 5 percent level.

to measure accurately (compared to the number killed), and that consequently the regression estimate on the number of people affected is attenuated by measurement error. Integrated Research on Disaster Risk (2015) reports that there may be uncertainty about what the number affected even captures: "The indicator *affected* is often reported and is widely used by different actors to convey the extent, impact, or severity of a disaster in non-spatial terms. The ambiguity in the definitions and the different criteria and methods of estimation produce vastly different numbers, which are rarely comparable" (14). In the aftermath of a major disaster it may be hard to collect comprehensive information on the number killed, let alone all the people who may be affected. Guha-Sapir and Below (2002) compared measurements of the numbers of people killed and affected from three studies and found that the studies agreed much more closely on their measurements of the number of people killed than on the number of people affected. Thus it may be harder to identify the underlying relationship with the number affected than with the number killed.

To the extent that the number killed does have a stronger effect on donations than the number affected, one contributory factor is likely to be media coverage. As shown by the results from Eisensee and Stromberg (2007), the number of deaths appears to be more strongly related to media coverage than the number affected, and media coverage has a causal effect on the aid response. In the next section, we present new evidence confirming that public appeals play a crucial role in driving donations.

12.4   The Importance of Publicity

We provide detailed insight into the week-by-week response of donations to public appeals, focusing on DEC appeals. The decision by DEC to launch an appeal triggers a set of actions by the Rapid Response Network. Specifically, national banks and the UK postal network are set up to receive donations; appeal videos, often featuring well-known celebrities, are broadcast via national news networks. Although the disasters will have been in the news, the appeals give the disasters—and the need for funds—additional nationwide visibility. We show that these appeals are important in driving donations.

We track donations before and after the launch of a DEC appeal on a high frequency basis. We do this by exploiting anonymized data on donations made through charity accounts administered by the Charities' Aid Foundation.[6] Important for our analysis, we observe the exact date of donations—as well as the recipient charity—for a panel of more than 100,000 donors. During 2009–2015, six disaster appeals were launched by DEC.[7] We report average responses to these six appeals; further analysis confirms that responses are similar across the six appeals. Tracking donations on a high-frequency basis allows us to study dynamics in the response to appeals. We also show that the appeal is crucial in triggering a response among donors: specifically, the timing of the response is linked to the date of the appeal, not the date of the disaster itself.

Figure 12.1 shows the dynamics in the response to appeals. The figure plots the estimated coefficients (and confidence intervals based on robust standard errors) associated with indicators for the weeks before and after the DEC appeal is launched. Weeks are defined as 7-day periods relative to the exact date of the appeal; week 0 indicates the first 7 days after the appeal is launched. The coefficients capture differences in daily donations to DEC (plus the 13 member charities) during the weeks before and after the appeal, compared to baseline (i.e., outside the disaster periods).[8] We track donations through

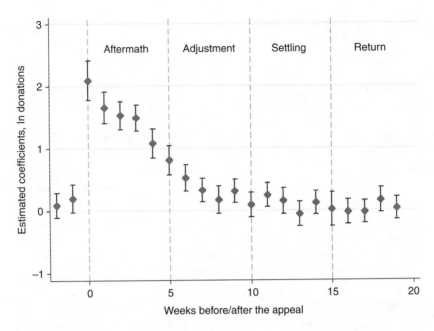

Figure 12.1

Estimated response to disasters, by week. *Source*: Figure is from Scharf, Smith, and Ottoni-Wilhelm (2017). *Notes*: Difference in daily (natural log) donations to the Disasters Emergency Committee and 13 member charities, relative to baseline of nondisaster periods. Estimated coefficients plus confidence intervals are shown. Regressions (estimated using ordinary least squares) include controls for trend, month, day of month, day of week, Christmas, New Year, Easter, bank holidays, and major telethons.

to week 19 (i.e., 20 weeks after the appeal), which allows sufficient time for the response to the appeal to play out.

The pattern of coefficients and standard errors indicates distinct phases in the response to appeals.

- *Phase 1* (weeks 0–4) is the **aftermath** period, during which there is an immediate and strong response to the appeal. In the 7 days following a disaster appeal, average daily donations to the DEC-13 are more than seven times ($e^{2.09} - 1 = 7.08$) higher than average daily donations to the DEC-13 during nondisaster period (i.e, outside the 22-week window surrounding each of the six disaster appeals) and about four times higher during the following 3 weeks ($e^{1.49} - 1 = 3.44$; $e^{1.66} - 1 = 4.26$).[9]

- *Phase 2* (weeks 5–9) is an **adjustment** period: donations to DEC-13 are still above their usual levels, but are lower than during the immediate aftermath and are beginning to return to their baseline levels.

• *Phase 3* (weeks 10–14) is a **settling** period: donations to DEC-13 are very close to baseline with no clear direction of movement.

• *Phase 4* (weeks 15–19) marks a complete **return** to baseline: the effect of the disaster appeal appears to have played out.

The results indicate that the response is initially strong but plays out fairly quickly, with donations returning to their baseline levels after a period of about 2 months.[10] This indicates that high-frequency data are important for looking at donation responses to this type of appeal.[11]

There is no evidence that the appeal causes time-shifting in donations to DEC-13 (i.e., that the increase in donations in the aftermath of an appeal is offset by any reduction in donations to the same charities at a later point in time), either during the 20-week period or subsequently. Instead, the appeal is associated with a significant increase in donations to DEC-13 compared to baseline.[12]

This analysis of the effect of the DEC appeals focuses on the date of the appeal rather than on the date of the disaster, which is consistent with the actual pattern of responses. We test this focus by looking for an effect of the date of the disaster rather than the date of the appeal. Four of the DEC appeals during the sample period were associated with a natural disaster that occurred on a specific date. Since there is typically a lag between the date of the disaster and the date of the appeal (between 3 and 6 days), this allows us to test whether contributions respond to the disaster or to the appeal by repeating the analysis but including an additional indicator variable for days after the date of the disaster, before the appeal is launched. The coefficient on this indicator variable is relatively small and insignificant: 0.165 (0.345). This contrasts with the very strong positive response to the appeal during the first 7 days after the appeal. Therefore we can dismiss that donations build up gradually after the disaster, because the response is immediate and large after the appeal, but not before. This provides striking evidence on the effect of public appeals on driving contributions.

12.5   Conclusion

Natural disasters often trigger strong donation responses. We show that the magnitude of the response is linked to the scale of the disaster, particularly as measured by the number killed. Our interpretation of this finding is that the number killed provides a more reliable—and directly comparable—measure of the severity of the disaster.

Analyzing high-frequency data on donations, we show that the appeals are important in triggering a donation response. The response to appeals is strong and immediate, but relatively short-lived: It tends to play out after 2 or 3 months. The evidence also suggests that appeals generate new funding for international aid, with no time-shifting in donations to DEC-13.

12.A   Appendix A

Table 12.A.1
Biggest natural disasters, 1968–2015.

Year	Type	Country	Number Killed	Number Affected
Twenty worst disasters, by number killed				
1970	Storm	Bangladesh	300,000	3,648,000
1983	Drought	Ethiopia	300,000	7,750,000
1976	Earthquake	China	242,000	164,000
2010	Earthquake	Haiti	222,570	3,700,000
2004	Earthquake	Indonesia	165,816	673,731
1983	Drought	Sudan (the)	150,000	8,400,000
1991	Storm	Bangladesh	138,866	1,5438,849
2008	Storm	Myanmar	138,366	2,420,000
1973	Drought	Ethiopia	100,000	3,000,000
1981	Drought	Mozambique	100,000	4,750,000
2008	Earthquake	China	87,564	4,743,7647
2005	Earthquake	Pakistan	73,338	5,128,309
1970	Earthquake	Peru	66,794	3,216,240
2010	Extreme temp	Russian Federation	55,760	11,000,000
1990	Earthquake	Iran	40,021	732,400
2004	Earthquake	Sri Lanka	35,399	1,019,306
1999	Flood	Venezuela	30,005	543,503
1974	Flood	Bangladesh	28,700	38,000,000
2003	Earthquake	Iran	26,797	297,049
1978	Earthquake	Iran	25,045	40,052
Twenty worst disasters, by number affected				
2002	Drought	India	0	300,000,000
1987	Drought	India	300	300,000,000
1998	Flood	China	4,250	242,714,300
1991	Flood	China	1,861	210,235,727

(continued)

Table 12.A.1 (continued)

Year	Type	Country	Number Killed	Number Affected
1972	Drought	India	0	200,000,000
2003	Flood	China	662	155,924,986
1996	Flood	China	4,091	15,4674,000
2010	Flood	China	1,911	140,194,000
1993	Flood	India	1,297	128,060,000
1995	Flood	China	1,618	126,570,411
2002	Flood	China	1,246	113,255,696
1994	Flood	China	1,564	111,539,385
2007	Flood	China	1,030	111,110,792
2002	Storm	China	108	107,403,094
1999	Flood	China	1,185	107,197,000
1989	Flood	China	2,000	100,010,000
1982	Drought	India	0	100,000,000
2011	Flood	China	628	93,360,000
1994	Drought	China	0	88,690,000
2008	Extreme temperature	China	145	77,000,000

Source: Data are from the Centre for Research on the Epidemiology of Disasters.

12.B   Appendix B

Table 12.B.1
Disaster appeals by the Disasters Emergency Committee, 1968–2015.

Date	Disaster Type	Country	Number Killed	Number Affected	Amount (£)
Feb 1968	War	Vietnam			360,000
Sept 1968	Earthquake	Iran	10,000	79,050	210,000
Nov 1968	War	Nigeria			240,000
Oct 1969	Floods	Tunisia	616	471,506	90,000
Nov 1969	Earthquake	Yugoslavia	15	286,116	60,000
Mar 1970	Earthquake	Turkey	1,086	83,448	370,000
Jun 1970	Earthquake	Peru	66,794	3,216,240	230,000
Jun 1970	Floods	Romania	215	238,755	110,000
Nov 1970	Storm	Bangladesh	300,000	3,648,000	1,490,000
Jun 1971	War	Pakistan			1,420,000
Dec 1972	Earthquake	Nicaragua	10,000	720,000	340,000
Oct 1973	Drought	Ethiopia	100,000	3,000,000	1,540,000
Sep 1974	Storm	Honduras	80,00	600,000	350,000

Table 12.B.1 (continued)

Date	Disaster Type	Country	Number Killed	Number Affected	Amount (£)
Feb 1976	Earthquake	Guatemala	23,000	4,993,000	1,300,000
Sep 1979	War	Cambodia			560,000
Nov 1979	Storm	India	594	1,605,772	870,000
Jun 1980	Drought	East Africa			6,100,000
Mar 1982	War	Central America			430,000
Jul 1982	War	Lebanon			1,030,000
Mar 1983	Famine	Ethiopia			1,970,000
Jun 1984	Famine	Africa			9,520,000
Oct 1984	Famine	Ethiopia			5,250,000
May 1985	Storm	Bangladesh	15,121	1,831,300	1,400,000
Jun 1987	War	Mozambique			2,480,000
Dec 1987	Famine	Ethiopia			2,690,000
Aug 1988	Flood	Sudan	96	2,500,000	8,890,000
Sep 1988	Storm	Bangladesh	2,379	45,000,000	5,810,000
Sep 1988	Storm	Caribbean	103	1,740,000	1,000,000
Dec 1989	Famine	Ethiopia			10,240,000
Sep 1990	War	Gulf			3,490,000
Jan 1991	Famine	Africa			7,930,000
May 1991	Storm	Bangladesh	138,866	1,5438,849	3,520,000
Jun 1991	Famine	Africa			2,600,000
Sep 1992	Famine	Africa			17,300,000
Oct 1993	Famine	Africa			2,530,000
Feb 1994	War	Yugoslavia			2,600,000
May 1994	War	Rwanda			37,000,000
May 1998	War	Sudan			10,500,000
Sep 1998	Floods	Bangladesh	103	1,000,000	5,500,000
Nov 1998	Storm	Central America	18,808	3,246,628	1,850,0000
Apr 1999	War	Kosovo			53,000,000
Nov 1999	Storm	India	9,843	12,628,312	7,000,000
Mar 2000	Flood	Mozambique	800	4,500,000	30,000,000
Feb 2001	Earthquake	India	20,005	6,321,812	24,000,000
Jan 2002	Volcano	DR Congo	200	110,400	4,650,000
Jul 2002	Drought	Southern Africa			16,000,000
Aug 2003	War	Liberia			2,500,000
Jul 2004	War	Sudan			35,000,000
Dec 2004	Tsunami	Asia	250,000	5,000,000	392,000,000
Aug 2005	Drought	Nigeria			32,000,000
Oct 2005	Earthquake	India/ Pakistan	74,647	5,284,931	59,000,000
May 2007	War	Dafur/Chad			13,600,000
Nov 2007	Storm	Bangladesh	4,234	8,978,754	9,000,000

(continued)

Table 12.B.1 (continued)

Date	Disaster Type	Country	Number Killed	Number Affected	Amount (£)
May 2008	Storm	Myanmar	138,366	2,420,000	19,500,000
Nov 2008	War	DR Congo			10,500,000
Jan 2009	War	Gaza			8,300,000
Oct 2009	Earthquake	Indonesia	1,202	9,806,076	9,300,000
Jan 2010	Earthquake	Haiti	222,570	3,700,000	1.07×10^8
Aug 2010	Floods	Pakistan	2,113	20,363,496	71,000,000
Jul 2011	Drought	East Africa			79,000,000
Mar 2013	War	Syria			27,000,000
Nov 2013	Storm	Phillipines	7,354	16,106,870	97,000,000
Aug 2014	War	Gaza			19,000,000
Oct 2014	Disease	West Africa	11,310	28,620	37,000,000
Apr 2015	Earthquake	Nepal	8,969	5,640,265	87,000,000

Source: Data on all natural disasters during 1968–2015 come from the database EM-DAT. Information on the appeals comes from the UK Disasters Emergency Committee (http://www.dec.org.uk/).
Note: Disasters analyzed in section 12.4 are shaded. Blank cells indicate no data available.

Table 12.B.2
Comparison of natural disasters and Disasters Emergency Committee appeals, 1968–2015.

	Breakdown of All Natural Disasters			Breakdown of DEC Appeals	
	% Disasters	% Deaths	% Affected	Number of DEC Appeals	% DEC Appeals
By area					
Africa	19.1	24.9	7.1	28	43.1
Asia	35.3	50.9	86.9	20	30.8
Australasia	4.5	1.9	0.3	0	0
Central America	16.8	13.8	3.8	8	12.3
Europe	14.4	6.2	0.8	5	7.7
Middle East	2.7	3.5	0.8	4	6.2
North America	7.3	0.5	0.4	0	0
By type					
Drought	5.0	19.4	30.6	5	7.7
Earthquake	8.3	36.8	2.6	11	16.9
Epidemic	10.7	6.5	0.4	1	1.5

Table 12.B.2 (continued)

	Breakdown of All Natural Disasters			Breakdown of DEC Appeals	
	% Disasters	% Deaths	% Affected	Number of DEC Appeals	% DEC Appeals
Extreme temperature	4.1	4.9	1.4	0	0
Flood	34.6	8.2	50.8	2	3.1
Landslide	5.3	1.1	0.1	0	0
Storm	27.4	22.4	13.8	13	20.0
Volcano	1.6	1.0	0.1	1	1.5
Wildfire	3.1	0.1	0.1	0	0
Famine				9	13.9
War				19	29.2
Number of observations	12,470	12,470	12,740	65	65

Sources: Data on all natural disasters over the period 1968–2015 comes from EM-DAT. Information on DEC appeals comes from Disasters Emergency Committee (http://www .dec.org.uk/).
Note: DEC, Disasters Emergency Committee.

Notes

Thanks to Ioannis Evangelidis for sharing the data used in his paper written with Bram Van den Bergh (Evangelidis and Van den Bergh 2013). Thanks also to the Charities Aid Foundation for allowing us access to their anonymized account data. All errors are our own.

1. DEC is an umbrella organization that brings together 13 leading UK aid charities to coordinate fundraising efforts in times of humanitarian crisis. The 13 member charities are large international aid charities, including Action Aid, Age International, British Red Cross, Catholic International Development Charity (CAFOD), Care International, Christian Aid, Concern Worldwide, Islamic Relief, Oxfam, Plan UK, Save the Children, Tearfund, and World Vision. Full details of all appeals launched from 1968 to 2015 are given in appendix 12.B.

2. Viewing data for 2015 and 2016 show roughly 15 percent more hours viewed in the days between Christmas and New Year compared to the rest of December and January (and higher levels of viewing in these months compared to the rest of the year). See http://www.barb.co.uk/viewing-data/weekly-viewing-summary/.

3. Evangelidis and Van den Bergh adopt a Heckman two-step procedure and use a logit model for the first stage. We use a linear probability model for ease of interpretation, but the results are similar.

4. In general, a high degree of overlap exists between the biggest disasters in the Evangelidis–Van den Bergh data and those reported in appendix 12.A, although the match is not perfect. In some cases, disasters reported separately in the Emergency Events Database (EMDAT) have been combined (e.g., the earthquake plus tsunami that occurred in Japan).

5. Another example: Wiepking and Van Leeuwen (2013) report evidence from Dutch data that the bivariate correlation between the number of people killed and the amount donated—both in levels—is 0, but using the same data, there is a strong correlation in logs (P. Wiepking, 2016, personal communication).

6. Scharf, Smith, and Ottoni-Wilhelm (2017) provide more information on the data. Charities' Aid Foundation is a charity that provides financial services to the sector. Its charity accounts are, in effect, checking accounts for making contributions to charities. Donors set up an account with a minimum £100 one-off payment or £10 monthly direct debit, and they use the funds to make contributions to any charity in a variety of ways. The rationale for such accounts is that they facilitate tax-effective giving.

7. The appeals were in response to the September 2009 Sumatra earthquake, the January 2010 Haiti earthquake, the August 2010 Pakistan floods, the 2011 east Africa famine, the 2013 Syrian civil war, and the November 2013 Philippines typhoon Haiyan. See appendix 12.B.

8. Further tests reported in Scharf, Smith, and Ottoni-Wilhelm (2017) confirm that this 20-week period is sufficient to capture the dynamics associated with the appeals. There is no evidence of significant differences in donation (relative to baseline) after this time. Further tests reject the presence of first-order serial correlation in the residuals from this specification.

9. The 13 member charities include the largest overseas aid charities in the United Kingdom. These attract a sizeable level of donations even during baseline periods.

10. This result is consistent with Eckel, Grossman, and Oliveiria (2007), who also report a diminishing of interest over time in the case of Hurricane Katrina.

11. Previous studies (e.g., Brown and Minty 2008) using data from the Panel Study of Income Dynamics have only been able to look at donations on a low-frequency (biennial) basis.

12. Our analysis assumes that the baseline level of donations is not affected by the appeals. Scharf, Smith, and Ottoni-Wilhelm (2017) show that, after each disaster appeal, donations return to the same baseline level. This supports the approach of modeling the effect of disaster appeals relative to a baseline appeal of giving.

References

Brown, P., and J. Minty. 2008. "Media Coverage and Charitable Giving after the 2004 Tsunami." *Southern Economic Journal* 75 (1): 9–25.

Eckel, C., Grossman, P. and A. Oliveira. 2007. "Is More Information Always Better? An Experimental Study of Charitable Giving and Hurricane Katrina." *Southern Economic Journal* 74 (2): 388–411.

Eisensee, T., and D. Stromberg. 2007. "News Floods, News Droughts and US Disaster Relief." *Quarterly Journal of Economics* 122 (2): 693–728.

Evangelidis, I., and B. Van den Bergh. 2013. "The Number of Fatalities Drives Disaster Aid: Increasing Sensitivity to People in Need." *Psychological Science* 24 (11): 2226–2234.

Fong, C., and E. Luttmer. 2007. "What Determines Giving to Hurricane Katrina Victims? Experimental Evidence on Racial Group Loyalty." *American Economic Journal: Applied Economics* 1 (2): 64–87.

Guha-Sapir, C., and R. Below. 2002. "Quality and Accuracy of Disaster Data: A Comparative Analysis of 3 Global Data Sets." Working paper prepared for the Disaster Management facility, World Bank, Brussels CRED.

Integrated Research on Disaster Risk. (2015). "Guidelines on Measuring Losses from Disasters: Human and Economic Impact Indicators." IRDR DATA Publication No. 2. Beijing: Integrated Research on Disaster Risk.

Loewenstein, G., and D. A. Small. 2007. "The Scarecrow and the Tin Man: The Vicissitudes of Human Sympathy and Caring." *Review of General Psychology* 11 (2): 112–126.

Scharf, K., S. Smith, and M. Ottoni-Wilhelm. 2017. "Lift or Shift: The Effect of Fundraising Interventions in Charity Space and Time." CEPR Discussion Paper 12338, Centre for Economic Policy Research, London.

Stromberg, D. 2007. "Natural Disasters, Economic Development and Humanitarian Aid." *Journal of Economic Perspectives* 21 (3): 199–222.

Wiepking, P., and M. H. D. Van Leeuwen. 2013. "Picturing Generosity: Explaining the Success of National Campaigns in the Netherlands." *Nonprofit and Voluntary Sector Quarterly* 42 (2): 262–284.

Contributors

James Andreoni Department of Economics, University of California–San Diego; National Bureau of Economic Research; and CESifo

Jon Behar The Life You Can Save, https://www.thelifeyoucansave.org/

Avner Ben-Ner Carlson School of Management, University of Minnesota

Ted Bergstrom Department of Economics, University of California–Santa Barbara

Greg Bose The Life You Can Save, https://www.thelifeyoucansave.org/

Sarah Brown Department of Economics, University of Sheffield

Catherine C. Eckel Department of Economics, Texas A&M University

Christina Gravert Department of Economics, University of Gothenburg

David H. Herberich Marqeta, Inc.

Samantha Horn Department of Economics, Yale University

Fangtingyu Hu Carlson School of Management, University of Minnesota

Dean Karlan Department of Economics, Northwestern University; Innovations for Poverty Action; Abdul Latif Jameel Poverty Action Lab, Massachusetts Institute of Technology; and National Bureau of Economic Research

Ann-Kathrin Koessler Institute for Environmental Systems Research, University of Osnabrück

Benjamin M. Marx Department of Economics, University of Illinois

Jonathan Meer Department of Economics, Texas A&M University

Michael Menietti Crowd Innovation Lab, Harvard University

Bradley Minaker Department of Economics, McMaster University

Mark Ottoni-Wilhelm Indiana University–Purdue University Indianapolis; and Indiana University Lilly Family School of Philanthropy

A. Abigail Payne Melbourne Institute of Applied Economic & Social Research, University of Melbourne

María P. Recalde Department of Economics, University of Melbourne

Kimberley Scharf Department of Economics, Birmingham Business School, University of Birmingham; National Audit Office Tax Centre; Center for Economic Policy Research; CESifo

Claudia Schwirplies Department of Economics, University of Hamburg

Marta Serra-Garcia Rady School of Management, University of California–San Diego; and CESifo

Sarah Smith Department of Economics, University of Bristol

Karl Taylor Department of Economics, University of Sheffield

Mirco Tonin Faculty of Economics and Management, Free University of Bozen-Bolzano; and CESifo

Mette Trier Damgaard Department of Economics, Aarhus University

Lise Vesterlund Department of Economics, University of Pittsburgh and National Bureau of Economic Research

Laura Villalobos Inter-American Development Bank

Index

Note: Page references with *f* or *t* indicate figure or tables, respectively.